.T CAMBRIDGE

A Men's University – Though of a mixed type

WOMEN AT CAMBRIDGE

A Men's University
– Though of a Mixed Type

by

Rita

RUTH McWILLIAMS-TULLBERG

corrected

London
VICTOR GOLLANCZ LTD
1975

ISBN 0 575 01969 7

PRINTED IN GREAT BRITAIN
BY EBENEZER BAYLIS AND SON, LTD.
THE TRINITY PRESS, WORCESTER, AND LONDON

CONTENTS

ILLUSTRATIONS

All unacknowledged photographs are reproduced by courtesy
of Newnham College, Cambridge.

ILLUSTRATIONS

All .... photographs ....

A NOTE OF THANKS

THE RESEARCH ON which this book is based was made possible by the generosity of the British Academy, who awarded me their "Thank-Offering to Britain Fund" Fellowship for the period January, 1970, to September, 1971. I am most grateful to them for financing twenty-one months of entirely pleasurable work. The Councils of Girton and Newnham Colleges gave me access to their archives and members of both Colleges have patiently answered questions and helped me in innumerable ways. A special word of thanks is due to Miss Ann Phillips of Newnham College, who cheerfully helped and encouraged me at every stage of this project, and who unfailingly coped with the many practical problems which followed my move to Stockholm. The staff of the Anderson Room of Cambridge University Library laboured hard to produce material for which I was searching, and Mr John Oates, both in his capacity then as Under Librarian at the University Library and as Librarian of Darwin College, contributed sound advice and touches of humour on many occasions. Miss Christine Hudson has never failed to produce beautifully typed copies of my much-corrected manuscripts. It is not possible to thank all who have helped with written material, recollections and advice, without producing a list running into several pages, but a glance at the references at the end of the book will reveal the names of those individuals and institutions who have given generously of their time and knowledge. Darwin College deserves special mention, since it was their request for an after-dinner talk which prompted me to explore the topic of women's admission to Cambridge and to discover that the story had not previously been told.

This book has, inevitably, a tinge of "women's emancipation" about it, and at Cambridge, where the topic is still given a

A*   9

A Note of Thanks

frivolous reception by some men, I was constantly introduced as a "Women's Liberationist". I am no great fighter for the Cause, since this has too often taken the form of woman moulding herself in the unfortunate image of tough, competitive men, or, more recently, of a psychotic hatred of all males. Modern emancipationists should be concentrating their efforts on assessment and adjustment of the roles of both sexes. However, to my mind, discrimination against women is an irritating waste of time which usually results in a waste of talent. It has not been easy to write about women's admission to Cambridge University without this sense of irritation at times rising to the surface. But the story is better told without unnecessary comment from me, and I am therefore most grateful to my husband, Hesse, who read the manuscript and censured some of my more extravagantly partisan remarks. However, the responsibility for the result remains entirely my own.

RUTH McWILLIAMS-TULLBERG,
STOCKHOLM, JUNE, 1973

WOMEN AT CAMBRIDGE

A Men's University – Though of a mixed type

I

INTRODUCTION

THE LARGELY UNEXPLORED topic of women's higher education at Cambridge is perhaps more directly relevant to the history of the University than to that of the movement for female emancipation. It is the story of how that great institution, from its generous and open-minded gestures of the 1860's and 1870's, when it provided women's education with the teaching and testing it so needed to set standards, sank into a peculiar mulish prejudice towards its women students which it maintained long after its fellow mules had stopped kicking. The University first agreed that schoolgirls could make use of the Local Examinations which it controlled; then it instituted a special examination for women over eighteen. Two women's colleges appeared within its precincts, lecturers went to the women's colleges, the women students attended men's lectures Tripos papers* were distributed to female students and informally marked until, in 1881, the University gave permission for them officially to sit the Tripos and to be classed. And then the door closed. Women who had taken the degree examination in exactly the same way as men were not to be allowed a degree or even a degree title and nothing was to be done by the University to suggest that women were more than barely tolerated intruders in its midst. Not until 1923 were women given the titles of their degrees and allowed to attend lectures by right and not simply as a privilege; not until 1926 could they take University posts and they had to wait until 1948 before they were given membership of the University.

There is a significance in the Cambridge story for the wider female emancipation movement. Firstly, despite its failure

* The Cambridge Honours degree examinations. Candidates are "classed", that is, given different grades on the basis of their examination results.

formally to accept women, the University was nonetheless giving them the highest academic training available and sending them into the world to educate generations of school-girls in an awareness of life and the possibility of their con-tributing to it. Secondly, since the voice of Cambridge was the voice of perhaps half the country's leaders, the attitudes of the University were the same as those which the women later faced in their campaign for the vote, and the degree struggles of 1887 and 1897 can be seen as rehearsals for the later contest. The fact that Oxford and Cambridge, and later just Cambridge, acted in the question of women's education quite independently from the other rapidly developing institutions of higher education does not mean that the controversies were simply parochial matters. The domination of public life by Oxford and Cambridge men ensured that the affairs of the old universities were of national concern and among the central domestic issues of the day, at least before the First World War. The issue of degrees for women at Oxford and Cambridge was also complicated by that of University membership and the right which every degree holder had to take part in the government of his University. Cambridge graduates in particular had considerable power over the academic and administrative organisation of their University, power which many of them were unwilling to share with women. Indeed, Cambridge men were never defeated on this point, since women were admitted to University membership only after the rights of graduates in University government had been severely curtailed.

The history of the foundation and early development of the women's colleges will be dealt with only briefly here, since the various college histories treat these in some detail.[1] Though a lot of colourful detail has remained unpublished, the women biographers of the colleges were happy to describe the process of education development while the relations between Newn-ham, Girton and the University remained good. However, a thick veil of reticence descended as soon as relations became strained; not simply because the ladies in question belonged to a generation which did not wash its dirty linen in public, but also because they were writing at a time when their freedom of speech was still circumscribed by the continuing uncertainty surrounding the place of women in Cambridge. The women and their friends made two major attempts in the nineteenth century, first in 1887 and then in 1897, to secure the degree for those who had succeeded in the Tripos, and the latter produced eighteen months of public debate in a campaign highly organised by both the supporters of women and their opponents. The work of the University was disrupted, friendships were strained and in the number of words written and the size of the M.A.s' vote the campaign outmatched the fury of the famous compulsory Greek row of 1904 and 1905. More curious, therefore, than the absence of accounts of the 1887 and 1897 controversies from the biographies and domestic histories of the colleges, is their abscence from two major works dealing with Cambridge in the second half of the nineteenth century. The books of D. A. Winstanley, are the standard histories of the University; yet in his *Late Victorian Cambridge*[2] no hint is given that women were established in Cambridge, informally attending lectures and taking Triposes from the 1870's. Indeed, the only mention made of Girton and Newnham is in Winstanley's description of the "Spinning House" controversy,[3] in that the presence of young women studying in the same town which housed so many monastic institutions for men further complicated the task of the University Proctors and city police in identifying prostitutes. Though not intending to extend his history beyond 1882, Winstanley did discuss the events leading to the Corporation Act of 1894, and the various controversies between the women's colleges and the University would have provided ideal material for an episodic chapter of the type which he liked to write. And to the contemporary reader, such a chapter would seem to have more bearing on the growth of the University than, say, the Master of Trinity's row with the Judges as to whether he would lend them his Lodge during the Winter Assizes, or whether Robinson tricked Jameson out of the St Catherine's Mastership. But Winstanley stuck strictly to the letter of the law. He was writing about Cambridge University, and in the nineteenth century women were not members of that body—nor were they in August 1946 when Winstanley wrote his Preface.

A more recent study, *The Revolution of the Dons* by Sheldon

Rothblatt,[4] similarly fails to deal with the advent of women in Cambridge, though the purpose of the book is in part to consider social change and the University. No doubt Mr Rothblatt felt only a limited number of topics could be dealt with, more especially since they were being considered for the first time, but if he had found space and time to consider women in Cambridge, it would have become clear that many of the "revolutionary" ideas of the dons on teaching techniques were first tested in the women's colleges. The careful organisation of personal tuition by the best available teachers, a practice firmly established in the men's colleges only in the 1890's,[5] was a central feature of the women's colleges from their foundation. Not that this form of instruction was the brain-child of any woman educationalist; special coaching was needed to remedy the inadequacies of their basic education and propriety demanded that the teaching of women should be strictly supervised. No doubt two of the Cambridge reformers, Sidgwick and Jackson, who had very strong connections with the women's colleges, were happy to try out their ideas of tuition in these newly formed institutions; the battle over compulsory Greek, for example, was first fought in the gardens of Girton and Newnham, as was the question of the Pass degree. The position of women at Cambridge was also of central importance when, in the twentieth century, the University took the highly significant step of turning to the State for financial assistance.

Most of this story refers to women of the middle class. To the Victorian mind, a clear dividing line existed below which a woman was not a "lady". The distinction was not necessarily a financial one. Indeed, the development in education of "ladies" rose out of the pressing economic problems faced by unsupported women, for their opportunities for paid work were far fewer than those of lower-class women. The unrelieved middle classness of the story is at times suffocating, but it must be remembered that the quality of education given to working-class children in State elementary schools without discrimination as to sex was, in some cases, far superior to that offered to the girls of the middle classes by their governesses and in their ladies' academies. Improvement in the education of middle-class women eventually benefited a very much larger group of school children than the privileged few who could go to university.

In the following pages, an attempt is made to trace the course of events from the conception of Girton and Newnham, to the formal admission of women to degrees and membership of Cambridge University nearly one hundred years later. Sadly this is a story of prejudice, of how some men, without offering any evidence in support of their opinion, insisted that women would damage their beloved Cambridge, and how others simply wished to keep its beauty and benefits for themselves. But not only is this the story of the paralysing power of conventional thought and fear of change, but also of the many men who, willingly or reluctantly, risked the uncertainty, and allowed women the education which had previously been the exclusive preserve of men. Fear of change had to be accommodated at the same time as progress was made, and it is left to the reader to judge whether the Cambridge women sacrificed too much to appeasement in order to reach their goal.

In the absence of previous accounts, it has been necessary to concentrate on producing a chronology of events, in a book of moderate proportions, and therefore little attempt has been made to provide a thorough-going analysis of the arguments used throughout the controversy. Possibly, then, as well as being of interest to the general reader, the narrative will prompt the specialist to further research. This study may also illustrate how a great issue was debated in one of our institutions of higher education; how, even in the halls of learning, fantasy was sometimes so much more influential than fact; how, over time, opinions did change, while the legacy of early attitudes lingered on; and how, through it all, the University lived and worked.

Despite the appearance of women on the scene, and, after eighty years of struggle, their admission to University membership, Cambridge survived the last century with its reputation intact and even enhanced. In the Senior Combination Rooms of today there are many who are fearful of the major changes which the University must face in the next hundred years.

It is hoped that tracing the history of one of the most significant Cambridge revolutions of the past century, might be of therapeutic value, helping to calm some of these anxieties and injecting a sense of proportion into today's disputes.

2

LOCAL EXAMINATIONS

IF THE PRECISE origins of the women's education movement
remain obscure for us, our ignorance is shared by a sub-
committee of the London University Convocation which in
1866, reported "a remarkable movement" in the improvement
of women's education since 1850:

> It is not easy to ascertain the causes which have produced
> this movement. The circumstance, however, that its origin
> cannot be distinctly traced, is itself the best evidence of its
> reality and that it was the natural expression of a subsisting
> undercurrent of feeling and not the temporary or spasmodic
> utterance of a few enthusiastic persons.[1]

The movement assumed a practical form in the establishment
of ladies colleges, and the opening of the first of these, Queen's
College in Harley Street, London, in 1848, provides a starting
point for an examination of the strands of thought and activity
which led to its foundation. By the second quarter of the
nineteenth century a new rôle had been evolved for the
middle-class women, reversing an earlier trend towards wider
participation in social affairs and concentrating instead on
home and family.[2] Continuing the moral and spiritual renewal
of the Church of England, middle-class women were assigned
the virtues of piety, absolute purity and innocence; their lives
were to be ones of patience and resignation. An unmarried
girl was expected to devote the whole of her attention to the
wishes of her family and since in this class of home all serious
domestic work was carried out by servants, her time was spent
on trivia which required neither physical nor mental exertion.
The demands of fashion meant that she was restricted in her
movements by complicated clothing; the open air could only

be faced veiled and gloved, and if, as a result of mental and physical repression, a girl had a fainting fit or hysterical attack, this was taken as further evidence of the fundamental inferiority of her sex. Marriage offered the only chance of escape from this dull idleness and was usually a girl's only ambition. However, it too had its pitfalls, for marriage was held up as a holy vocation, demanding life-long sacrifice and submission. Through her constant attention to her husband's wishes and deference to his opinions, a woman was expected to show her appreciation of his God-given, masculine superiority. Any intellectual gifts which she might possess were to be concealed and repressed for his sake. Whereas papers and periodicals for women in the eighteenth century had attempted the serious cultivation of the mind, papers of the post-1825 period tended to a pattern of "fiction, fashion and miscellaneous light reading of a superficial kind".[3] Ignorance and innocence were confounded, and while the latter remained enshrined as the essential civilising antidote to the depravity of man, women who sought knowledge were held to be unnatural. With the position of women so ordained, it was inevitable that they should be wholly dependent on their men, possessing no income and few resources themselves. Indeed, this was the law in the case of married women, until the Married Women's Property Act (1882), but unmarried women were equally dependent—and there were many of these.

Untenable though most women would regard it today, it was not the position of married women which was the main-spring of educational reform, but the plight of her unmarried sister. The emancipation of the married woman is a movement of the 1960's and 1970's. A century earlier, the reformers, though sympathising with her legal disabilities, felt she had a certain security and important work to perform in the maintenance of a home and the upbringing of her children. The unmarried woman, on the other hand, was frequently little more than a parasite, and when the host died or failed she also foundered. In those days of high competition and wild speculation, fortunes were rapidly made and lost; disease would swiftly deprive a family of a breadwinner and whilst society dictated that the daughters of professional men were "gentlewomen", professional salaries could not support many unmarried daughters. And it was the number of these unmarried daughters which created the problem. The fiction of the feeble, dependent female which the Victorian male had chosen to create, no doubt with the acquiescence of many an idle woman, was an expensive one to maintain and not all men were willing to face up to their responsibilities. Many women were left without a husband and it was often assumed that this was due to the migration of single men to the U.S.A. and the Colonies or to service in the Army or India. However, the actual excess of women over men in the twenty-plus age group was, in mid-century, about 4%;[4] a more likely explanation of spinsterhood was the failure of men of suitable fortune to come forward as prospective husbands. In 1861, 20% of women over twenty years in England and Wales were unmarried.[4] A contemporary commentator, J. D. Ackland of Oxford University, was reported in the *Western Times* of October 1863 as saying,

> A great number of men, from foolish conventional ideas of fashion and other causes, are constrained to lead a single life and numbers of women are unable to find the partners whom they are fit to support and comfort, and to whom they might naturally look for support.

Fathers looked for financial security for their daughters and it was not easy to find a man of appropriate wealth who was prepared for the drain on his pocket that a wife and family would entail. In Victorian society it was quite easy for a man to buy *ad hoc* any comforts he might need or fancy without encumbering himself with a wife, and possibly daughters. Women, on the other hand, trapped by the current social mores, were of necessity forced into matrimony.

The plight of those who did not achieve this goal attracted the attention of groups of reformers in the 1840's (F. D. Maurice and Charles Kingsley among them). When circumstances forced a gentlewoman to earn her own living she turned to the one profession open to her—that of a governess. In theory, by doing this, she did not lose class; but, even so, her position was frequently intolerable. She was neither a guest nor a member of the family with whom she worked; by birth a lady, she was economically in the position of a servant. Rarely did she gain the respect of her employers, her pupils or even the lowest chambermaids, since all too often she was manifestly bad at her job. Her own education would have consisted, beyond learning to read and write, of the cultivation of "accomplishments". An ability to recite a few simple sentences of French, to sing, to embroider, to walk and dance gracefully and to ornament the drawing room was all that was necessary for a girl who wished to capture a husband. Any intellectual achievement was regarded as a distraction and even a positive disability in the central ambition of matrimony, and of no value after the catch had been landed. Jane Harrison, the famous archaeologist and one of the earliest beneficiaries of the reforms in women's education, describes how as a little girl she was happily absorbed in a Greek grammar when a favourite aunt stripped the gilt off the gingerbread by remarking, "I do not see how Greek grammar is to help little Jane keep house when she has a home of her own".[5]

A girl forced to take up work as a governess not only did not know how to teach but did not know what to teach. In 1841, the Governesses Benevolent Institute was founded in Harley Street, "to afford assistance privately and delicately to ladies in temporary distress"; its main purpose was to help governesses in periods of unemployment. Soon pathetic case histories were being amassed from which it became clear that the status of governesses would not improve until they could command respect by their expertise. Some training for their work was essential. Yet the solution could not simply be a college for the training of governesses. The very essence of the problem was that the middle-class woman and her family could not be brought to anticipate the need to acquire teaching skills. A middle-class girl did not turn to teaching until it was forced on her. Instead it was recognised that education for all middle-class girls would have to be improved as an insurance against later distress.[6]

In 1848, a group of people assisted by some of the lecturers at King's College, London, and in particular by the Christian

Socialist F. D. Maurice, founded Queen's College, for the education of girls over twelve years, in day and evening classes. The College might more correctly have been described as a school than an institute providing tertiary education, since it took girls from an early age, and few of its students had more than the most elementary education on which to build. Nor was it in any way connected with the University of London, which at this time was an examining body rather than a corporate university. Though the academic future of Queen's was not so glamorous as that of Bedford (founded the following year as a non-denominational institution), or of the women's colleges of Oxford and Cambridge, important advances in girls' education can be traced directly to the work done by early students of the College, among them the famous Misses Beale and Buss.[7]

It is not enough, however, to attribute the reform of women's education to the recognition of economic needs and professional disabilities.[8] After all, if the demand by parents was simply that their daughters be drilled in drawing-room deportment, governesses would not have had to enrol for the relatively rigorous intellectual courses offered them by Queen's. In opposition to the deadening nineteenth-century view of women as helpless though adorable creatures of inferior mental and physical ability, a small group of writers, following the lead of Sydney Smith, believed that women shared a common humanity with men and should be allowed to realise their intellectual potential. Certain nonconformist groups questioned the contemporary treatment of women, and in Unitarian and Quaker families girls were often given an education and sometimes treated as the equals of their brothers.[9] Yet another school of thought stressed the rôle of women as wives and mothers and valued intellectual training above "accomplishments" for its importance in character development. This latter view, however, was widely different in its implications from the first, for within it were the seeds of the theory of "separate development"—that women should have disciplined study in certain "feminine" subjects, leaving men unchallenged in their traditional rôles as the leaders in public and professional life. Initially support was welcomed from anyone who believed that, for whatever reasons, women's brains could and should be trained, but the "separate development" school which blossomed so strongly in Cambridge in the 1880's and 1890's was a constant distraction to the main aim of the women's educationalists, which was to secure facilities for the highest intellectual development for women. It also provided a convenient smoke screen behind which the real opponents of women's advance could hide. More truly substantial support for women's education came, in the 40's and '50's, from the growing public concern for the quality of education given to both sexes and to all classes which manifested itself in Royal Commissions and schemes for reform.* The quality of teaching in elementary schools receiving Government aid was questioned and in 1846 the system of pupil teaching was introduced—a sort of five-year apprenticeship from the age of thirteen, followed by two years at a training college after a Queen's Scholarship had been gained. But attempts to open up the profession of elementary school teacher to middle-class women failed, since their basic education was so imperfect that none could attain the standard required for a Queen's Scholarship. Other schemes, such as getting women to work as genteel shop assistants, did not succeed because of their inability to add up. Clearly, the teaching of middle-class women was in need of a thorough-going reform.

Examinations were to play a major part in the advance of women's education, and it was in this connection that Cambridge University first became involved. These too, were part of a wider pattern of educational reform and in the 1850's examinations administered by the Royal College of Preceptors, the Royal Society of Arts as well as Oxford and Cambridge were opened to schoolboys. The women at Queen's College were subject to internal examinations and great stress was laid on training women in disciplined study, a feature so much lacking in women's education. As the improvements in education began to filter through into a few girls' schools, some mistresses felt the need for a public standard by which

* Royal Commission on Popular Education 1858; Clarendon Commission on the Public Schools 1861, Schools Inquiry Commission 1864.

to measure the progress of their pupils and as an encouragement to mental discipline. There was an unerring instinct for "quality" in these middle-class women despite their own economic position, which was often close to indigence. Only Oxford and Cambridge possessed the necessary degree of respectability, for educational institutions, like people, were judged in terms of breeding rather than current performance, and it was to these institutions that the women naturally looked for support. The idea that public examinations should be equally available to boys and girls was also popular among those of the women's education movement who were concerned with education as a yardstick by which the ability of women could be compared with that of men—and shown to be the same.

From the very outset of schemes for the education of women, two factions appeared: those for whom education was an end in itself, and those for whom it was a means to a particular end, proof of equality with men. This discord must later be considered in detail; at this point it can be said that despite the energy dissipated in the controversies between the two groups, both were essential to the rapid and successful development of the movement. While the "educationalists" kept before themselves the high ideals of academic excellence and mental development for all (middle-class) human beings, irrespective of sex, the "emancipationists" provided the dynamic for the rapid expansion of academic opportunities which were vital to the aims of both groups.

The leader of this latter group was Emily Davies, who was later to found Girton College. Daughter of a clergyman and sister of Llewelyn Davies, F. D. Maurice's close associate, she hid a stubborn and aggressive spirit behind a plain exterior, that of "a rather dim little person with mouse-coloured hair and conventional manners".[10] A student who knew her in her old age—she lived to be ninety-two—wrote that her appearance in later years suggested a fairy godmother rather than a lifelong fighter in the cause of women's rights in education and the Parliamentary vote.[11] If her appearance misled any of her acquaintances, they quickly learned their mistake. She was quite single-minded in her pursuit of the identity of educational opportunities for women and men, and bombarded her opponents and her more hesitant associates with consistent arguments devoid of the soft words and graceful compliments by which a Victorian lady was expected to soften her opponent's heart. Emily Davies bullied those around her with a ruthless logic so tartly expressed that it can surprise a reader even today. She was an opportunist, seizing each and every chance to promote the cause of women's education—but she was quick to see that women could only challenge men's intellectual dominance if they matched them at their own tests. The inflexibility of her views is understandable in the face of the demands for "separate development" which grew with the years and she saw all attempts to solve the special academic problems of women students—and there were many in the early days—as capitulation to the enemy. She had no knowledge of tact or compromise and caused as much if not more discomfort among her fellow workers as amongst her opponents. Yet her determination was of great value to the women's movement in its early years, and her single-mindedness can be readily appreciated in the face of the complex, unpredictable and sometimes devious behaviour of other workers in the field.

It was through a chance contact with Emily Davies that Elizabeth Garrett formed her vague aspirations into concrete plans to study medicine. Emily Davies stood by her side during the first ten difficult years, inspired her, fought and planned on her behalf and although Elizabeth Garrett was not able to acquire full medical qualification in Britain, her struggle won the cause many friends and paved the way for the admission of women to the medical profession. Emily Davies had gained valuable experience helping her protégé; above all she learnt that though a woman could, without too much difficulty, buy herself education of the highest quality, her chances of having her intellectual achievements attested were nil, and so, in consequence, were her chances of challenging the male monopoly of the professions and public life. Emily Davies was determined to alter this, and from the very beginning it was her organising ability which played such an important part in the opening of the Cambridge Local Examinations, the predecessors of today's 'O' and 'A' level, to schoolgirls.

Many of the men and women who were concerned with the advancement of female education had made each other's acquaintance at the meetings of the National Association for the Promotion of Social Science (N.A.P.S.S.). This movement, founded in 1857 and modelled on the British Association but with a rather more radical outlook, had from the first allowed women to become members. It proved to be a great platform from which women and their friends could address the sort of people who would be inclined to assist them in furthering their cause. It also provided women with immensely valuable experience in the arts of organisation, writing papers in a clear and convincing style and, for the very brave, addressing and debating with mixed audiences. The success of the examinations run by the two universities, Oxford and Cambridge, for upper and middle-class boys since 1858, led some members of the N.A.P.S.S. to the view that they ought to be extended for use by girls. The task of organising this minor revolution was left to Emily Davies.

In the summer of 1862, Emily Davies made informal inquiries in both universities regarding the position and attitude of the authorities towards examining girls. From Oxford she heard that the University had given the Local Examination Delegacy authority only in respect of boys. It was not competent to examine girls and in the opinion of Miss Davies' correspondent, John Griffith, there was no point in asking it to bend its rules, since he believed "that the University would think the examination of young ladies a matter altogether beyond its sphere of duty". Having thus delicately but no doubt accurately expressed the University's attitude towards the somewhat improper suggestion that it should concern itself with the education of females, Griffiths himself gave Miss Davies a little encouragement by suggesting that she might canvass the support of Dr Temple of Rugby, who had originated the movement for examinations for boys of the middle-class.[12]

The reply which Emily Davies received from Cambridge was much more hopeful.[13] Her correspondent there was G. D. Liveing, a man who throughout his long life remained a strong supporter of the women's education movement. He offered his services as presenter of the women's case to the Local Examination Syndicate, the body of University men responsible for running the examinations. At first he had believed that girls could apply to be examined in the normal way without any special case being made out for them, but later a careful examination of the regulations he concluded that this was not the case and that the consent of the Senate, the University's government, would be required. The Cambridge examinations, like those of Oxford, were not held at the University, but in centres all over the country, and administered by local committees. One of the strongest objections to the examinations of girls was the indelicacy of bringing them together at all—girls whose families were not acquainted with each other—entrusting them to the authority of persons other than their parents and making them the centre of public interest. Since it was the local committees who would bear the heavy and novel responsibility of conducting the examinations for these middle-class girls, Liveing wisely advised Emily Davies to sound their opinions and, if possible, secure their support. Liveing also suggested that the well-established method of pleading one's case at the universities—the carefully-phrased and well-supported petition, or Memorial, as it was known, should be used to bring the women's request to the attention of the Senate.

Emily Davies acted on the advice of both her correspondents. Her approach to Dr Temple was not very successful; he wavered in his opinion, being convinced that girls should have "privacy and modesty" and would be harmed by competition. He did, however, suggest that girls' *schools* might be examined, thus reducing the attention given to individual students, adding the proviso that such examinations should not, of course, be carried out by "unmarried University men".[14]

In drawing up the Memorial for Cambridge and sounding the opinions of the Local Examination centres, Miss Davies was involved in labour scarcely imaginable in these days of telephones, dictaphones and typewriters. She wrote letters by the score, personal letters, not stereotyped circulars, demanding information or begging support. Such a flow of correspondence characterised every step of the women's struggle for academic recognition. Her own outlook was ambivalent: she was the embodiment of middle-class propriety and refinement, a reactionary, one of the last to accept any relaxation in the codes of conduct which surrounded the behaviour of middle-class women. Yet there was one unexpected streak in her make-up, one area in which she was a radical. She was not exceptional in condemning the frivolous, husband-catching behaviour which, with the encouragement of their mothers, was indulged in by some girls. What marked her out was her belief that a girl's mind ought not to be made subordinate to the demands of her family in general, and some man in particular. Though every propriety was to be closely guarded, even strengthened, there was no reason why a woman's intellect should not be encouraged to grow, equal and even outstrip that of a man. Her creed was to be perfectly expressed in the college which she founded: residential, thus taking the girls away from the distraction and petty demands of their homes, intellectually as demanding as any man's college, yet physically as far removed from the life of the University as possible. This paradox of vision and conventionality runs through all her letters; her persistence in pleading her cause in the most unenlightened quarters is impressive, though this was in part due to her inability to recognise that others could genuinely hold views differing from her own.

In 1863 her task was to produce evidence that examinations for girls could be organised without causing any offence and that the Local Examination centres were willing to undertake the task. The Royal Society of Arts (R.S.A.) had for some years been running examinations for both boys and girls and they told Miss Davies that they had encountered no difficulties in organising their examinations. However, the R.S.A. examinees were not of the same social calibre as the students whom Miss Davies had in mind and their experience was hardly relevant. She well appreciated the reservations which were expressed about girls having to travel thirty or forty miles to an examination centre. Her plea was simply that girls whose parents were prepared to make the necessary arrangements to get them to a centre "should not be arbitrarily shut out from the examinations merely on the grounds of sex".[15] Again, when it was objected that "it would never do" to examine boys and girls "of that rank" together, her answer was to place the responsibility for considerations of rank on the parents. "No girl can be examined without the consent of her parents, and they might surely be trusted to take all reasonable care of their daughters in these respects."[16]

The replies from the centres were mixed; the most significant were from London and Liverpool. The latter was strongly opposed to any suggestion that girls and boys should be allowed to take the same examinations, since this would ruin their status in the eyes of the boy candidates; the Cambridge-London centre, whose secretary, H. R. Tomkinson, was a member of the N.A.P.S.S. and who co-operated in many of Emily Davies' later schemes, returned an encouraging reply and could see no objection to examining girls, though he too recognised that this would require careful organisation. A trial run was said to have been helpful in securing the establishment of Local Examinations for boys at Oxford and Emily Davies and her associates believed that such a trial could be used to demonstrate that the problems of organising an examination for girls were not insurmountable. However, the London Committee for the Oxford Local Examination was rather hostile to any suggestion of examining girls and so, as the plan evolved, it seemed more probable that a trial run would take place in connection with Cambridge through its London centre, though Miss Davies still hoped to catch the attention of both universities.

In June 1863 friends of the cause invited her to Cambridge where she learnt that, though the trial examination might be permitted to take place privately, there were grave doubts that the Senate would then consent to the formal opening of the Local Examinations to girls; indeed, there was still quite a lot of opposition to the organisation of such examinations for boys. In the same month, Mr Tomkinson applied to the Cambridge Local Examination Syndicate for permission to use their examination papers for girls and requested that their scripts be marked by the appointed examiners. The Syndicate could see no objection in principle to the examination of girls, but were concerned that the examiners would be overburdened with scripts. The boys must be given priority—perhaps the girls could have different examiners?[17] Fortunately this suggestion was withdrawn, as no doubt Emily Davies would have refused to accept separate examiners for girls and the story of women's education in Cambridge would have taken a different turning.

The Syndicate's final decision was that examiners were to be asked to mark the girls' papers in a private capacity and had to be approached individually: Emily Davies won their support and reported that they were sending her "delightfully kind letters".[18] By the time all the necessary permissions had been granted only six weeks remained before the examination in which to find and prepare candidates. The organisers of the scheme circularised the better girls' schools and thought they would be satisfied if perhaps half a dozen girls came forward. Instead, they found they had eighty-three candidates from such schools as the North London Collegiate, Queen's and Bedford, Sydenham College and the Chantry School, near Frome. The girls were entered for a wide range of subjects and in both higher and lower age groups. The examinees acquitted themselves well in the circumstances and were found on average equal to the boys in all subjects, except arithmetic. The quality of instruction in the subject benefitted greatly from this unpleasant revelation and within two or three years it was not possible to detect any inferiority in the average arithmetic results of the girl candidates. In writing a report on the examination,[19] Emily Davies made great play of the fact that an external examination had revealed both good and bad points in girls' education and that the examiners' reports were of great value to the teachers. Nor did she miss the opportunity to point to something else which was lacking in the education of women:

> In order to secure that the less showy branches of education shall receive their due share of time and attention, it seems to be necessary that the teachers be sustained by some external agency, which shall at once test and attest the soundness of their work.[20]

Her report was read and discussed at the meeting of the Social Science Association on Friday, 29th April, 1864, and in general, the members were highly pleased with the success of the experiment. Yet even among this group, some doubts were raised as to the suitability of the subjects set for examination. Two speakers declared that the mental organisation of the sexes was totally different. Women should be taught, and well taught, music and needlework, but should not be encouraged to "fly after chemistry, political economy and other things of that kind, but first of all to adhere to those things which are suitable to the female brain—and female life. . . . That education is best for a woman which fits her to become a friend and a companion, a mother and also a nurse."[21] Such sentiments only stiffened Emily Davies' determination to allow no difference of treatment in the education and examination of men and women. Other speakers could see no evidence for the suggested mental difference between the sexes and ridiculed the view that if girls were encouraged to use their brains, the excitement would bring on insanity. On the contrary, an improvement in mental and physical health might be expected, and a member from north of the border pointed out that girls there were admitted to public examinations as a matter of course and that there was no suggestion that Scottish girls were unsexed on this account. Mr Tomkinson, who had supervised the arrangements, testified that the examinations had been conducted with great propriety and privacy and that the girls themselves had been excellent examinees.

The meeting agreed to join in a petition to Cambridge University for the formal opening of the Local Examinations to girls. When presented to the University the following October, it contained over 1,200 signatures of people concerned in the education of girls. The petition was supported by several influential University men, notably Dr Liveing, Mr Markby and Professor Fawcett, and the following month, the Council of the Senate appointed a Syndicate, a special committee of University men, to investigate the request. The following February they reported that they saw no objection to the extension of the Local Examination scheme to girl candidates for a three year trial period. The girls were to be cared for by special Committees of Ladies attached to the Local Examination centres and examined in different rooms from the boys. No names or class list of successful candidates were to be published. The Syndicate also specifically dismissed a suggestion which was to be made repeatedly in the early years of the movement, that women should be offered examinations in subjects considered specially suitable for the female intellect and at the same time should be excluded from examinations in others. Emily Davies was from the first firm in her opposition, and pointed out that it was illogical not to allow girls to enter for Greek or Higher Mathematics, even though there might be very few candidates for these examinations. As for introducing special "girls' subjects" she complained,

> I'm afraid that if we began with alterations in the scheme, we should be in a sea of difficulties. Almost every individual that I meet has a different theory about what is 'apposite to the female mind' and to reconcile them all would be quite impossible. . . . My strongest objection is that the girls' certificates would not—in the present state of opinion— *could not* have the same value.[22]

It was this latter point which weighed most heavily with Emily Davies throughout her struggle to gain entry for women to the highest levels of educational attainment and it set her on a collision course with those who were more concerned with the academic content of women's education. But this early acceptance by Cambridge of her viewpoint was important in establishing the seriousness of the venture in the public eye.

As was customary in Cambridge, a date was appointed for the discussion of the report in the Arts' School by members of the University. After the Syndicate had reconsidered the report it was to be voted on by all registered M.A.s who were able and willing to attend in Cambridge on the given day. Usually the debate on a report was not confined to the meeting in the Arts' School; University men circulated their opinions in flysheets and interested outsiders lobbied the voters. In this case, however, there does not seem to have been much controversy, though one strongly worded objection was received from the Liverpool Local Examination Committee. They opposed the admission of girls on a variety of grounds, but the main purport of their argument was that it would bring the examinations into ridicule, so that they would be shunned by the best boy candidates. By opening the examinations to women, the University was implicitly approving the identity of education for boys and girls, and boys could be expected to prefer Oxford to such an "emasculated institution"—an idea which was to crop up again in later years. On the day of the discussion, several points were raised in favour of the report. It was said that the examinations were good for girls because they needed some stimulus which would bring their critical faculties and judgement into play. Robert Potts, who was Emily Davies' chief correspondent in Cambridge at that time, replied to objections that there was no need for examinations for "that class of girls", pointing out that "that class of girls" requiring the examinations would probably become teachers and therefore the examinations were most valuable. The University should not be afraid of losing its dignity by organising girls' examinations; instead he urged it to step forward as the leader of female education. Although not much opposition had been expressed during the discussion, supporters of the scheme feared that the country clergy would be organised to come up to Cambridge to vote against the measure. In the event, the voting was very close, fifty-five to fifty-one in favour of the examinations for women, but the measure had not really aroused much interest or passion. The scheme was reviewed in 1867, and made permanent.

Meanwhile at Oxford, the women's prospects rose and fell by turns. Emily Davies was faced with the University's complicated administration, an effective defence against intruders such as she. Her letters show that she was anxious to make a "correct" approach to the University, to be sure that requests were laid before bodies in the proper order of precedence, and that officials were given their proper titles. All this care was, however, to no avail. The Examination Delegacy were prepared to consider similar but not identical examinations for girls, a proposal which Emily Davies could never have accepted.[23] Griffiths, the Secretary of the Examination Delegacy, was more hopeful and encouraged Miss Davies to make a formal approach to the Vice-Chancellor. The time was ripe for such a move, since the Statutes governing the examinations were due to be renewed, but despite Emily Davies' efforts to raise support amongst Oxford men, the proposed admission of girls to examinations was firmly rejected by the Council barely a fortnight after the favourable Cambridge result. They were said to have been strongly influenced by the opposition expressed by the Liverpool Committee and were prepared to let Cambridge take the risk of such a novel experiment, no doubt believing that in view of the Cambridge decision boys would now turn to the Oxford examinations.*

Thus it was that Cambridge stepped forward as the enlightened leader of educational advance for women, not in any deliberate way, but with a degree of tolerance and willingness to experiment which Oxford could not match. Emily Davies' approach had coincided with a movement for educational renewal among a small but energetic group of young Cambridge dons; for the most part, University men were indifferent to the matter of female education, as the size of the vote reveals. Even the opposition did not perceive any real threat to the privileged position of men. They were patronising and jocular; this new feminine whim amused or irritated them according to the state of their digestions. A few women would spoil themselves, but there would be plenty who were prepared to remain empty-headed and docile, permanent proof of the superior brain-power of their menfolk. Education-seeking women could be ignored, dismissed by the epithet of Adam Sedgwick, the renowned Professor of Geology who, hearing of the success of their petition, described them with a growl as "nasty forward Minxes!".[24]

---

* See above, p. ▓.▓▓. The Oxford Local Examinations were opened to girls in 1879.

3

THE SCHOOLS INQUIRY COMMISSION AND PLANS FOR A COLLEGE FOR WOMEN

WITH THE OPENING of Cambridge Local Examinations to girls seventeen years after the foundation of Queen's College in London, official recognition of female secondary education was made by one of the two ancient universities. But the movement was to receive even greater acknowledgement that year when by the courageous persistence of Emily Davies and her friends, girls' schools were included in the terms of reference of the Royal Commission on Secondary Education[1] (usually referred to as the Schools Inquiry Commission) which was concerned chiefly to examine those schools for boys of the middle class which had escaped scrutiny in the earlier Commissions on Popular Education (1858) and Public Schools (1861). The first of these had dealt mainly with the education of the lower classes and neither specifically included nor excluded the education of girls in its terms of reference. The Commission was remarkable in that, for the first time, women were invited to give expert or professional advice in answer to a written circular, though none of them was examined *viva voce*. The twelve female witnesses were questioned because of their activities in running elementary ragged or charity schools, rather than for any special interest which they had in girls' education, and though one witness, Barbara Leigh Smith (Madame Bodichon), took the opportunity to deliver a tirade against the inferior legal and social position of women, the remainder seemed to agree that girls need only be educated to their subordinate positions as sisters, daughters, wives and mothers.

Emily Davies was determined that the opportunity presented by the inquiry into middle-class education should be fully exploited for the benefit of girls. Revelations of the horrible

36

inefficiency of most existing girls' schools could only, she reasoned, help her campaign, and she was also anxious to have the question of charitable endowments publicly examined. Some charitable foundations were spending their income primarily or entirely on boys' education in opposition to the letter or spirit of the founders' intentions. But it was by no means clear that girls' education was to be considered by the Commissioners; their terms of reference were vague, but it seemed unlikely that time could be spent investigating the education of young ladies. Fresh from her experience of canvassing supporters for Elizabeth Garrett's unsuccessful approach to London University, Emily Davies began again to collect a suitable list of names on her petition to the Royal Commissioners. Her Memorial, which asked the Commissioners to consider the state of middle-class education for girls and possible measures for improving it, was successful, though not without a great deal of back-stage manoeuvring. The Commissioners agreed that though their chief duty was to investigate the education of middle-class boys, a little time could be spent on girls.

Fortunately, several of the investigators were converts to Miss Davies' cause and they did a magnificent job in revealing the low standards existing in the majority of girls' secondary schools. One of the most perceptive Commissioners, James Bryce, wrote in despair:[2]

Although the world has now existed for several thousand years, the notion that women have minds as cultivable and as well worth cultivating as men's minds is still regarded by the ordinary British parent as an offensive, not to say revolutionary paradox.

In their report the Commission described the evidence of parental indifference to girls' education as "abundant and consentaneous". "There is a long-established and inveterate prejudice, though it may not often be distinctly expressed, that girls are less capable of mental cultivation and less in need of it than boys; that accomplishments and what is showy and superficially attractive, are what is really essential for them and, in particular, that as regards their relations to the other sex and the probabilities of marriage, more solid attainments are actually disadvantageous rather than the reverse." Boys are educated for the world, girls for the drawing room. Any academic knowledge which it is felt they should have, is imparted by teachers who simply are not competent for their work. For this, Bryce blamed the "want of any institution for supplying a high education to women" or for training them as teachers. Schoolmistresses lived in isolation from each other and from new ideas. Teaching was rarely a freely chosen profession for women; too often it was a necessity to be dropped as soon as possible. Another Commissioner, J. G. Fitch, judged that only 6 or 7 % of governesses deliberately planned to take up the work:

> Schools are started by a widow or two sisters who think schoolkeeping a shade more genteel than millinery. . . . For five or six years the school goes on, the girls learning nothing from a teacher, who is only fit to ask questions out of Blair's catechism. . . . Then the schoolmistress marries or goes to keep house for a brother; the school disappears, and another one like unto it arises in its stead.[3]

But Bryce laid the greatest blame at the door of the parents,

> The thing most needed is to get rid of that singular theory o girls' education by which parents are at present governed— to make them believe that a girl has an intellect just as much as a boy, that it was meant to be used and improved and that it is not to refinement and modesty that a cultivated intelligence is opposed, but to vapidity and languor and vulgarity of mind, to the love of gossip and the love of dress.[4]

The report of the Commission echoed the points so strongly brought out by Bryce. "It cannot be denied that the picture brought before us of the state of Middle Class Female Education is one the whole unfavourable. . . . Want of thoroughness and foundation; want of system; slovenliness and showy superficiality; inattention to rudiments; undue time given to accomplishments and those not taught thoroughly or in any scientific manner; want of organisation." In the opinion o^f the Commission "there is weighty evidence to the effect that the essential capacity for learning is the same, or nearly the same, in the two sexes". Parents must be encouraged to regard the education of their daughters as worth-while and women must be offered the opportunity to stretch themselves intellectually. They specially commended the attempts at higher education carried on at Queen's and Bedford, the advanced classes for girls run in Oxford,* the new examination schemes and the plan of Miss Emily Davies to organise a college for women which would give them the equivalent of a university education. The Commission recommended that girls' schools, modelled on the lines of Miss Buss's North London Collegiate should be established in every town of four thousand inhabitants or over. The curriculum should include arithmetic and perhaps further mathematics and Latin. In the reallocation of endowments which was considered by a Government enquiry of 1869, it was accepted that girls' schools should receive some share.[5] The watchword of the new order was that the mother's education was possibly of greater importance to a family than that of the father.

Following the report, great advances were made in the field of secondary education for girls. In 1870 Miss Maria Grey founded the Women's Education Union and two years later the first schools of the Girls Public Day School Company (later Trust) were opened. By 1890, there were thirty-four such schools. Other schemes involved Church schools and in many towns local day or "High" schools were founded. The preparation of girls for public examinations became common-place and the curriculum generally followed that of the best boys' schools. Though there was some tendency for the women to ape the attitudes and priorities set by the boys' schools, especially in their enthusiasm for competitive games and *esprit de corps*, this has some explanation beyond the search for

---

* An experiment started by Mark Pattison which seems to have failed through lack of support and financial difficulties. Half a dozen University men were involved in the scheme; over half the students were from University families. (See his evidence to the Commissioners Q 17,823.)

equality with men. In their mania for tennis and hockey, the girls were not so much comparing themselves with boys as contrasting themselves with their grandmothers, whose attacks of the vapours had often been the result of tight corseting and inadequate exercise. Young women revelled in their new-found health and freedom. In the matter of curriculum the women were concerned to take the men's advice. The fountainheads of academic excellence were the great universities of Oxford and Cambridge. Though in need of reform in matters of detail, the academic standards which they set were supreme. The curriculum of the public schools was a prelude to that of the universities and not surprisingly the girls' schools took their standards from them. Logically, no University man could advise them otherwise, if they interpreted the word "education" in the same way for both sexes.[6] Further, Oxford and especially Cambridge were the major sources of teachers for these reformed girls' schools, and schoolmistresses were naturally anxious to send their best students to their old colleges. Then as today, the universities influenced the course of secondary education for a vast number of children, only a few of whom were to see inside their walls.

As well as giving evidence in person to the Schools Inquiry Commission, Emily Davies had sent the Commissioners in July 1867, a memorandum on the "Need for a Place of Higher Education for Girls". The absence of a "public institution for women analogous to the Universities for men" was regretted and it was requested that in any recommendations concerning school endowments or other charities which the Commission intended to make, that the need for such an institution should not be overlooked. Strictly speaking, the matter lay beyond the Commissioners' brief, but as Emily Davies had already in hand a scheme for a college for women up to university standard, the publicity was no doubt valuable. Late in 1866, she had circulated a programme for a College for Women and in her letters at this time, she wrote optimistically of raising £30,000 and employing Waterhouse, the architect of the Manchester Assize Court "with its gardens and grounds and everything that is good for body, soul and spirit",[7] to design the college buildings.

Emily Davies' plans to gain university education for women coincided with a reform movement within the universities themselves and in part explains the interest taken by some young dons in the women's education movement and the foundation of two women's colleges in Cambridge instead of one. There existed at this time a group of University men passionately concerned about the quality of education given at the universities and the way in which these ancient foundations exercised their authority over the whole spectrum of education for children and adults. Their concern was justified; on many counts the universities were failing in what was held to be their responsibilities. Singled out for special criticism was the low standard of the Ordinary Degree, the excessive emphasis placed on the study of Latin and Greek to the detriment of modern languages, science and social science, and the exclusiveness entailed by association with the Established Church.[8] Reform at Oxford and Cambridge has never been easy to effect, but several university men saw in Emily Davies' plans a possible vehicle for their own pedagogic ideas. Here was something which they could mould from the start; both the college and the schools from which the students might come could be an ideal testing ground for their theories. They discovered, however, that Emily Davies was not to be so easily manipulated—*her* college was not to be a laboratory for educational experiment.

The circular of 1866 was not her first attempt to organise higher education for women. As early as 1862, Emily Davies had formed a committee to press for the admission of women to universities, following the unsuccessful attempts of Elizabeth Garrett to matriculate at London University as a first step towards sitting for a medical degree. Legal opinion had been consulted in 1856 when Miss Jessie Merton White had asked leave to matriculate, and in considering Elizabeth Garrett's request, the Senate confirmed "that it saw no reason to doubt the validity of Counsel's opinion in (that) case", which was that under the existing University Charter the Senate had no power to admit women. However, London University was about to receive a new charter, and Emily Davies rapidly set in motion a campaign to have women's right to its examinations and membership included in the new articles. It was decided to press in the most general way for admission to degrees without singling out the controversial subject of medicine. Emphasis was given to the need to improve the quality of female education in general, the issue of professional qualification being kept in the background.[9] Despite an impressive list of supporters, the clause admitting women to degrees was defeated by one vote in the Senate. In 1866 London was again asked to permit women to matriculate. The reply was to offer an examination specially adapted for women, an offer which Emily Davies and her committee firmly rejected.

Forming yet another committee of carefully selected "names", Emily Davies set about implementing the plan for a women's college which she had outlined in her programme of 1866. She lacked tact, but was skilled in tactics, and knew exactly whose support should be canvassed and whose rejected in order to give her schemes an aura of solid respectability and allay the fears of those who hesitated to champion so revolutionary a move. The patronage of known feminists was kept to a minimum, nor could the names of people of doubtful reputation, such as George Eliot, be accepted. When a supporting committee of dons was formed in Cambridge Emily Davies expressed fears about their youthfulness:

> If we could get a few more old ladies like Lady Stanley of Alderley, who has six grown-up daughters and a multitude of grandchildren, they might counterbalance the levity of young Cambridge.[10]

The most daring factor in the scheme, and the one which had to be promoted with the utmost care and delicacy, was not that young women would be given the opportunity of advanced learning, but that they would do it in a college, away from their homes and families. Though many girls of secondary school age had been sent away to boarding schools, the idea of having young women of marriageable age away from home was novel and somewhat shocking. At a meeting in April 1867 of the Committee which had worked for the opening of the Cambridge Local Examinations, there was criticism of the plan to take girls away from their homes to study. Bolder spirits suggested mischievously that the really weak point in the scheme was that girls would want to come to college and would not want to go home. Two male supporters, Mr Clay and Mr Tomkinson embarrassed Emily Davies by their enthusiasm for a residential college. It was to be a paradise— "they insisted that the girls should have breakfast in their own rooms (instead of all together like a school) as if the whole thing depended on it".[11]

After a conference held the following year to discuss the college proposals and attended by over two hundred people, a participant reported that *the* objection had been that girls would be taken away from home. However J. R. Seeley, a great power in the reform of the teaching standards of Cambridge, maintained that while it often happened that boys had "too little home", girls had "too much". In any case, they would only be away for half the year, though in his view, it was important to situate the college in the country where they would have greater privacy and freedom than was possible in a town.[12] His opinion was firmly shared by Emily Davies, but as she had suspected, the delicacy of the situation was not appreciated by the young dons in Cambridge, who pressed her to locate her college in the city.

Despite her determined and somewhat aggressive nature, Emily Davies was extremely conservative in matters of propriety, and it must be remembered that Cambridge at this time numbered very few women in its academic community. Only Professors and Heads of Colleges were free to marry; the colleges were monastic communities and until 1882 when the rule was changed, a man had to resign his fellowship on marriage. A man might easily spend his undergraduate years speaking to no other women than his bedmaker, and any young woman found in college precincts was likely to be arrested by the Proctors, who were very nervous about the possibility of prostitution. For these reasons, while quite openly declaring that the model for her institution was no less than Trinity College,* Emily Davies insisted that the girls should

* See quotation from N.A.P.S.S. meeting p. ▮.▮1.

be housed at a distance from Cambridge. In addition, she was not certain which University, London or Cambridge, was the most willing to forward her schemes, and in choosing a house at Hitchin, about half way on the railway line between London and Cambridge, she no doubt felt she had the best of both worlds.

The location of the College was not the only matter on which she crossed swords with the Cambridge Committee. At least one of its members, Henry Sidgwick, opposed her on two counts. Sidgwick was by this time involved in religious doubts which led him, in 1869, to renounce his fellowship and to fight the prescription that all who took College Fellowships should subscribe to the Thirty-Nine Articles of the Church of England. Since he was prepared personally to sacrifice so much to bring freedom of conscience to the Cambridge colleges, it is hardly surprising that he refused to support any formal subscription to the tenets of the Church of England in the new college for women, as the London Committee had planned. His second quarrel was with the decision by Emily Davies and her London Committee to encourage girls to enter for the Cambridge Ordinary or "Poll" degree. On the face of it, the plan seemed quite reasonable, since the degree was of a supposedly general nature and of a considerably lower standard than the Honours degree; in fact it seemed quite a suitable goal for girls who would come to college with very little educational grounding. But Sidgwick was beginning a campaign, which he carried on throughout the century, against the poverty of the Poll degree and also the Previous Examination, which was compulsory for all degree candidates, and which involved them all in an examination of Greek and Latin.* The standard required in the Classical languages was very low, but nonetheless some knowledge of both of them was an essential prerequisite for a Cambridge degree. Not only did Sidgwick object to the low standard of knowledge required in the examination, which made a mockery of the exercise, but

* The Poll degree was often referred to as the General, the Pass, or the Ordinary; the common name for the Previous Examination was the Little-Go. See Appendices A and B for a fuller explanation of these examinations.

he also dissented from the prevalent view that a classical education was the only one of any real worth. He, and others like him, saw that schools must make a place for mathematics, science and modern languages in their curricula and that the University's insistence on Latin and Greek for all degrees positively discouraged schools from developing other subjects. Instead of leading educational advance, the University was hindering it. A Classical scholar himself, Sidgwick did not seek to eliminate the study of Greek and Latin from the schools nor the University; but at least for those students whose bent was scientific, he felt the substitution of French and German for Greek would be of greater value. He knew he would have a difficult task persuading the University and schools of his viewpoint; but in the new girls' schools, there was no existing tradition of Classical scholarship and Sidgwick was determined that nothing should force them into this outdated mould.

James Bryce, who had worked so diligently to reveal the inadequacies of girls' schools to the members of the S.I.C., engaged in a lengthy correspondence with Emily Davies on examinations. He was a man with wide experience in the educational field and acutely aware of the faults in university education. Though sympathetic towards Emily Davies' demands for the authoritative testing of women's intellectual attainments, he condemned the Pass degrees of both Oxford and Cambridge as "very bad . . . little better than a farce . . . and quite unworthy of a University".[13] He cautioned Emily Davies against making teaching subordinate to examinations.[14] "In reality the University degrees are to a great extent a gross imposture . . . the one thing both girls and boys want is teaching of the highest and most stimulating kind rather than certificates and degrees."[15] He discussed the point with Henry Sidgwick who agreed that the standard of the Poll degree was too low to be of any value and that of the Honours degree too high, not too high for the natural abilities of girls, but too high for the training which they could receive in any school at that time or were likely to receive for several years to come.[16] But Emily Davies was unmoved by such suggestions and accused them of wanting separate systems of education for

45

boys and girls. Bryce replied that he and his friends thought it a pity to load a new institution at the outset with "the very vices whose existence they opposed in the old one". He realised however, that she was not to be convinced, and was not without admiration for her strength of mind, for he concluded the debate with the comment, "very likely you are right and we (Henry Sidgwick and I) are wrong".[17]

Religious affiliation was another stumbling block in the plans to found a new college. Emily Davies' own position was much more liberal than some of her opponents chose to believe, but she had constantly before her the problem of raising money for her new college as well as securing sound moral support from the "right" people. And the right people socially were, inevitably, members of the Established Church. By promising to exclude religious instruction and practices from the College, Emily Davies could have attracted radical support, but at the expense of all the rest.[18] Instead, at a time when there was a movement towards separating the schools and universities from their official connections with the Church of England, she chose to stand against the tide. In her circular on the proposed college, she stated that religious instruction would be given and services held according to the principles of the Church of England, but students could be excused these where conscientious objections were entertained. In this matter of religious affiliation she was, however, less sure of her ground and more open to suggestion. On the advice of James Bryce, she altered the text to read that attendance at religious instruction and services would not be obligatory, wording which was held to be more liberal and less condescending.[19]

In allying her college to the Church of England, Emily Davies believed she was acting realistically; personally she was a little uncomfortable with the arrangement and felt the less said about it the better.[20] She had a clear appreciation of the destructive power of religious controversy and this was an added reason for committing her college firmly in one direction. She insisted that the clause on religious instruction and services be incorporated in the trust deed of the college where it could not be changed without considerable difficulty. She felt bound by the promises she had made to supporters of her scheme and explained:

> I should like the matter to be considered *settled* for the moment. If it were known that the members of the college *could* make a change at any moment, some restless person might feel it his duty to be continually proposing it and we should be in constant hot water.[21]

It is difficult to judge just how significant the Church of England allegiance was in the dispute between Emily Davies and Henry Sidgwick—it was one of many areas in which they held different views. Girton may well have had (and still have) a more religious tone than Newnham (it has, for example, a college chapel which Newnham has not) but it was no less liberal in religious matters. Girton accepted two Quakers among its first five students and Newnham from the first insisted on recording the place of worship a student would regularly attend and permission was to be sought before the student could go elsewhere.

Following Oxford's failure to open its Local Examinations to girls, Emily Davies dismissed that University as a possible promoter of female education. Cambridge seemed to hold out the best promise of support and while the college was to be situated in "a healthy locality between London and Cambridge, thus putting it within reach of the best teaching in all subjects of the College course", application was to be made specifically "to the University of Cambridge to hold examinations at the College in the subjects prescribed for the Ordinary Degree". Sidgwick was critical of this decision, urging that ultimately women were likely to get at least as much help from Oxford as from Cambridge and recommended the siting of the college at Bletchley. In any case, what reason had she to suppose that Cambridge would recognise the college and agree to examine its students?—Cambridge people did not in the least expect it.[22] If Sidgwick thought he had made a telling point, Emily Davies was not in the least disturbed. In 1868 at a N.A.P.S.S. meeting, she was even more specific about her intentions for the college:

It is an essential feature of the institution that it will be, as far as possible, officially connected with the University of Cambridge. It is not proposed to set up a new female University standing on its own basis exclusively and under-taking to confer degrees by its own authority. The College is intended to be a dependency, a living branch of Cambridge. It will aim at no higher a position than, say, that of Trinity College. That the University will adopt the daughter, cannot, as yet be positively asserted, but past experience gives good ground for hope.[23]

Again and again during the months of planning and preparation, Emily Davies returned in her correspondence to the proposed relationship of her college with Cambridge University. There was, however, a perceptible shift in her attitude; in her circular of 1866 Emily Davies talked of applying to Cambridge for use of their degree examinations and described her college as holding a position "analogous to that occupied by the Universities towards the public schools for boys". By 1869 she regarded the college "simply as a measure of University extension" and the exclusion of women from education and examinations and attestation an "unfor-tunate accident" on the part of the University which she and her colleagues proposed to remedy. It would be necessary at first for the college to undertake the education of its women students, but this would be done under the same conditions of syllabus and residence as the University exacted from its members. As she commented to Tomkinson "this may be a wrong idea, but it is at any rate clear and intelligible and one deliberately adopted at starting".[24] *The Times* correspondent, commenting on the N.A.P.S.S. paper of 1868 was certain that the idea was wrong; collegiate life was desirable for men because it fostered independence and boldness and "it was a singularly good rehearsal for their future life in the world", a world of perpetual competition with other men. The life of most women would be quite the reverse; their duty was at home tending their families—their very virtue was dependence. Feminine virtues could only be learnt at home and it was therefore especially unsuitable to take girls away from their homes at the time when they should be preparing for marriage. He conceded that there might be exceptional cases in which college education could be serviceable but

> . . . anything would be mischievous which tended to place the standard of female education in intellectual excellence, in mutual competition and in any kind of public exhibition. That education will always be the best for girls which is the most domestic, and English homes will always be the schools in which English wives and mothers can best be trained.[25]

Emily Davies had reasoned that it was not good for future generations to demand of wives and mothers nothing more than complete absorption with petty cares and "good sound ignorance". Even as mistresses of households, their work suffered from want of discipline and knowledge acquired in their youth, and few reasonable men could complain if steps were taken to remedy such deficiencies. However, home was a most unsuitable classroom and an impossible base from which to challenge the intellectual dominance of men. As Emily Davies shrewdly appreciated, such a struggle could only take place within the walls of a University.

4

THE FOUNDATION OF THE CAMBRIDGE COLLEGES FOR WOMEN

HENRY SIDGWICK'S RIFT with Emily Davies widened when he began to take an interest in the activities of another group of women educationalists—the North of England Council for Promoting the Higher Education of Women—and to help them secure from Cambridge University an examination especially planned for them.

The enthusiasm for women's education had not been confined to the south of England. In the north, activity revolved around the figure of Anne Jemima Clough, though she herself would have been the first to remark on the quality and quantity of her helpers. Born in Liverpool in 1820, there seemed little in her background to indicate the important rôle she was to play in the development of higher education for women. She was the sister of Arthur Hugh Clough, the poet, and, like Emily Davies, it was through her brother that Miss Clough was brought into contact with the London circle of men and women who were dedicated to the improvement of the lot of women. Until she was sixteen she lived in Charleston, South Carolina, and when her family returned to England, she occupied herself teaching at the Local Welsh National school in Liverpool, where her father was a cotton merchant, and instructing older girls at her family house. In 1849 she went to the Borough Road School, Middlesex for a few months, to study the theory and practice of teaching, and at this time met many of the women's education activists. After her father's death, she moved with her mother to Ambleside, and formed a school there. Yet she remained constantly dissatisfied with her own teaching methods and what she regarded as her low academic ability.[1] She was aware of her own intellectual potential and even more so that of other, younger women, and knew that it must remain underdeveloped and wasted until they could be trained to use their minds. Arthur Hugh Clough died in 1861, and the following year Anne Clough moved down to London to live with her sister-in-law. In this house, she was surrounded by the intellectuals and educationalists of the day. She was in London throughout the agitation for Elizabeth Garrett's admission to London University, the opening of Local Examinations to girls, the Memorial to the Schools Inquiry Commission and the early days of Emily Davies' plan to found a college for women.

Her own ideas for the practical improvement of girls' schools were taking shape and she submitted to the Commissioners a memorandum "Hints on the Organisation of Girls' Schools" which was later substantially reproduced in *Macmillan's Magazine*. Her scheme involved senior girls from every school in a town coming together for special lectures and classes given by qualified lecturers.[2] By this means, one of the major weaknesses of girls' schools—their small size and therefore lack of specialist teachers—could be overcome. Since it was assumed that the girls would always be accompanied by their teachers, the plan also sought to alleviate the isolation which hindered the work of schoolmistresses.

She returned to Liverpool in 1866 with a letter of introduction to Mrs Josephine Butler who, before her work against the Contagious Diseases Act removed her from the field, was an ardent worker for the women's education movement. Miss Clough first tried to organise a series of twelve lectures on Italian history to be given in February 1867 to senior girls from the Liverpool schools by F. W. H. Myers of Cambridge University. The plan fell through, but led to the foundation of the Liverpool Ladies Educational Association, with Anne Clough as secretary. It received a further airing when Miss Clough was invited to give a paper at the Manchester Association of Schoolmistresses. There a more elaborate scheme took shape, which was to include several big towns, employing between them an itinerant lecturer. Manchester, Sheffield, Leeds and Liverpool pledged their support. Anne Clough was already in touch with Henry Sidgwick and she approached the Cambridge don for advice on the selection of a lecturer.

On the first occasion he had recommended J. W. Hales whom he had described in a letter to his mother in December 1866 as

> 4th Classic in my year, and extremely well read in History and English Literature. He took a very strong interest in female and middle-class education when here and was one of the chief promoters of the girls' examination. He is enthusiastic, humorous, ready, fluent and has in fact, just the qualities that make a good lecturer—I ought however to say he wants to be married and therefore money is of importance—but as he would supplement whatever other income he gets by literary work, it seems to me that such a post as her schemes would create might just suit him. He has friends in Liverpool and could get very good testimonials.[3]

The advice arrived too late since, through the good offices of Mr and Mrs Butler, Anne Clough had already secured the services of Myers. The lectures were never given and Sidgwick was called upon again, this time to give his opinion on the merits of a candidate for the new job as itinerant lecturer in historical, literary and scientific subjects. James Stuart had been mentioned by Mrs Josephine Butler, but Anne Clough, though not wanting to seem to distrust Mrs Butler's advice, felt she might be too enthusiastic about her friends.[4] Clearly, he was not Sidgwick's choice:

> I do not think Stuart so good a man (for such a post as you describe) as *Hales* whom I mentioned before. Hales is older, has much more varied educational experience and has taken for some years English History and Literature for his special study. Now Stuart's university course has been mathematical not literary and though he is a well read, cultivated man, I do not *know* that he has given any special study to the subjects on which he would lecture. But if they do not mind his age (he only took his degree a year and a half ago) his inexperience and (as far as I know) want of any special qualification in the way of reading—in every other respect the choice would be an admirable one. Stuart is bright,

eager, clever, writes an effective English style, has a clear, self possessed impressive delivery and moreover has a quaint simplicity and a naïve independence of thought which, if it does not quite deserve the name of originality is the next best thing to it. He is a thoroughly good fellow, and is sure to be liked by everyone who has anything to do with him— I think that is a pretty good statement of the pros and cons.[5]

Providentially Sidgwick's doubts were set aside and Stuart was selected for the scheme which he was to foster and develop into that other great movement for adult education in the nineteenth century—the University Extension Lecture movement.

Sidgwick was fortunately not disturbed by this failure to follow his advice, and indeed, Hales was soon employed in the lecture scheme. In his reminiscences, James Stuart says that the lectures he gave in the winter of 1867 were on Astronomy. His course was advertised as the "History of Science, including Astronomy, Light, Heat etc." and press reports also mention magnetism and electricity.[6] Certainly the course was not one which convention would have decreed suitable for the minds of young ladies. Yet they flocked to hear Stuart and at the lectures in the four towns of Liverpool, Manchester, Sheffield and Leeds, the total attendance was over five hundred and fifty women, and the circulating libraries and booksellers could not keep pace with the demand for recommended books. Clearly women had an appetite for learning, especially from those to whom the great universities had given their seal of approval.

The success of these first lectures led to the formation of the North of England Council for Promoting the Higher Education of Women, with responsibility for the organisation of lectures in the major Northern towns. Anne Clough acted as secretary and by 1870 the number of these lecture centres in the North was twenty-five. At the Council's very first meeting in November 1867, support was expressed for Miss Davies' proposed college, though many were opposed to the specific religious affiliation that Miss Davies and her London Committee envisaged. Support was also expressed for a scheme to examine women over eighteen years old at a level higher than that of the Cambridge Local Examinations. Miss Clough and her associates were concerned that women should do more than just listen to lectures. They needed some goal, some examination towards which they could direct their energies and, at the same time, some standard by which they could measure their intellectual advance. They were, however, too old and perhaps too mature for the schoolgirls' examinations. Directing herself particularly to the problem of establishing a standard amongst women teachers, Miss Clough was anxious that some respected academic body should take the problem in hand.

In a memoir, preserved in the Sidgwick papers, Henry Jackson describes how a meeting was held in London in December 1867 to discuss the establishment of a private association to examine women. Some ladies were there and a group of Cambridge men, but Sidgwick was not at first one of the scheme's active promoters; the prime mover was Myers, inspired by Josephine Butler. Miss Davies was also present, but opposed any suggestion of "examinations for women". She thought that after school examinations girls, like boys, should take University examinations and a degree. New examinations were not needed; the point was to gain access to the existing ones. Jackson continues his account, "Myers and I discussed this and not seeing how soon women would be ready for Tripos examinations and fearing the low standard of the Pass Examination, we decided to resist Miss Davies in all ways".[7] Jackson hoped from the first that Cambridge would take up the scheme, but initially a private association was planned which included men from both Oxford and Cambridge. It is not clear how this co-operation came about, and it did not survive, but Mark Pattison at Oxford had tried to run a series of advanced classes for ladies there and the Sidgwick brothers represented a strong link between the Universities. Henry Sidgwick cannot have been far from the centre of activity, despite Jackson's memories, for he wrote to his sister Mary, on 4th February 1868, that he was "violently engaged in a scheme for improving female education" and referred to the board constituted of Oxford and Cambridge men—no end of swells—to examine governesses and schoolmistresses. The association was to be a voluntary and informal one and members of it were not simply giving their approval to a scheme to examine women but were to be responsible for arranging the examinations and appointing examiners. As Sidgwick put it in a letter to his mother, a member's reputation depended to a certain extent on the scheme's being good and on the examiners being competent.

However, the association was determined that its responsibilities should be taken over by the Universities. Sidgwick felt the best way of achieving this end was to start the scheme and to demonstrate by its success that there was a real demand for such examinations. It was at this time that London University was offering Emily Davies its examinations for women* and there was some apprehension that the Oxford and Cambridge plan would become redundant. But Sidgwick pointed out that both Oxford and Cambridge independently ran examinations for middle-class schoolchildren without any suggestion of duplication, and felt there was probably room for two examinations for women.

Meanwhile, the North of England Council continued to discuss plans for an examination for teachers and governesses, and during the early months of 1868 were preparing a Memorial to be addressed to Cambridge University asking for their assistance in the matter. There seems to have been a large body of opinion among resident members favourably inclined towards the women's request, and, the legend goes, the rest were won over by the charm and sincerity with which Mrs Butler pleaded the case when she arrived in Cambridge to present a petition signed by five hundred and fifty teachers and three hundred other women. A Syndicate was appointed in May 1868 to consider the request and it reported in October of the same year. It was agreed that an examination, calculated to test the higher education of women could be undertaken by the University without inconvenience; it was to be of a more advanced character than the Local Examinations and on a plane suited to the greater age of the candidates. The plan

* See above p. ██.

was approved with little opposition, and after a three year trial became permanent. Two years later, the examinations were opened to male candidates. Though conceived as a qualification for schoolteachers and governesses, the examinations were open to any woman over eighteen whether or not she intended to teach.

With the North of England scheme of lectures well under way and the beginning of examinations, Sidgwick conceived a plan to tap University lecturing talent for the benefit of women in Cambridge itself. In December 1869, a meeting was held in the drawing-room of the home of Professor Henry Fawcett, the Professor of Political Economy, and his wife, Millicent. Among those present were F. D. Maurice, then Knightsbridge Professor of Moral Philosophy; the fierce tempered Dr B. H. Kennedy (of *Latin Grammar* fame) and his two daughters; James Stuart; Dr John Peile (later Master of Christ's) and his wife; Mrs J. C. Adams, wife of the astronomer; Mrs Venn; Mrs W. H. Bateson, and Thomas Markby, the secretary of the Local Examinations Syndicate. Several accounts remain of this momentous meeting and of how it was deliberately kept informal and low-key. Mrs Fawcett was a Garrett, sister of Elizabeth who had tried to open the medical profession to women; the Fawcetts and Sidgwick are said to have had an ambitious residential scheme in mind which they kept to themselves for fear of shocking more moderate opinion. In the notice convening the meeting, the necessity for providing some "hall or lodging" was mentioned for women coming from outside Cambridge to attend the lectures, but little was made of it, for, as Mrs Fawcett explained, "wishing to establish a college for women in Cambridge was like wishing to establish it on Saturn".[8] The plan was to organise a series of lectures for women in Cambridge, and this was done with astonishing speed, starting the following term (Lent 1870). Courses were offered in English Language and Literature, English History, Arithmetic, Latin and Political Economy, and in the first term were attended by between seventy and eighty women. Great care was taken not to excite public ill-feeling, but, as Sidgwick reported to his mother, the scheme was easily accepted.

There is a good deal of zeal here for women's education, not much fanaticism and not much serious opposition. The fact is *all the jokes have been made.*[9]

The next stage, however, had to be handled with great delicacy. From the beginning, there were applications from women outside Cambridge and a few non-Cambridge students were housed by some of the Cambridge ladies. But the amount of private hospitality which could be given was limited and as no real "lady" could take lodgings, the problem of accommodating the non-Cambridge students forced itself on the group of dons and their wives who had formed a committee to manage the lectures. The subscription of a few small scholarships, including one from J. S. Mill, to be awarded on the results of the examination for women, strengthened the possibility that a few women might be able to leave their homes and become full-time students in Cambridge. As Sidgwick wrote to his mother in January 1871,

We are just now in a rather peculiar position. We have given exhibitions and induced one or two young persons to come to Cambridge, but the Committee as such does not provide them any accommodation—this is done advisedly, because some of us, though they do not object to girls coming up to Cambridge to attend lectures, yet do not wish formally to encourage them, still less to be responsible for them. The result is that I have semi-officially to make arrangements for the comfort of these persons, or at least to see that no difficulty is thrown in their way by the absence of provision.[10]

In the summer of 1871, Henry Sidgwick, having foregone his holiday, took and furnished at his own expense No. 74, Regent's Street, where he intended to house the first of his resident students. From the outset he hoped that Anne Clough would come to Cambridge to run the house for him, but it seemed for a time that she was committed to the rector of Bishopsgate in London to become headmistress of a girls' school there. This plan fell through from lack of funds and

Miss Clough consented to come to Cambridge "for not more than part of the year".[11] She stayed with the residential scheme, which was to grow into Newnham College, until her death in 1892. She was a fussy and at times almost incoherent woman, who throughout her life regretted her own lack of intellectual training and who did all in her power to secure its benefits for the girls in her care. Like Emily Davies, she had a determined streak in her nature, but she employed it more on the administrative and domestic front and was prepared as time went by to leave academic matters to those whom she felt were better qualified to deal with them. From the first, her own opinions were in harmony with those of Sidgwick, for she knew that women should not be expected to run, academically, before they could walk. Her aim was to improve the education of women teachers so that, like leaven in the lump, they could produce a generation of schoolgirls better prepared to fend for themselves and to follow the new academic and professional avenues which were opening to them. She was prepared to wait for the cumulative effects which the better education of girls would gradually bring, so that she came to Cambridge with no fixed notions of women fighting to prove their equality by taking men's degrees. For Emily Davies the goal was quite clear, but it does not seem that Anne Clough, at this time, had any idea of women taking degrees and being admitted to the University. As Emily Davies put it, "Miss Clough and her section don't want degrees".[12]

Sidgwick's early intentions in this direction are difficult to establish; from the beginning he probably had no other motive than to give women the opportunity to widen their intellectual horizons, gaining whatever they could from proximity to the University. Emily Davies, however, found it hard to believe that Sidgwick had no masterplan which would settle women in an inferior position in the University for all times. As her own scheme for Cambridge education for women was realised in Girton College, her letters reveal that she was very much harassed by the competition which the "Newnham people" presented. Though absolutely certain of the rightness of the "Girton way", she felt herself, as a London-based woman, considerably at a disadvantage when up against Sidgwick, who had the ear of the University. At one point she described Sidgwick's schemes as "the serpent gnawing at our vitals".[13]

In October 1871, five young women came into residence at 74 Regent Street. The quarters were cramped with little privacy for individual students; they shared a sitting room, and sat round the table together with Anne Clough in the evenings, reading or attending to the household linen. They had no garden, and such vigilance was exercised over their every move that they looked with envy at the freedom of the small boys playing on Parker's Piece, the big open common outside their back window. In a sense, the very fact of their living away from home, from their parents and relatives, meant freedom for these young women. But they were by nature adventurous souls who had had to face and overcome considerable opposition to their plans for further education, and they found it difficult to accept the discipline which the fussy Miss Clough felt she must impose on them. But for the sake of the venture, it was best if the women remained as inconspicuous as possible, and adhered strictly to the behaviour conventionally expected of a young lady. There were occasional bouts of rebelliousness. In a letter to Myers on 20th December 1871, Sidgwick wrote:

As for my Garden of Flowers (Myers explains this as Sidgwick's "harem or collection of girls reading at Cambridge") peace reigns again I believe; the only point that has occurred of an inharmonious bearing is that Miss Kennedy yearns to attend Ward's Anglo-Catholic ritual by herself and we refuse—that is Miss Clough does, I being Jorricks. My own feeling is that we ought to run all risks that Liberty brings with it; but I keep silence, assuming no responsibility that is not thrust on me. Restraint of Liberty is our rock ahead, I foresee.[14]

The house of residence was run in conjunction with the Cambridge lectures for women, and it was expected that women would prepare themselves for the newly instituted Higher Local Examinations. On the other hand, some of the women who were accepted for residence were awarded scholarships on the *results* of this examination; quite what Sidgwick had in mind for them is not clear. Emily Davies, whose scheme for a women's college had come into being in 1869, had already started her students on the road to Tripos examinations. Whether or not Sidgwick consciously also aspired to this goal, he was from the first pragmatic about the needs and ability of women, and the programme for the early students was deliberately flexible. They were often widely read, but they were unused to the discipline of regular study and a course was mapped out individually for each student to meet her requirements.

One of the first five students, Mary Paley, who later became the wife of Alfred Marshall, Professor of Economics in Cambridge from 1885-1906, illustrates, in her delightful reminiscences[15] the aspirations of these early students. Mary Paley was the great-granddaughter of Dean William Paley (of Paley's *Evidences* fame) and daughter of Thomas Paley, the Rector of Ufford near Stamford in Lincolnshire. Even though he was a strict Evangelical, her father shared with his children his love of literature and took it upon himself to teach them Latin, a little Hebrew and some Euclid. At eighteen, Mary became engaged to an army officer who immediately left for a three-year tour of duty in India. To fill in her time, she began preparing for the Cambridge Higher Local Examinations for women which had come into being in 1869. She and her father worked together at Divinity and Mathematics, her French and German were already good, and she went up to London in 1870 and 1871 to take the examinations. She writes in her memoirs, "Professor Liveing invigilated and Miss Clough came and comforted me when I was floored by the paper on Conic Sections and was crying over it".[16] The army officer returned, but they discovered that they had grown apart in their interests and the engagement was broken, leaving Mary free to accept the scholarship in Cambridge which she had been offered on the results of her examination, Conic Sections notwithstanding.

Mary Paley came to Cambridge with no idea of reading for a Tripos. She wished for "general cultivation" and chose Latin, History, Literature and Logic—this last at the advice of her father since he felt it was such a *safe* subject. Persuaded by a friend, she went along to the lectures in Political Economy given by Alfred Marshall. It is not clear under what arrangement these lectures were given, since the opening by individual dons of their lectures and laboratories to suitably chaperoned young ladies had not yet begun, and yet the classes given to Mary Paley and her companions were above the standard of those given under the lectures for women in Cambridge scheme. According to Mary Paley, it was Marshall who persuaded her and her friends to prepare for the Moral Science Tripos. Until 1848, there were only the Mathematics and Classics Triposes at Cambridge,* and in that year the Moral Sciences and Natural Sciences Triposes were introduced, though the former had not proved very popular. However, it was felt that it was the most suitable for girls to follow, since it required neither Classics nor Mathematics. When Mary Paley came to take her Tripos in 1874, she wrote her papers in the drawing room of Dr Kennedy's house in Bateman Street.

> As we [she and Amy Bulley] were the first of Miss Clough's students who attempted a Tripos, we were made much of. The Miss Kennedys gave us very delicate light lunches, and after it was over they took us to stay with them at Ely until the results were known for fear the excitement might be too great for us.

She describes how until the very end the ywere not sure they would be allowed to use the papers nor whether all four examiners would consent to look over their answers. Finally they agreed.

> The Tripos papers came by "runners" as we called them, who after getting them at the Senate House hurried to Bateman Street; among these runners were Sidgwick, Marshall, Sedley Taylor and Venn.[17]

* There were also degrees of Bachelor of Medicine and Bachelor of Law but the examination requirements for these were minimal. The Law Tripos was established in 1854.

Two of her examiners voted Mary Paley in the first class and two in the second.

The problem of obtaining leave to use the University's examination papers had already been faced by Emily Davies on behalf of the students whom she had settled in a hired house in Hitchin in 1869, twenty-seven miles from Cambridge and thirty-five from London.[18] Following an entrance examination, five candidates had been chosen to start on the course which in ten terms was to lead them through the Little-Go* to a Tripos. The young women had four lecturers in the first term, three of whom came out from Cambridge by train, to tutor them in the English literature, Greek, Latin, Divinity and Mathematics they would need to pass the Little-Go. The girls had no grounding in the subjects needed for matriculation and Emily Davies' insistence that they do everything "like the men", especially keeping to the time limits imposed on male students, was a great cause of strain and tension. No student at Miss Davies' establishment was *obliged* to enter for a University degree examination, but if she chose to make it her goal, then she must adhere strictly to the University regulations governing the examination. Alternative courses of study and examinations were offered to the students, though few seemed to have made use of them As one student put it, "no allowance was made for our colossal ignorance of the special subjects required. . . . Three years and one term was in those days the time allowed to men in which to take the Tripos, and Miss Emily Davies scorned all compromises and her students must conform to the same rule."[19] After a year's hard preparation, it was felt that five students were ready for the Little-Go and two of these were also ready to tackle the Additional Subjects in Mathematics. But it was by no means certain that they would be allowed to use the University examination papers and, on top of their anxieties about their academic abilities, the students and staff had to face the possibility that they had spent a year preparing for an examination which they would not be allowed to take. Miss Davies applied to the Council of the Senate for leave to use the papers. The Council felt it

* See Appendix A.

was not within their province to give this permission, but did not object to a private arrangement being made with the examiners.* The Senior Examiner, James Cartmell, was approached, and through his good offices the services of the other examiners were secured. The descriptions which the young women students gave of their experience during the examination period are an odd reminder of how isolated they were in their Hitchin house from the real life of the University. Carefully chaperoned by Miss Davies, they went to Cambridge to sit the examination and to see for the first time some of the sights and the way of life of the University whose regulations dominated their studies. Fortunately, these distractions did not prevent them from succeeding in the papers they took. But the Additional Subjects of the Previous Examination continued to present a very difficult hurdle for some of the students who were not able to clear the examination until October 1871, leaving themselves only four terms in which to work on their Tripos subjects. Two students had chosen the Classical Tripos and one the Mathematical, having been discouraged by Miss Davies from other Triposes with lesser reputations, by which she meant Moral and Natural Science.

In the autumn of 1872, Miss Davies began a correspondence with the Senior Examiner on the question of admitting women students unofficially to the University's Tripos examinations, a process which was to be repeated annually with the same uncertainty as to its outcome, until 1881. Sufficient examiners were found who were willing to look over the papers of the Tripos candidates, but when later in the term Emily Davies applied on behalf of five new Little-Go candidates, the situation had become more complicated. A W. M. Gunson, of Christ's College had approached the Council of the Senate with a Grace authorising the admission of women to the University's examinations. This had been rejected and the Senior Examiner was placed in an awkward position when Miss Davies' now familiar request for informal examination of her students

* During the 1897 controversy, Sidgwick was privately informed that the Council's decision to reject Miss Davies' request was made by a vote of six members to five. N.A.

came before him. For a time it seemed that the use of the examination papers would be refused, but by reminding the Senior Examiner that the Council had in no sense reversed their decision of Michaelmas 1870, when they had accepted that the college could make its own private arrangement with the examiners,* his co-operation was secured. The students were successful; not only did five pass the Previous, but two of the Tripos candidates were unofficially given a second class and one a third. When the news reached Hitchin, the students set to ringing the fire bell—so loudly that the local brigade was alerted.

But the strain which working for a Tripos in such a short time had involved could not be overlooked, and as the students themselves became aware of the deficiencies of the Little-Go examination, they appealed to Miss Davies and the College Committee in February 1873 to allow students to proceed to a Tripos without having passed the Previous Examination. They were supported in their plea by seven college lecturers and individual members of the College Committee, but Miss Davies rejected their advice for the sake of maintaining the comparability of her students' work with that of their male counterparts, an aim which she set above the intellectual needs of individual students. She was extremely angry that the lecturers should have given the students their support behind her back and was absolutely incensed that the students themselves should have any opinions in the matter. As she wrote to one of the Classics lecturers, E. C. Clark:

> . . . with regard to the students' Memorial, I think it was felt by the Committee generally, that as persons *in statu pupillari* and most of them very young and inexperienced, they were scarcely in a position to make as a body, a formal suggestion to the Committee on a grave question of general policy. Some certainly signed, knowing very little about the matter. And we cannot help regretting that some of the Lecturers should in this case have discussed the College policy with the students, apart from the Committee, and

* See above, p. ▮.▮.

endorsed *their* action, instead of addressing the Committee, if they thought it desirable to do so, on their own account. I feel however, that in doing so, the Lecturers were quite unaware of the difficulties we have had to contend with in the internal management of the College.[20]

The students, she felt, did not need any encouragement to express their own opinions on how the college should be run—there had already been trouble in that direction. One student had tried to sabotage the marking of the morning register by deliberately and systematically absenting herself from it. "Two years ago we had far worse trouble, of a different sort, in which all the students but one were involved.* I feel sure that in that sad case you would have agreed with the authorities and would have been astonished and grieved at the spirit shown by some of the older students."[21] Emily Davies was wrong on two counts. The lecturers had not discussed the issue with the students, but had acted quite independently of them. This was not the first indication which Miss Davies had received of the lecturers' dissatisfaction with the college syllabus. In August 1870, Professor J. R. Seeley had withdrawn his teaching support, since he was no longer prepared to give his time to Emily Davies and the college while they insisted on "stationary" education. "I cannot take any pleasure in attending to the details of a College where the old and to me obsolete routine goes on. I do not cease to wish it success. . . . I hope for times when you may feel able to be bolder and more progressive."[22] Nor were the students as inexperienced as Emily Davies claimed; many of those who signed the petition, had already passed the Previous. She was right when she pointed out that the students were not *obliged* to take degree certificates, but could take college certificates in single subjects instead, but her students rejected these on the very grounds which she herself rejected the Tripos-without-the-Previous—that is, lack

* This presumably is a reference to an incident in 1871 which almost closed the college. The students performed some amateur theatricals "taking male parts and dressing accordingly". The college authorities were shocked, but the students did not take kindly to being reprimanded.

of a recognised standard. What she failed to appreciate was the spirit of her students; the individual drive which had led them to take the unorthodox path of a college education. She could never reconcile intellectual growth with spiritual growth and continued to regret the independence of spirit of her students.* Her letters rarely betray any warmth or even interest for her students as individuals and she cared little for personal popularity, though she revealed a certain jealousy of Anne Clough and of the affection which the students at Newnham had for her. Dame Louisa Lumsden, the first Girton student to become a college lecturer, resigned after differences with Emily Davies especially over what she regarded as neglect of the students' welfare. Students, she complained, were merely cogs in the wheel of Emily Davies' great scheme; " . . . it was plain we counted for little or nothing except as we furthered her plans".[23]

It was this same question of the Previous Examination which so sharply divided Emily Davies from others who were working for the advancement of women's higher education. When Sidgwick had first contemplated the problem of accommodating women students in Cambridge he had corresponded with Emily Davies on the possibility of amalgamating their two schemes. The lease on the house in Hitchin was due to expire in Michaelmas 1872 and, as early as 1870, Emily Davies and her committee were considering plans for building a college, the location of which was again a point of controversy. Sidgwick pointed out the advantages of joining forces; a college built in Cambridge meant a ready supply of lecturers and the chance for women to attend the lectures of University Professors. The Hitchin scheme had proved very expensive and this had been a deterrent to many students. But Emily Davies could not agree with Sidgwick; she objected strongly to the use made of the examinations for women and had very definite views on the dangers of siting her college in the University town. For his part, Sidgwick objected to the use of

* "Is it not vexing to see such a spirit shown? I am afraid we shall have no lasting peace while any of the pioneers (i.e. first students) remain." Emily Davies to Barbara Bodichon 8.2.1873. G.A.

the Previous, and the official connection which the Hitchin college had with the Established Church. Co-operation was impossible; Emily Davies and Henry Sidgwick went their own ways. Land was acquired at Girton, a village felt to be suitably distant from Cambridge to deter casual visitors, and the now famous buildings were ready for occupation by Miss Davies and her students in Michaelmas 1873.

Sidgwick proceeded independently with his plans for No. 74 Regent Street. Soon, his "little garden of flowers" grew too large for the confined space of the house and Miss Clough moved with her students to Merton Hall, a larger and very beautiful house situated near St John's College at the top of the Backs. The students revelled in the seclusion of the garden, but as the Hall accommodated only fourteen students, a supplementary house was taken in Trumpington Street in 1873. But such arrangements could only be temporary; the landlord of Merton Hall was not able to renew the lease beyond the summer of 1874. Another suitable house could not be found and the decision was taken to build on land leased from St John's College. After a year spent cramped in a variety of temporary accommodation, Newnham Hall, taking its name from the surrounding village, was ready to accept a Principal, a resident lecturer and thirty students in October 1875. From the outset, it was unable to take all the students who wanted to live in Cambridge, and for very many years, Newnham's "out" students were accommodated with responsible women in the town. They shared most of the advantages of students actually resident in Newnham, and though technically those running the Lectures for Women in Cambridge, which prepared women for the Higher Locals and cared for these out students, were a separate group from those running Newnham Hall, the same band of enthusiasts were involved in both schemes and co-operated fully with each other. The college took the first step on the path it was eventually to follow, when two students were entered for a Tripos in 1874; and in 1875 Mary Paley returned to the post as resident lecturer, a development which was to set the College free from its dependence on male lecturers, and remove some of the teaching load from the shoulders of the men who had generously given so much of their time and talents to start the new venture. In this era of educational reform, young dons like Sidgwick undertook college lectures, inter-college lectures, extension lectures, lectures to women, advanced classes to resident women, and in some cases acted as correspondence tutors,[24] as well as serving on various University Syndicates and College Committees. It might be argued that their own work suffered—it seems inevitable—but they undoubtedly made a vital contribution to the higher education not only of the men for whom they were directly responsible but of their sisters and less privileged brothers.

About the appearance of two colleges for women, Sidgwick wrote to a friend " . . . we are accustomed in Cambridge to a complexity of systems and there are plenty of fine old arguments to prove that it is rather a help than a hindrance."[25]

For many years Emily Davies remained bitter over the presence of Newnham, its success and its ideals—or lack of them as she thought. It seemed to her that she and her college so often made all the sacrifices in the struggle to gain recognition for women's intellectual abilities, while Newnham students were happy to reap the gains.* Girton had a reputation as a woman's rights foundation[26] and was regarded with resentment and suspicion by many Cambridge people; Newnham was more in tune with liberal Cambridge ways, the "cause" was kept in the background and the atmosphere in the college was in consequence more harmonious and congenial. Emily Davies' irritation was understandable, but her jealousy of Newnham was often childishly expressed. She was quite gleeful when she heard reports that the rooms at Newnham were smaller than at Girton[27] and that a distant relative by marriage to Anne Clough might send his daughter to Girton rather than Newnham.[28] A mature student approached Girton and coolly accepted a study loan of two hundred and fifty pounds without security and without interest as if she was receiving no special favour. Emily Davies grumbled that it was rather too much to do for one student of no special

* At a later date the suffragettes who used militant tactics in seeking the vote, felt much the same about the suffragists, who favoured only peaceful and legitimate tactics.

promise "but it may be worth while to rescue her from the Newnham net".[29]

Newnham and Girton continued in their separate approaches to the higher education of women, though in time there was little to distinguish between them. Girton continued to insist that students passed the Previous examination and proceeded to the Tripos within the appropriate time limit, while Newnham for many years accepted students who could reside for only short periods and who aimed solely at the Higher Local Examinations, which met the urgent demand for teachers faster than was possible under the Girton scheme. Newnham also allowed its students to take Triposes without having taken the Previous Examination, though they had to prove themselves in the Higher Locals.[30] As the Cambridge educated women returned to the schools as teachers and the general standard of girls' education began to rise, the practice of admitting girls to Newnham solely for the purpose of taking Higher Locals was discontinued and the pattern of education in Newnham and Girton became similar. That is, girls came to Cambridge for the purpose of taking degrees.

5

1881 ADMISSION TO EXAMINATIONS

DURING THE 1870's the two women's colleges went quietly about their business, avoiding the limelight and taking immense pains to give their critics no cause for complaint. Though their existence was in no way recognised by the University authorities and they were never certain that they could use the degree examination papers, the women's presence was becoming a factor in University life. The students at Hitchin had been taught by men coming out from Cambridge by train and their teaching schedule had been largely dictated by the railway time-table. Sidgwick had less difficulty in persuading men to lecture to his young ladies in rooms conveniently situated in the middle of town, but it soon became tiresome for some of these hard-pressed young dons to repeat their lectures for the small numbers of women students who were preparing for a Tripos. A more economical solution, both in energy and money, was to invite the young women to the Tripos lectures given for the male undergraduates.

The organisation of the University at that time was quite different from the familiar faculty structure of today. A Professor was paid by the University to give lectures which were open to any member of the University; his lectures were regarded as public property, in contrast to college lectures where more detailed Tripos teaching was given by a Fellow solely for the benefit of the men in his college. There were seventeen men's colleges in Cambridge at the time and the disadvantages of the fragmented teaching effort was beginning to be appreciated; a movement towards intercollegiate lectures had begun, and students from several colleges joined together to listen to lectures. In this spirit of rationalisation, it did not prove difficult for Sidgwick to persuade several dons to open their lectures to women, and the number of dons willing to

admit women increased each year. Of course, great care had
to be taken over the arrangements for mixing the sexes in the
lecture-rooms. The women students were accompanied by a
chaperone—despite strong protests from some quarters that a
chaperone would simply provoke flirtation[1]—and their details
of their arrival and departure from the men's colleges had to be
given careful consideration. As Henry Sidgwick wrote, " . . .
they might even be allowed to attend my lecture course in one
of the ordinary lecture-rooms [in Trinity College] provided it
were fixed at an hour when there would be no crowding on
the staircase.[2] Nor was it too difficult for women to gain
admission to Professorial lectures, and by 1873, when the
Girton buildings were ready for occupation, twenty-two out of
thirty-four Professors were prepared to admit women to their
lectures. Facilities for science study were less easy to organise,
as the women were not welcome in the already heavily over-
crowded University laboratories. Both Newnham and Girton
were obliged to build their own laboratories, to the great
benefit of their students, who were usually lacking laboratory
experience from their girls' schools. Some of the women who
were successful in the Tripos stayed at their colleges as
lecturers, but in the early years, the women's colleges were
still heavily dependent on men coming in to coach their
students, and such tutoring was a not unwelcome source of
income for many young dons. They were less enthusiastic,
however, about the long walk out to Girton and would have
preferred to teach the girls in town. Miss Davies could not
overcome her suspicion of the distractions and possible dangers
her students would meet if they received their teaching in the
city, though as a gesture towards the lecturers' complaints, she
did make a shed available for their tricycles.[3]

The lives of the women students were ordered by innumerable small rules of behaviour, and it is only possible to understand how the students bore with these constraints by
considering the narrowness of the lives they would have led
had they stayed at home. Miss Davies tried to avoid giving
ammunition to the ready critics of women's education by
keeping her students in the country, well out of the public eye.
But to some the very idea of women pursuing a course of higher

education produced outburts of disgust, alarm or incredulity. A clergyman traveller in a railway carriage was heard to exclaim as the train approached Hitchin, "Ha! This is Hitchin and *there* I believe is the College for women. That infidel place!"[4] Later when the College moved to Girton, it aroused much curiosity amongst some of the ladies of Cambridge who didn't think it could possibly be "nice" for a young lady to be filling her head with classics and mathematics. Such things were to spoil her. One woman, who with some misgivings had invited a Girton student to dine, remarked afterwards

> My dear, she was such a *nice* girl, with rosy cheeks and nice manners and nicely dressed and you wouldn't have thought she knew anything.

At Newnham, the problems were even greater, since the students were more often on view. Sidgwick's early students were very independent spirited—naturally enough since they had agreed to risk ridicule from family and friends and the certain loss of all hopes of marriage in order to be educational pioneers, (though, in fact, 30 % of the students in the first ten years are known to have married). Three of the first five were exceptionally good looking and wore fashionable "tied-back" skirts. Sidgwick wished they could move around Cambridge unobserved and that they could not was "all the fault of their unfortunate appearance".[5]

However, the women students were soon attracting attention for reasons other than their good looks. In 1880, a Girton student, Miss C. A. Scott was informally bracketed with the Eighth Wrangler* in the first part of the Mathematics Tripos. This was a great success for the women, more especially as it had come in a subject which was supposedly beyond their mental capacity. But Miss Scott received no recognition of her success from the University. Unlike her co-Wranglers, she could never look forward to the day when she could write the initials "B.A." after her name. The injustice of this situation

* That is, eighth in order of merit, the "Senior Wrangler" being the first.

was heightened by the fact that it was now possible for women to graduate from London University, which two years previously had opened its degrees to women. Forces outside Cambridge felt that the time had come to attempt to secure some formal recognition by the University of the work of educating women which was going on within its precincts. A Memorial was got up, principally on the responsibility of Professor and Mrs Steadman Aldis. Aldis was at that time Professor of Mathematics at Durham College of Science in Newcastle. The couple had lived in Cambridge a great deal, and Mrs Aldis was fond of giving a lively description to curious audiences on Tyneside of the reading of the Tripos results in the Senate House. She would arouse the sympathy of her listeners for the women students "who had to steal about Cambridge in such an unrecognised manner".[6] Her sense of injustice at the position of women in Cambridge was clear in the wording of the plea which was addressed to the Cambridge Senate. It was suggested that women were in Cambridge on sufferance and the arrangements for their informal examinations were unsatisfactory. The University could remedy this by granting "to properly qualified women the right of admission to the Examinations for University Degrees and to the Degrees conferred according to the results of such Examinations".[7]

The existence of the Newcastle Memorial, which received over eight thousand signatures, was unknown to the women's leaders in Girton and Newnham until it had been in circulation for some time. It caused both sets of authorities some embarrassment, since they had not themselves been contemplating any action at that juncture. Their problem was whether to ignore the representations made on their behalf, to support them or to use the opportunity to make their own representations to the Syndicate. From the start, Sidgwick hoped Newnham and Girton could work together, presenting a united front—but he wanted this on his own terms, that is that they should ask for no more than formal admission to examinations and that women be excused the Previous. As one of Miss Davies' supporters warned her, Sidgwick's idea was "a joint letter or representation—what the diplomatists call 'an identical note' ".[8]

Emily Davies' rage at what she felt was the unprincipled success of Newnham could be contained no longer. She boiled over in a stream of lengthy and forthright letters to Sidgwick in which she utterly repudiated his suggestion that they should work together for "the common cause". She was bitter over Newnham's successes in the Tripos examinations, since Newnham students reached their goal without the discipline of the Previous Examination and the University's strict time-table to which the Girton girls were subject. There was also great confusion in the minds of the public over the standard reached by Cambridge women and they could not be convinced that it was a common standard with men while Newnham continued to disregard the examination regulations. Girton and Newnham, she declared, had as much in common as Gladstone and Lord Salisbury.[9] She attacked Sidgwick with venom and he, characteristically, after the initial shock of having his polite and carefully reasoned approaches thrown back in his face, used his expertise and influence in University affairs to outmanoeuvre her. Miss Davies always tried to keep her disputes on an impersonal level, but she scarred her opponent with the memory of an impetuous and vicious fighter. Even more damagingly, Sidgwick could not have failed to notice that there was considerable truth and justice in many of the points she made.

Sidgwick's first reaction to the news of the Newcastle Memorial was that it should be stopped. Emily Davies concurred with this and used her connections on Tyneside to see if this could be done. But the Memorial had already been in circulation for some time and its authors were not prepared to set it aside. In March 1880, Newnham decided they would send in a Memorial supporting the sentiment of the Newcastle Memorial, which was that women should receive some formal recognition from the University, whilst dissociating themselves from the specific request for degrees made by the Newcastle paper and its rather tactless criticism of the existing, informal examination arrangements. The draft of the proposed Memorial was sent by Sidgwick to Emily Davies—marked private and confidential—in the hope that Girton would decide to make a similar approach to the Senate and that the wording of the two Memorials could be harmonised. Sidgwick asked Miss Davies to suggest any wording which was likely to conflict with her Committee's view.[10] Unfortunately, Miss Davies chose to lay the Newnham document before her Committee, who then sent Sidgwick a formal reply hostile to the Newnham draft. Sidgwick was angered by what he felt was a betrayal of confidence and the brusque way in which Girton[11] had interpreted his efforts at diplomacy, yet he tried hard to remain friendly and co-operative.| He suggested that each college should ask for its own examinations practices to be regularised, neither college asking for degrees at that stage, since he felt these were certain to be refused and could jeopardise the whole position of women in Cambridge. He also suggested that the Girton Committee had overlooked the extent to which the Newnham Committee abstained in their draft Memorial from putting forward what they considered the strong points of the Newnham system. The Girton point was that they faithfully copied the University course laid down for men; the corresponding Newnham point was that they loyally followed the lines laid down by the University in the official action it had taken regarding the education of women, that is, by making instruction for the Higher Locals an integral part of the Newnham scheme of instruction.[12] Emily Davies was not in the least bit penitent; she hit back, hard.

I am glad to know of the abstinence shown in not dwelling upon the loyalty to the University expressed by Newnham in preparing students for the Higher Locals, which we had certainly quite missed seeing. There were perhaps two or three reasons for our blindness. 1. We were not aware that Newnham took its stand on the platform of separateness; this policy has been rather represented to us, I think, as expediency for the present and so on, not as a deliberate preference for special examinations for women. 2. It seems to me that the point is untenable insomuch as that the University does not, so far as I know, lay down that the Higher Local is specially suitable for women as such. On the contrary it says, this is what we consider suitable for men and women who are unable to reside at Cambridge and study in the way we expect from undergraduates. As the examination is expressly non-gremial, to claim credit for preparing for it at the University itself, seems inappropriate.[13]

She also spoke bluntly on Sidgwick's proposal that they should ask only for certificates from the University and not mention Degrees.

As to your expectation of converting us to the policy of asking for Certificates, I can only say that it strikes me as showing an admirable strength of hopefulness founded no doubt on much experience of success in persuasion. If it had been a question of regularising *our* system *only* . . . but to regularise yours also, would be to aggravate and perpetuate the misconceptions as to the difference, or absence of difference between us and Newnham, under which we had laboured all these years. Evidently you have no conception of what we have gone through. No doubt you have been misled by our patient endurance and because we have not made an outcry, you do not realise our sense of injury, nor see how unlikely it is that we should lend ourselves in any way to an attempt to obtain the sanction of the University for a system which causes us incessant annoyance.[14]

Sidgwick tried again to persuade her that no harm could come of his suggested approach—it would merely involve exchanging the University's existing impartial indifference to the two schemes for its impartial recognition.[15] Miss Davies stormed back; Girton could not help it if the Tripos examiners "with a want of principle which we can only lament, examine candidates as women, who, if they were men, would be summarily dismissed"[16] but at least such a pernicious state of affairs had no official University approval. If Girton did anything which helped Newnham's "separate scheme for women" to be officially recognised, even if Girton also received recognition, they would have done an evil thing. Then came Miss Davies' open admission of her cause—

We, who are interested in Girton, do not care for it alone—
Girton is a detail, for the moment the most prominent, but
not so important as to justify us in forgetting everything else
for the chance of hastening its progress . . . we would rather
delay, if necessary, than snatch at what might look like an
advantage if it involved furthering anything contrary to our
essential principles.[17]

But it was to the Mistress of Girton, Miss Bernard, that she
explained the real meaning of her "cause", an explanation
which might more usefully have been given to Sidgwick:

We are not fighting for the existing Little-Go any more than
for one part or another of any of the Tripos Examinations.
What we fight for is the common standard for women and
men without in the least committing ourselves to the opinion
that the ultimate best has as yet been reached in any
examination.[18]

Sidgwick could do no more; each college made its own
petition to the Council of the Senate. Girton claimed no part
in the circulation of the Newcastle Memorial, but supported
its request for formal admission to degrees and to the University.
In their Memorial of 16th April, 1880,[19] Girton reminded the
Council that they had asked their permission ten years
previously to make use of the papers for Little-Go and to allow
them to make arrangements with examiners to correct papers
and conduct vivas. The Council had replied that they didn't
consider it within their province to give such permission, but
they did not disapprove of private arrangements where these
were practicable. The Girton Committee submitted that the
informal experiment had now been carried on for long enough
for the University to consider the formal admission of women
to the B.A. degree. They also added a few sentences on an
issue which was to take a central part in controversies of later
years. They wrote:

The Committee wish to point out that the certificate given
by the College though to a great extent recognised as

substantially equivalent to a degree, can only be regarded as a temporary resource. It lacks the official sanction of the University; it confers no title that can be conveniently used to indicate the holder's real position; and it fails to constitute a formal qualification for educational work.[20]

The Association for the Promotion of Higher Education of Women in Cambridge, the official title of the group which had founded the lectures for women in Cambridge and Newnham College, dissociated itself from the Newcastle Memorial and asked only that the examinations and academic instruction provided for women be put on a firmer footing. This was supported by a flysheet signed by 123 resident members. The Memorial offered a detailed description of the "Newnham way" and a history of its success under the previous decade. Newnham students were not put forward as Tripos candidates unless they had completed a course of study at Cambridge in the Tripos subject and gave evidence of "general intellectual culture". This latter could be demonstrated by a pass with Honours in the Higher Local Examination, an examination which the University itself had introduced to test the education of girls over eighteen. Two students had been allowed to offer a pass in the University's Previous Examination but the Newnham authorities did not wish to make this latter examination a compulsory part of their system "because of the influence that their action might be expected to exercise on [girls'] schools". Since 1874, twenty-one students had been entered for a Tripos and all had succeeded. Four had been placed in the First Class and none of the six most successful candidates had exceeded the normal period of residence.[21]

Sidgwick was a member of the Syndicate which was appointed on 3rd June, 1880, to consider the women's case.[22] When it met, it had before it fifteen Memorials[23] two asking for formal admission to examinations and lectures, three asking admission to examinations and degrees and the remaining ten asking for admission to degrees. When the syndicate issued its report in the Lent term of 1881[24] it left aside the issue of the admission of women to degrees for reasons which its members felt unable to discuss, but they advocated the formal opening of the Tripos examinations to women who had fulfilled the normal residence requirements and had been recommended by their college. On the successful completion of their examination, they would be given a certificate and their names published in a class list, though separate from the men. They would be allowed to substitute certain passes in the Higher Local Examination for the Previous and they would not be admitted to the Poll degree.

It is not difficult to perceive the hand of Sidgwick in these recommendations; and they did not satisfy Emily Davies. When asked by Sidgwick to support the Syndicate's proposals, she revealed her disappointment and discontent. Miss Davies had every right to feel thwarted, for Sidgwick had in fact produced a scheme which exactly reflected his own ideas of educational reform; he had succeeded in removing the evils, as he saw them, of both the Previous and the Poll degree from the arena of University education for women in Cambridge, a success which he strove throughout his life to repeat for the benefit of men students. She could not accept the idea of certificates given indiscriminately to Girton and Newnham students and talked of Girton awarding its own certificates, or even of allying itself to London University, though this was an "extremely distasteful" idea.[25] Clearly she was prepared to make a stand against the Syndicate's proposals, but she accepted the point made by her Cambridge friends: that a defeat would men the end of informal examinations and the end of the relationship with the University.[26] Instead, she accepted the step forward, the right to be examined and the printed class list, and continued to harbour a deep resentment against Newnham, its ways and its leaders.

When the report went for discussion in the Arts School on 11th February, 1881, one of the members of the Syndicate described how easy it had been to agree over it. Another speaker retorted that this was not surprising in view of the membership of the Syndicate. Indeed, the women had been very fortunate and the proposals of the Syndicate represented an enormous advancement of their aims, since they would now have an official connection with the University. The discussion of the report was brief and confined to the mental and physical strain which Tripos work might impose on women, and expressions of regret that a residence clause had been included in the proposals. Why not open the Tripos examinations to any woman no matter where she lived and studied? But this view received little support, since it was feared it might lead to a demand by male students for the same privilege. The supporters of the scheme were so surprised at the lack of opposition that they felt bound to raise (and refute) possible objections themselves. The first was the suggestion that this concession would lead to further requests from women—but then the University was quite at liberty to reject these as they arose. Surprise was expressed that no one had raised the matter of a University solely for women. The women's supporters scorned it as an impractical suggestion used merely as a cover by those who simply wanted to keep women from the benefits of higher education.

Though little opposition had been encountered during the discussion, it was still felt that the forces of reaction would be rallied against the women at the vote.

Dr Perowne, who as you know is the leader of the Conservative party here, has virtually given notice that he will oppose the measure. He said that he trusted the Senate would consider well before it adopted any such proposals and dwelt on objections to anything of the kind, his objections being really *fundamental* to the admission of women in any form.[27]

But Dr Perowne and his party did not sway many votes. In a letter to his sister, Sidgwick describes the "triumph of the 24th" (of February) and how he would never forget the astonishment with which he realised that the Senate House was full with about four hundred M.A.s and that, so far as he could tell, they were all going to vote on the right side. "Ultimately, with great trouble, I discovered the enemy seated in a depressed manner on a couple of benches in one corner, about thirty in number."[28] The Graces were passed by 366 votes to 32, and the news caused great jubilation among the women, at Newnham at least. One of the Newnham students

Miss Emily Davies, Founder of Girton College.

Miss A. J. Clough, first Principal of Newnham College.

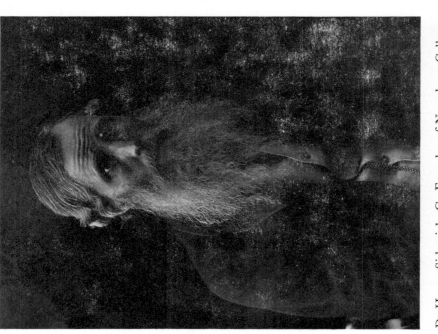

Dr Henry Sidgwick, Co-Founder of Newnham College.

went on horseback to the Backs, another stood on a bridge half-way between her and the Senate House, and a third on the steps of the Senate House; and when the joyful result was published, the latter waved a white handkerchief to the watcher on the bridge, who signalled the victory to the horse-woman, who galloped home to the assembled Newnhamites.[29]

The male undergraduates do not seem to have been greatly disturbed by the ladies' success, though the Union debated and substantially defeated the motion, "That this House strongly approves of the recent action of the Senate in opening the Examinations to women and hopes that it is only a step towards granting them degrees"*, and Sidgwick wrote light-heartedly to his sister that he was being "chaffed in Hall" because his nephew was said to have proposed a motion "That the Higher Education of Women is Undesirable", at the King's College Debating Society. "There is a charming breadth of statement here! He tells me that it was carried 11–10."[30] But the women had their champions; Professor Richard Jebb, the great classical scholar, who was fond of composing small verses, sent the following lines to Sidgwick in celebration of the women's success:

The votes by which the ladies won
　　Were as a Leap Year's days.

A month's brief tale would all but tell,
　　The number of the Nays.

Thus, as the sun in heaven, our cause,
　　Is clear to men of sense.

The adverse tide is little more,
　　Than lunar influence.[31]

The absence of opposition to the encroachments which women were making on the male preserve aroused some contemporary curiosity, and since the passing of the 1881

---

* In 1869, the Union had debated the motion, "That this Society views with interest and sympathy the career of the Ladies College at Hitchin". An amendment "For 'interest and sympathy' read 'Amusement' " was defeated.

Graces seems to have marked the end of a honeymoon period for the women in Cambridge, the point requires closer examination. Since 1863, women had been making successful overtures to the University for a share in its educational advantages. Their share was no doubt small, but it represented much more than the "thin end of the wedge" which their later opponents so much regretted. They used the services of the University Examination Syndicate at junior and senior level and had had instituted for their own special benefit examinations for students over eighteen. They had quietly and unobtrusively encamped on the walls of the University citadel, slipping in through back doors to attend lectures and examinations until, in 1881, they were given an official place in the examination room. Writing after Sidgwick's death in 1900, G. O. Trevelyan commented:

> Retrospectively, I am astonished at so great and cardinal a success. I should have thought the same base influences would have defeated it [the admission of women to exams] as have prevailed of late. [meaning the 1897 defeat][32]

Women owed much of their early success to a spill-over from the "revolution of the dons", and though the University reformers had to fight entrenched attitudes in teaching methods, contents of courses, the place of the Church in University education etc., where women were concerned they had at the outset no sacred cows to slaughter beyond the belief that women could not or should not be educated—a view which few even of the most reactionary of University men could conscientiously maintain. They were also greatly assisted by the revelations of the Schools Inquiry Commission which had spelt out in awful detail just how young ladies were "educated". The Commissioners had appealed for a change of attitude in families towards the education of their girls; their words touched the consciences of people already in the field and almost out of the dust arose a fine structure of secondary education for (some) young ladies. It was on this wave of enthusiasm and concern that women had founded their colleges in Cambridge.

Yet it must be noticed that the University in 1881 had granted the women very little of what they had asked. There was to be no membership, no degrees, not even the right to attend lectures. The question of University membership and degrees had not even been considered. Opinion, it seemed, was unfavourable and since Sidgwick felt that a request for membership and degrees would end with the women's total exclusion from University examination and teaching, he no doubt played down the suggestion during the Syndicate's discussions.[33] There is no evidence to support or contradict Sidgwick's judgement on this point, but failure to make firm provision for the teaching of women students indicates their case received no really thorough consideration by the Syndicate, who did not think through the consequences of their decisions. By opening Tripos examinations to women without providing for their teaching, Cambridge was acting as no more than an examining body, on the pattern of the often despised and criticised London University, whose degrees could be taken by students who never set foot in the capital. Cambridge men were most careful to stress that it was the three years spent in the University learning from great teachers and from each other which was evidence of a student's education, not his degree certificate. It was true that the women students were to be present in Cambridge for ten terms, but propriety required that they lived excluded from social intercourse. Now, according to the University's decision, their chance of receiving teaching was to continue to rest merely on the goodwill of University men, and their own inadequate resources. On the other hand Cambridge had not followed London's lead in awarding its women students degrees on the successful completion of their examinations. They chose instead to create a graduate without a degree, a wingless bird which was to plague their consciences for many years. With hindsight it is possible to say that the University acted at this point in a casual and incautious fashion; admission to examinations was undoubtedly the thin end of the wedge, and the University's later disputes with the women can be traced back to this decision of 1881. At the time, however, the move was welcomed as an advance by most Cambridge women, for whom the uncertainty surrounding admission to examinations had been a great burden and the progressives amongst the don were able to congratulate themselves on their liberalism and generosity in the cause of women's education.

6

THE DAMP SQUIB 1887

THE 1887 TRIPOS lists produced a success for women's education which could not pass unmarked. There was only one candidate placed in the first class of the Classical Tripos that year, and she was a student of Girton, Miss Agnata Frances Ramsay (later wife of Montague Butler, Master of Trinity). A committee was quickly formed in London with Emily Davies and her friends as members to press for the admission of women to degrees. From the start they seemed so certain of success that they felt they could dictate terms. At a meeting on 26th May, 1887, they resolved that "while we are prepared to accept for women such abatements of the privileges of graduates if any, as may be deemed expedient, we will not support any measure excluding women from the Ordinary Degree or admitting them to Degrees on other conditions than those laid down for undergraduates generally". And in a hopeful footnote, they also resolved that Sidgwick, among others, should be invited to join the Committee.[1]

Their first circular on the subject suggested that Cambridge women suffered a professional disadvantage because they did not have degrees. But their main argument was that women had shown themselves able and willing to follow the same curriculum as men—they should therefore receive the same recognition as men and be admitted to membership of the University with at least some of its various privileges and obligations. Any hope that Sidgwick would join such a Committee was a pious one; he rejected their invitation on the grounds of timing, alarmed by what he considered an unwisely precipitous demand. Possibly he felt that even at this stage, the women's education movement had a great deal to lose by asking the University further favours which he felt it was not ready to grant. For although women had been formally admitted to examinations, in 1881 they were still only permitted to attend lectures and laboratory classes with the permission of the individual lecturer, and an ill-timed request for admission to degrees might result in the withdrawal of these privileges. It seems that Sidgwick's fear of antagonising the University was exaggerated, a camouflage for his real objection to Miss Davies' proposals which was the inclusion of the Ordinary degree and the Previous in the scheme of women's education. The London Committee's proposals sought the complete identification of examinations and degrees for men and women in Cambridge. Men and women would sit the same Previous examination and then proceed to either the Poll degree or Honours. To Sidgwick this was anathema; he believed that both the Previous Examination and the Poll degree were without value and continually campaigned for their amendment. Sidgwick felt that to admit women to these examinations would not only lengthen their lives, but, in the case of the Previous examination, which demanded a knowledge of Latin and Greek, would put pressure on girls' schools in the direction of classics and away from the modern subjects he favoured. And he could now claim the authority of the University in support of his viewpoint, since in their official action in 1881, they had forbidden women the Poll examination and allowed them an alternative to the Previous.[2]

To counter the London Committee's activities, Sidgwick, together with three colleagues, A. Cayley, N. M. Ferres and Coutts Trotter, circulated a letter to those people who he believed had supported the admission of women to Tripos examinations in 1881, inviting them to a private meeting at Gonville and Caius Lodge on Thursday, 9th June at 2.30 p.m. The letter was less than impartial, claiming that the resolution of the London Committee passed on 26th May "would involve a reversal of the action that the University has hitherto taken in relation to the higher education of women", and casting doubt on the expediency of pressing for the degree only six years after the Tripos examinations had been opened. If the opinion of those who had supported the women in 1881 was now opposed to the activities of the London Committee, "representation" was to be made in the hope of persuading them to suspend their operations. On the other hand, if a decided majority appeared to be in favour of the proposed movement, the meeting would consider "how far the present conditions of the admission of women to Tripos Examinations will require modification if the degree is granted to women who pass them". Sidgwick also asked those who could not attend the meeting to let him have, in writing, their views on the desirability of pressing at the present time the claims of women for admission to degrees.

A surprising number of replies favoured women's admission to degrees and rather took Sidgwick to task for his reaction to the activities of Miss Davies and her friends. R. D. Archer-Hind objected strongly "to throwing cold water on the designs of the London Committee . . . I cannot forget that but for very strong pressure from without,* the formal admission of women to the examinations might even yet have been unaccomplished". Though he did not personally insist on admission to the Ordinary Degree, he felt women should have the degree "however and whenever it can be obtained" and he was prepared to give his active support to the London Committee.[3] A. J. Tillyard made a similar point, criticising Sidgwick's approach to the reform. "If the friends of women in Cambridge are timorous about speaking out their minds at this juncture, I hope they will at least not hinder their more courageous brethren in London."[4] Other correspondents were more docile. They supported the admission of women to degrees, if not membership of the university, but they offered no real opinion on the expediency of asking for a concession at that moment in time, preferring to rely on the judgement of others. T. J. Lawrence summed up the problem:

> To my mind it is entirely a question of tactics. I have always felt that the logical result of the previous action of the Senate in the matter would be the formal admission of women to the degrees they are at present allowed to win but not to possess. Sooner or later, the full concession must

* Presumably a reference to the Newcastle Memorial. See above p. ▪.▪.

be made; and I would rather it were sooner. But I quite see that it would be unwise to court defeat by raising the question prematurely. On the other hand, if those who have good opportunities for feeling the pulse of the Senate are of opinion that the change could now be carried, I hope the attempt to complete what was so well begun six years ago will be made without further delay.[5]

For some correspondents, the main problem was not timing but the insistence of the London Committee on admission to the Ordinary Degree and the equality of conditions, which meant the Previous examination with its Latin and Greek. Even this last, however, was not without its supporters. As A. F. Tovey put it, a moderate study of Classics and Mathematics as required for the Previous and the Ordinary was what was most lacking in female education.[6] Even so opposition to these examinations remained an article of faith for Sidgwick and his followers and the London Committee must have known, after their 26th May resolution, that they could not expect his co-operation.

Alfred Marshall, who had helped Newnham so much in its early days and had later married one of its first students, Mary Paley,* had been an early deserter from the women's side. He had been one of Sidgwick's disciples in the cause of women's education and university reform, but by the time of his return to Cambridge to the Chair of Economics in 1885, Marshall was ready to dismiss many of his previous enthusiasms as youthful fancy. He no longer had any great reverence for Sidgwick's opinions on university affairs[7] and his early views on female emancipation had changed considerably.[8] Marshall had not supported the opening of examinations to women in 1881 on the grounds that women should study locally and not be encouraged to leave their homes[9]—he was at that time Principal of University College, Bristol, where both men and women students were accepted. His contribution to the new debate was characteristic; writing in a style of liberal enlightenment, he advocated a wait-and-see policy which effectively

* See above p. ▉.▉.

blocked all possibility of reform. "My wife and I think it would be a mistake to ask the Senate to admit women to degrees until the great changes of recent years have had more time to establish themselves and to work out their full effects." Speaking personally, he also objected to Cambridge becoming a mixed University for if women took part in the government of Cambridge it would cease to be fully adapted to the wants of men and would degenerate. Women could take part in the "government of Cambridge" because graduates had a right to vote on many University questions and also for two University Members of Parliament. The fear of women "interfering" in men's affairs was to become the major objection to women's advance at Cambridge; Alfred Marshall was one of the first to mention it. Although not in agreement with much of what had been written, Sidgwick made extensive use of the first part of Marshall's letter in his campaign against the London Committee. This is some measure of the lengths to which Sidgwick was prepared to go to stop the scheme, since in the small Cambridge community, he could hardly have been unaware of Marshall's real views on the position of women, and the differences between the two men on a variety of matters were no secret.

Some Cambridge men from whom Sidgwick solicited opinions were more open as to their reasons for opposing any advance by women. Positive opposition came from those who interpreted any move by women towards the degree as a move to share in the government, wealth and privileges of the University. W. Skeat wrote,

> If given the B.A., they must next have the M.A. and that would carry with it voting and perhaps a place on the Electoral Roll; a vote for the University Livings and all the rest. Even the B.A. degree would enable them to take 5 books at a time out of the University Library on a ticket countersigned by "their tutor". I am entirely opposed to the admission of women to "privileges" of this character. And I honestly believe they are better off as they are.[10]

Skeat's reasoning was a little inconsequential; had women

been admitted to membership of the University, they could no more have claimed the Parliamentary vote on this count, as Skeat suggested, than could an M.A. who was disenfranchised because of his status as an alien, Peer, felon or lunatic. As for women taking part in more parochial affairs, to which those of the University could be likened, the concept was not a novel one. Though women did not have a Parliamentary vote, women rate-payers had, since 1869, been able to vote in local government elections and be themselves elected. In the twenty years which followed, women had become familiar figures on School Boards and acted as Poor Law Guardians and Inspectors. Many of these jobs, however, were regarded as women's work, dealing with lower-class children and the destitute, hardly central to the real affairs of men. Care of the artisan and his children could be left to women, suitably superintended by the wiser sex, but the education of the middle and upper-class young male was held to be an exclusively masculine affair. A great many University men felt it self-evident that a women could no more have anything intelligent to contribute to a discussion on the content of a degree course for a young man than she could suggest ways in which the Government should levy and spend taxes. Even worse, it was feared she might attempt to meddle in men's education, altering it, in some unspecified way, to her own advantage.

Views like those of Skeat were often repeated in the ensuing struggles, but it was rarely felt necessary to explain why women should not be given responsibilities and privileges at the University, why they should be excluded from University government or even Library tickets. One of Sidgwick's correspondents said that the basis of his objection to University membership for women, was that such a proposal was founded on a principle of society and a concept of human nature which he believed to be untrue[11]—no doubt a reference to the egalitarian demands of women. For some, the difficulty could be solved by divorcing the degree from University membership and all that that implied in terms of voting rights. Women would not be allowed to graduate, but be given instead the title of a degree, that is they could write "B.A." after their names, but would not be members of the University. The art of making simple things difficult has long flourished in Cambridge and the idea of degree titles fitted well into this pattern and was to become one of the central solutions to the "women problem" at the University in the years to come. Curious though it seems today, the suggestion was at the time in line with the generally disenfranchised position of women in the community and the granting of a degree title to women in 1887 might well have been a valuable stepping stone to full membership.

No record of the meeting at Caius Lodge remains, but two days later, Sidgwick was addressing a letter to those who had been invited to attend the meeting, enclosing a Memorial for their signature which would then be sent to the London Committee. "We the undersigned, being resident members of the Senate who supported the admission of women to Tripos examinations are of the opinion that it is undesirable at present to raise the question of admitting them to degrees." Sidgwick added to this excerpts from the letters he had received opposing the plans of the London Committee, but did not include any of those in favour. The meeting had also resolved that it should be left to the conveners of the meeting to give such publicity to the memorial as seemed desirable, should the London Committee decline to suspend its operations. The delivery of such an ultimatum was not in Sidgwick's usual style and it is difficult to decide what he felt he could achieve by it. He must have appreciated that the opposition of Cambridge men could not have stopped Emily Davies *trying* to get the degree for women at that time; all that he was doing was ensuring that she did not succeed. And this is all the more curious in the light of a letter from Millicent Fawcett, the widow of the Professor of Political Economy, who later in the month informed him that she supported Emily Davies' approach to the University and reminded him of how, the previous month when she had talked the matter over with him and his wife, "we agreed that such a step should be taken when a favourable opportunity arose and that such an opportunity would occur when a woman distinguished herself in one of the old Triposes".[12] It was also Mrs Fawcett who, Emily Davies claimed, had stimulated the Girton people into action. In the autumn of 1886, Mrs Fawcett had given an address in which she cited the withholding of Cambridge degrees as a grievance. Emily Davies wrote:

> I was agreeably surprised to find any one so closely connected with Newnham taking this line, and afterwards had a talk with Mrs Fawcett on the subject. She said that Dr Sidgwick would be ready to work with us for Degrees if, in his judgment, the time was fitting, and that his policy was the same as ours, *i.e.* to wait for some remarkable achievement by a Girton or Newnham student and then to turn to account the sympathy then called forth. She said his aim from the beginning had been to get Degrees and everything else for women, but added the disclosure that it was to be on his own terms, *i.e.* with dissimilar conditions. This startling revelation was what set us to work. We were hoping that Miss Ramsay would gain distinction; but without counting on help of that kind, it seemed to some of us that the time had come for us to move. We felt that we should be in an awkward position if, a success having been won by a Newnham student, we were while, so to speak, trading on it, to be strongly opposing Dr Sidgwick's views, and that we had better move at a time when we could take the initiative and the lead. Before any step was taken, however, we consulted Prof. Liveing and it was on his opinion that we decided at once to take action. He took the view that it was not well to let things remain too long at a standstill and that, with a view to ripening opinion, it was better to risk defeat than to go on doing nothing.

But she had no illusions about Sidgwick's ability to make his opinions felt in University circles:

> I have greatly feared a repetition this time of the former experience [1881] *i.e.* that when we had secured the appointment of a Syndicate, Dr Sidgwick would get a report in favour of his views and we should again be in the position of having to support his scheme or none.[13]

Sidgwick's explanation to the London Committee of his objections centred round the vague issue of timing. He suggested that the Previous might be reformed within a few years and that if Cambridge women were at any real disadvantage vis-à-vis women in the newer Universities who were receiving degrees, this would become more obvious. In addition, Sidgwick felt, though he gave no reason, that they ought to wait for Oxford to catch up with them, so that "the academic education of women should continue to be effectively carried on without any serious check in both the older Universities".[14]*

Emily Davies was unimpressed. At the meeting of the London Committee at which the Cambridge Memorial was read and considered, the feeling in favour of continuing the campaign was very decided. She did not believe that Sidgwick and his friends really represented Cambridge opinion for she had "heard of more support at Cambridge than [she] had ventured to count upon and [was] by no means hopeless of success". Sidgwick had also passed on to her the view that if women pressed their demands, lecturers might withdraw permission for them to attend lectures. Emily Davies retorted tartly:

[this] would show a spirit so unlike that of Cambridge men generally that we need not be seriously afraid of it.[15]

So far Emily Davies had had the better of the contest. The issue of timing was a red herring; the dispute would have been more productive had Sidgwick concentrated on his opposition to the Previous and the Pass Degree. The timing of a reform can never be "right" in the sense that it will meet with no opposition; the right time for a reform is when the opposition is at a minimum and the case in favour is very strong. Neither Sidgwick nor Miss Davies were to know that 1887 was more "right" than any year for the next sixty would prove to be; more important, before the movement for degrees for women could hope to have any success, the women's group would have to agree on the questions of the Previous and the Pass.

* For a brief sketch of events at Oxford, see p. ■.■ and ■.■.

The dispute caused confusion amongst the women at Newnham. Sidgwick's influence was very strong there; his wife, Eleanor Mildred Sidgwick,* was Vice-Principal of the College and shouldered an increasing amount of responsibility as Miss Clough grew old. If the University was going to receive Memorials from groups supporting and opposing women in Cambridge, Newnham could hardly stay silent. But their dilemma was, as Helen Gladstone (at that time Mrs Sidgwick's secretary) put it "to compose a memorial so as not to *ask* for degrees, but not to appear to reject them if they are offered".[16] Sidgwick made this delicate situation even more difficult by bringing the dispute into the open. In a letter to the *Daily News* on 1st July, 1887, he explained his opposition to the London Committee's plans. He was not opposed in principle to the identity of conditions for the two sexes in University examinations and he supported in principle the idea of a mixed university. But he believed that the demand for degrees was inopportune and impolitic, since it was too soon to judge the effect of Newnham and Girton on the life of the University. Further, if women gained admission at the expense of having to take the Previous examination, they would have struck an extremely bad bargain. He suggested that the matter be dropped for four or five years, by which time the Greek of the Little-Go might have disappeared and there could be less talk of "inexperience" in the effect of women on the University environment. The issues were now becoming clearer; Sidgwick wanted the women to have their degrees, his real worry was that imposing the Previous on women candidates would lengthen the life of the examination which he was so committed to change. But the opposite interpretation was quickly pointed out to him by Emily Davies' brother, Llewelyn Davies, who replied to Sidgwick in the columns of the same paper, four days later. He too was opposed to compulsory Greek, but in his opinion the prescription would be abolished all the sooner if women were involved in it, since it would then be very clearly unreasonable. Who might have been right is a matter for conjecture, though Llewelyn Davies was quite mistaken if

* Sidgwick had married Eleanor Mildred Balfour in 1876.

he thought sweet reason would be the guiding star in Cambridge disputes about Greek.

This correspondence did serve the purpose of isolating the real point of disagreement between Sidgwick and the London Committee, and it also gave Henry Jackson, a close friend of Sidgwick but a supporter of the "Girton line", a chance to mediate between the parties. He appreciated that the Girton people could make no headway against Sidgwick's active or even passive opposition; perhaps "*they* [Newnham] should include Poll examinations amongst the Examinations which entitle to degrees, and *we* [Girton] should allow their stipulation for an alternative for the Little-Go".[17] He pointed out that exceptions were already being made to the Previous for those whose educational background was unusual and that this practice would probably grow.* Emily Davies found it hard to swallow such a compromise and lectured Jackson on the importance of "the common standard":

> Our fanaticism on this point arises perhaps chiefly from looking at it with reference to women's questions generally as to which it has been felt to be of extreme importance to maintain the principle "fair field and no favour" which would generally be understood as excluding competition on dissimilar conditions. It has been our flag and we feel great hesitation in accepting anything that looks like a deviation from the general policy, even when the immediate point may seem to be of small importance.[18]

However, she too appreciated that they could not succeed against Sidgwick and, while giving nothing away herself, she admitted that the Committee *might* decide that the dissimilarity of conditions was not worth fighting about.[19]

When the Committee met at the end of September, they made a tactical withdrawal. They would not insist that the Higher Local option should be abolished, simply that the women who used that route to the Tripos should continue to be awarded a certificate rather than a degree. This must have

* See Appendix A.

95

pleased Miss Davies, who had long been irritated by the lack of distinction made between the examination successes of Girton students and those of Newnham. The scheme presented to the University in a revised Memorial in October[20] incorporated even further modifications which this time cannot have satisfied Miss Davies. Membership of the University was no longer requested, nor any stipulations made about the conditions on which the degree would be awarded. The Committee were perhaps hopeful that the University would never agree to give its degrees to women on any conditions which differed from those on which it awarded them to men. There were now no longer any real grounds on which Sidgwick could oppose the approach to the University, and by November 1887 the *Manchester Guardian* was reporting that Sidgwick and the London Committee had accepted a common platform on the details of the demand. The objection that the proposals would irritate the University authorities seemed now to have disappeared.[21] In a letter to Archer-Hind the following month, Sidgwick expressed the hope that the University, while opening fully to women the advantages of its teaching and examinations, would avoid forcing on them a curriculum precisely identical with that prescribed for male undergraduates. Identity of conditions had, he believed been an essential feature of the platform of the London Committee, but their latest Memorial did not reflect this "extreme point of view". Admitting women to teaching and examinations seemed in Sidgwick's mind synonymous with admitting them to membership and he explained to Archer-Hind that he was satisfied that the question of admitting women to membership under such conditions and limitations as might from time to time be determined, could be separated from the question of just what these conditions and limitations might be. He himself would certainly answer the first in the affirmative and trust to the wisdom of the University to settle the second "with a single minded regard to the true interests of the education of women".[22] And so for the time being harmony was restored between the two factions, each privately placing its trust in the wisdom of the University to come up with a solution favourable to its own side.

But the University was not to be allowed to play the role of Solomon at all. At Sidgwick's change of heart, a body of resident members feared that the movement, now moderately and influentially led by him, would be successful. Men like Alfred Marshall who, when the demands of the women and their supporters had seemed too immoderate to cause any anxiety, had written that women might be granted the degree title, now signed the following two Memorials:

A. (*i*) That to tie permanently the Higher Education of Women to the Higher Education of Men by granting the Membership and Degrees of the University of Cambridge to women would be detrimental to the interests of the Education of Women and (*ii*) That if Degrees are granted to Women in connection with the examination of the University of Oxford and Cambridge, they should be conferred by some independent authority, in a position to consider the various educational problems which would arise from the point of view of women's education especially.

(Signed 9th January, 1888, by 180 resident members)

B. We the undersigned Resident Members of the Senate of the University of Cambridge beg leave to express our earnest hope that no step will be taken by the University towards the Admission of Women to Membership and Degrees in the University.

(Signed 9th January, 1888, by 69 resident members)

The latter group gave a detailed list of objections to the presence of women in Cambridge, objections which were to become so familiar in the following decade, serving as the dress uniform of a variety of unexpressed fears. It was held that if women were admitted to the Tripos, they could not for long be excluded from the Ordinary Degree. "The result of having a considerable number of young women resident in Cambridge with no other occupation than reading for an Ordinary Degree might be very serious"—i.e., a threat to discipline. At that time

n Cambridge the majority of undergraduates were Poll men*
for whom the three University years were usually a time of
leisure and amusement before they settled down to the business
of life. Undeniably, their wild and undisciplined behaviour
gave the dons sufficient headaches, without adding a group of
leisured ladies to their number. However, the Memorialists
had absolutely no reason to expect that the women's colleges
would not have exercised, as they had always done, the
strictest control over the women students, keeping them closely
to their books. It is also clear that the wild, though well-bred,
University bloods would instantly revert to gentlemanly
behaviour at the slightest whisper of "ladies present". The
code was strongly maintained and any young man who mis-
behaved himself in the presence of a lady was roundly condemned by his peers. Indeed, the growth of student opposition
to women in Cambridge was due in part to the restraints
which their presence exerted on undergraduate behaviour.
Even if the dons in 1887 could not see that more women might
have eased their discipline problems rather than have added
to them, they might have noticed their own condemnation o
the Poll degree as the refuge of the idle—"with no other
occupation than reading for an Ordinary Degree"—and used
their energies in reforming it. And if none of these points had
occurred to them, they might have remembered that the
University had already barred women from the Poll Examination in 1881 and had the power to do the same again. Similarly
criticism can be levelled against many other points which
were raised against women in this and later controversies.
It was held, for example, that women would flood to Cambridge
in large numbers, both to the women's colleges and as non-
collegiate students. Now the University strictly controlled the
number of non-collegiate male students, and there was no
reason why it would not have also controlled the number of
female non-collegiate students. And when the University
finally acknowledged the existence of women's colleges, they
exercised and continued to exercise until the 1960's, control
over their size.

* As late as 1902, only 53% of degrees were for Honours (given
in Rothblatt, *op. cit.*, p. 185). See Appendix B.

However, one very sensitive point was raised in 1887. Memorialists in favour of the women's case had referred to the growth of opportunities for women at other universities, where they were freely admitted to degrees, and this was the sort of implied criticism which few Cambridge men could swallow. The idea that real educational progress was being made in the newer institutions, and that Cambridge was no longer the leader in the field hurt the men who loved and took a great pride in their university. But they were always able to take refuge in the peculiarities of their own institution which so inhibited academic, organisational and administrative change, and in the belief that because of these special features the education they gave their undergraduates was the best in the land.

The signatories to Memorial B mentioned two of these special features in particular: compulsory residence and the privileges and powers given to graduates. In late Victorian Cambridge, residence as a member of a college for a stipulated number of weeks in a year was held to be the major feature of an undergraduate's education. Here he learnt to rub along with his fellow-men (in the narrow sense of the expression) and from a position of freedom and responsibility it was hoped he would develop a capacity for self control and self reliance.[23] This was the ideal of college life. As has already been suggested, three years at Cambridge represented the last fling of irresponsible behaviour for many undergraduates; yet living a communal life away from one's family is a valuable experience and Cambridge students gained in a way that students residing at home and attending the provincial universities did not. Unfortunately, in the case of women, the possibility of their living away from their parents' home was neither favourably viewed nor generally accepted, and many men genuinely felt that the Cambridge rules, which insisted that uninterrupted residence be maintained for certain weeks of the year, would rest rather heavily on a woman student. At the same time, it was felt that the women in their colleges were isolated from University life and therefore could not benefit from the "real" education of the academic community, though any attempts by the women to share in this life would have been regarded as an unseemly and presumptuous intrusion. The special privileges and responsibilities attached to the degrees of the old universities also distinguished them from their newer rivals. The most important of these were the right to vote for the University M.P., and the right to vote on many issues concerning the running of the University, decisions which in other institutions were taken by small Councils or Governing Bodies. A Cambridge graduate who paid an annual fee to keep his name on the books—and many did not—had the right to vote on issues which ranged from the establishment of a new Chair, and the extension of a laboratory, to the founding of a new Tripos and the purchase of a collection of fossils for the Museum. The extension of such powers to women would have been a move against the tide of public opinion, which at that time was reacting against any further involvement of women in the democratic processes. The counter-argument still pertained—the University could withhold any privileges it so chose and from the outset the London Committee had assumed there would be "abatement of privileges". But to suggest that women should be granted membership in any form was enough to set many Cambridge men on the defensive. The women, in mentioning it, had made a tactical error which they tried to correct in their next confrontation with the University—but it was a mistake which could not easily be erased.

In February 1888, the Council of the Senate met to consider the Memorials which had been placed before it. There were ten in all, but since it was held that the request for admission to degrees by women would involve a change in the constitution of the University, no weight could be attached to the signatures of non-members. Since a majority of the M.A. signatures was against any further concessions to women, and included many of those who were teachers and supporters of the women's movement, the Council declined to take any action. And so, for the time being, the matter was dropped.

7

INTERLUDE

IN HER WORK on the women's emancipation movement,[1]
Ray Strachey describes the years from 1889 to 1897 as a period
of deadlock and discouragement. Public opinion was growing
bored, irritated and indifferent to emancipationist propaganda,
and this was particularly noticeable in the field of education.
Great improvements had occurred following the Schools
Inquiry Commission;* good schools were opened for girls and
there were many opportunities for higher education. London
University had opened its degrees to women in 1878, the
Scottish universities, the Royal Irish, Wales, Durham and the
new provincial universities or university colleges all awarded
their degrees to women by 1895. With these successes came
public complacency, then reaction. The second inquiry into
secondary education,[2] which opened in 1894, had little to say
on the specific subject of girls' education, beyond noting a
"most marked" improvement in girls' schools, proprietary
and private as well as endowed. The universities were con-
gratulated for producing a large supply of competent teachers—
"no change in recent years has been more conspicuous than
this, nor any more beneficial"—but were not called on to
make any greater contribution. In reply to questions on the
relationship between schools and the universities, only Henry
Sidgwick's brother Arthur, from Oxford University, felt it
necessary to spell out how tenuous was the foothold women had
in the ancient universities.

This feeling that all was well with women's educational
opportunities allowed many men, not only nature's reaction-
aries, but many who had given the women pioneers moral
support and practical assistance, to oppose their advance at

* See above, Chapter 3.

Cambridge. There was no special need for women to continue knocking on the doors of Cambridge University; there were plenty of other institutions where they would be welcome—they could even found a university of their own. Why should they share in the male inheritance of seven centuries? Cambridge was tired of change after a quarter-century of reform and was no longer able to respond to the ideals of education and justice set before it. Women's education was no longer its responsibility—they could go somewhere else. Nor was it just against the development of women's education that the University set its face; Sidgwick, who throughout his life had done so much to revitalise the academic life of Cambridge, was near to despair in the 1890's and, in her *Memoir* of her husband, Eleanor Mildred Sidgwick wrote that he felt Cambridge had "become hidebound in a kind of stupid conservatism", and he anticipated "a long period of slow decadence in which, from failure to adapt itself to the needs of the times, it would gradually fall into disrepute".[3]

In their search for equality of opportunity in the field of higher education, the women at Cambridge certainly faced very positive barriers of opposition. They continued, however, to make full use of the facilities which were available to them and to excel in their degree examinations. One spectacular success in Cambridge aroused a great deal of public interest. Philippa Fawcett, daughter of Henry Fawcett and his wife Millicent Garrett, was classed above the Senior Wrangler* in the 1890 Mathematical Tripos lists. In the same year, Margaret Alford of Girton College was bracketed with the Senior Classic; but her success was overshadowed by Miss Fawcett's result, for it had long been held that women were incapable of such abstract thought as Mathematics involved. In later years, some writers referred back to this event as the one which had convinced them that women should have the same educational opportunities as men. On the other hand, though it is hard to pin down, the resentment of women competing with men begins to grow from 1890 onwards. The

* Described then as "the most famous mathematical honour in the world". In Part II of the Tripos, which was less competitive, she was also placed in the First Class.

pattern of opposition which grew up around Elizabeth Garrett's effort in the 1860's to receive a medical education was to be repeated in Cambridge following the success of her niece. For when Miss Garrett had first attended the medical classes at the Middlesex Hospital, her fellow (male) students had greeted her kindly. But when she incautiously revealed that she was both an able and ambitious student, they had her turned out.[4]

It was still necessary to convince certain sections of the public that advanced study was not harmful to the female constitution. The rumours of girls "ruining their health" while at college reached such proportions that Mrs Sidgwick was obliged to undertake a major statistical study of the health of Cambridge and Oxford women students compared with that of their non-student sisters.[5] Her conclusion was that as large a proportion of women students enjoyed good health after going through college as had enjoyed it before. Further, there was a clear indication of an improvement in health during the three years of college study compared with the preceding five years, an improvement which could not be observed in women who were not students. As mothers of healthy families, women who had been to university were found to be more satisfactory than their sisters who had not. One man, at least, was convinced, and in writing to Henry Sidgwick to thank him for a copy of his wife's *Statistics*, Sir Francis Galton, the geneticist, proposed a scheme to encourage the early marriage of girls who had proved the soundness of their physical and intellectual health:

As Honours girls are now shown to be no less healthy than others of the same rank, there is a strong reason for encouraging their early marriage and consequent early and large families, who would, on average, be hereditarily gifted. They are the last persons to whom so-called 'prudential checks' should apply. We want to swamp the produce of the proletariat by a better stock. . . . I heartily wish it were possible to institute a dower fund as an equivalent to Fellowships. It is a monstrous shame to use any of these gifted girls for hack work, such as bread winning. It is as bad as using up the winners of the Oakes in harness work.

Francis Galton's dower-fund was to be used in rewarding candidates who had been selected by a Board of women for their good physique and morale, "especially such as appeared to have been hereditarily derived and therefore to be the more probably transmissible", with "£50 on marriage, if before the age of twenty-six and £25 on the birth of each and every living child". Such an award "would suffice to affirm the principle in an outspoken manner and to assure marriageable men that marriage with such girls was *safe*".[6] Galton urged Sidgwick to give the matter some thought, but the latter must have been too aware of the delicacy of the women's position in Cambridge in the midst of so many men to want to give the scheme any consideration.

The authorities of the women's colleges never forgot the precariousness of their existence and were forever vigilant lest their students' behaviour might give offence. All contact between male and female students was potentially dangerous and had to be kept to the minimum. As one Newnham student put it,[7] their definition of "danger" was somewhat narrow-minded and tedious. The girls were chaperoned in any place where men might be encountered and a large part of the river was out of bounds for fear men might be bathing there. A student once caused a great panic by being seen walking in the College gardens with a man. The offending male proved to be the girl's brother, but she was reminded by the Principal that "the brother of one was not the brother of all". Hockey was played, but in the most secluded part of the garden, hidden by the College buildings—a necessary precaution since hockey skirts were six inches from the ground. The caution of the Cambridge women was neither appreciated nor shared by other institutions; one visiting women's hockey team brought a man with them to umpire the match. He was made to leave the College at once. Yet, generally speaking, the students accepted the limitations of their activities as laid down by their elders. As the Newnham student put it:

> We filled our lives with work and play within the college, regardless of the thousands of young men who were living nearby. College societies abounded and in debates and in the Mock Parliament many students acquired a facility in

speaking which was to be useful to them in their future lives. We read papers to one another; we danced and acted; the musical ones played and sang.[8]

If the young women did not find the restrictions on their movements too irksome, the women teachers certainly did. These women were doing important work preparing their students for the University examinations, and they were often themselves anxious to follow up lines of research. Their work was continually hindered by their isolation from the other University teachers and their exclusion from all matters concerning the organisation of the Triposes; their enthusiasm for research was dampened by the absence of funds for advanced work, and they were barred from University prizes and scholarships which might have helped them financially. One big inconvenience was the restriction placed on their use of the University Library. In 1891 the teachers of the two colleges combined in a petition to the Library Syndicate for some relaxation of the rules, which limited their use of the Library to the hours between 10 a.m. and 2 p.m. During these hours, the women were usually teaching and the Syndicate were "respectfully requested" that subject to payment of the necessary fee, the women might receive permission to use the Library from 10 a.m. to 4 p.m., an extension of two hours. Permission was refused.[9]

Since a recognised academic career was closed to them at the University, some women sought another avenue for their teaching talents which would enable them to retain their links with Cambridge. The members of the University Extension Lecture Syndicate* included several strong supporters of women, not least of whom was the Secretary, Arthur Berry. In February 1893 he informed the women's colleges that the Syndicate was prepared to receive applications from women for appointment as Lecturers, provided they showed exceptional fitness for the work. This was a new departure and the Syndicate was anxious that the experiment should in the first

* The Syndicate appointed by the Council of the Senate to take charge of the extension lecture scheme which had developed from James Stuart's activities in the 1860's, above p. ■.4.

instance be a conspicuous success. A First in a Tripos, it was agreed, should be a *sine qua non* and in addition, a woman applicant would have to show a marked aptitude for the art of lecturing. Ellen McArthur, a Girtonian who had gained a First in the History Tripos in 1885 and who had several years' experience as a lecturer at Girton, was appointed as an Extension lecturer in December 1893, just after the Syndicate had published its annual report for the previous twelve months. When her appointment became known Alfred Marshall complained to the Vice-Chancellor in his capacity as Chairman of the Extension Syndicate that the appointment was underhand and that the Syndicate did not have power to make it under the existing Ordinances.[10] In Marshall's opinion, a career of public lecturing to largely male audiences was unsuitable for a woman and would damage her character.* But no one seemed prepared to join Marshall in his objections. Arthur Berry replied that the appointment had not been concealed and that it would appear quite properly in the next report. He added, with assumed indifference, that the matter would not be given any prominence, since the Syndicate felt it might give a false importance to what they considered a trivial matter.

Despite this rebuff, Marshall continued to obstruct the appointment of women as Extension lecturers. Another Girtonian, who had gained a First in Mathematics and then, as a student of Marshall, a First in Moral Science, worked as a clerk on the Royal Commission on Labour of which Marshall was a member. This was an unusual job for a woman to gain and when the Commission was finished she returned to Cambridge as a coach, but her aim was to become a University lecturer. As a start she wrote to the Secretary of the University Extension Board asking to be considered. She asked Marshall for a reference, but he was so strongly opposed to the idea that he wrote a personal letter to every member of the Board urging her non-appointment. She was, in his opinion, too young and feminine to be suitable for audiences almost wholly masculine. He was prepared to believe that she would be able to hold the attention of her audience but, from a psychological point

* As Principal of the newly founded University College at Bristol, Marshall had allowed his wife to lecture to mixed classes.

of view, would this holding influence be the kind of influence which was altogether satisfactory?[11]

While Marshall was conducting his own private war against the advances of women, the Board of Trinity College, Dublin, were opposing the admission of women to their institution for reasons which they gave with an unblushing honesty. Not for them a delicate reference to "discipline problems" nor the concern over the cruder parts of the Latin Classics expressed by many Cambridge men, who hoped to shield a woman's innocence by keeping her in ignorance. In Dublin, women were devils in skirts. As the Board put it in their reply to the women's request for admission to the educational benefits of the College, parents placed their sons in residence at Trinity College in the persuasion that their morals would be subject to some supervision and such supervision would become impossible if women were allowed within the walls of an institution intended for the residence of young men. It had been suggested that any female who entered the College gates would be chaperoned—but it could not be left to the discretion of the gate-porter to determine whether, of two women passing through, one was of sufficient age to be a suitable guardian to the other. The Board added forthrightly,

> . . . if a female had once passed the gate, it would be practically impossible to watch what buildings or what chambers she might enter, or how long she might remain there.[12]

The leaders of the Irish women, though they had the support of the majority of teachers and Fellows of the College, had a particularly frustrating time in their dealings with the Board who used a variety of tactics to delay the moment of refusal.* Their tribulations were not without some benefits. During their campaign, the women had amassed, often with the aid of women at Oxford and Cambridge, facts, figures and opinions on the presence of women in British universities— useful groundwork for later campaigns.

* The women first made their request for admission at the time of the tercentenary of the College in March 1892. They were refused in July 1895.

The women at Oxford were the next to try their luck. The events which led to the foundation of women's colleges there, were similar to those which had produced Girton and Newnham at Cambridge. A lecture scheme was successfully established in 1873 and by the end of the decade, Somerville College and Lady Margaret Hall, the one non-denominational and the other connected with the Church of England, were receiving students. Other women resided privately in town. By 1884, most Honours Schools and other examinations were open to them, though like their sisters at Cambridge, Oxford women were not awarded a degree. Though differing greatly in points of detail, there was a similarity of constitution between the two universities, marking them off from the newer institutions and casting them in the roles of both conspirators and rivals in the affairs of women. Rivalry led them each to reject women on the grounds that a "mixed" University would result in an exodus of the best men to "the other place". As conspirators, they came close to expelling women from both their sacred precincts to a woman's university, possibly sited at Bletchley, mid-way between Oxford and Cambridge.

> We hear on good authority that the reason why Bletchley will be chosen as the site of the Women's University which will be founded after the Senate has rejected the present proposals for a Degree, is that no fast mails stop there. *Granta*, 8th May, 1897.

Fortunately, old habits of independence could not give way even before the deadly peril of academic women and the plan never materialised. The women at the two universities were no less independent and there were elements of both support and rivalry in the action of women at Cambridge in beginning their own agitation for degrees, following the lead taken by Oxford women.* The women at Oxford were refused their degrees by a vote taken in March 1896. In Cambridge at that time, hostilities had just begun.

* Henry Jackson wrote to Henry Sidgwick in 1895, "I regret exceedingly that the Oxford people have moved without warning us". (11.9.1895. G.A.)

8

A NEW CAMPAIGN

THE EXAMPLE OF the women at Oxford in seeking degrees raised the topic once more at Cambridge. The experience of 1887 was fresh in their memories, and the old campaigners hesitated to reopen the issue. Both colleges, however, now had a large corpus of old students whose voices could not be ignored, especially in Newnham where the Associates, an elected body of old students and teaching staff, had some share in the government of the College. In the late summer of 1895, Emily Davies approached the Sidgwicks, having by this time appreciated that despite her own personal feelings in the matter, she could do nothing about degrees without their co-operation. The Sidgwicks were in no hurry to act. Their proposal was to do nothing until the question had been settled at Oxford, and then to approach Cambridge with a joint Girton-Newnham Memorial, asking for full membership and all which that entailed. If the boldness of such a move delighted Miss Davies, she was quickly brought down by the admission that the Sidgwicks intended to try to get "special conditions" for women, that is, for them to be excused the Previous. On hearing this, Miss Davies rejected the idea of a joint Memorial, pointing out that inconvenience and embarrassment was likely to arise from having a Memorial signed by people who wanted fundamentally different things.[1] Henry Jackson, to whom Emily Davies had written an account of her meeting with the Sidgwicks, concluded that without their full support it was inexpedient to open a campaign.[2] But younger voices were determined to force the issue. At the annual meeting of the Newnham Associates held on Saturday, 2nd November, 1895, it was agreed that the following resolution should be submitted to the Council of Newnham College for their comments: "that in the opinion of the Associates of Newnham College, the Senate should be asked to admit women to membership of the University and to University degrees".[3] In phrasing their resolution this way, the Associates made it clear that they were fully aware that it was possible to separate the matter of a degree title from the membership of the University, with all the privileges which the latter entailed, and that as far as they were concerned, they wanted both. Their bluntness was to lead them into difficulties as the campaign advanced, yet it is clear at this point that even the more cautious of the women's leaders did not feel that they were asking for too much. Miss Davies had been privately informed by Marion Green-wood, one of the Newnham Associates, that in discussing the question of University membership, the issue of "identity of conditions" had not come up, adding that in any case, year by year, more Newnham students were obtaining identity of conditions by taking the Little-Go.[4] The implication that an important body of Newnham people would accept the Little-Go raised Miss Davies' spirits, and she rounded on a correspondent who suggested there was no support for the women's case amongst University people. In 1887, the women's colleges had taken opposite paths; if this time Girton and Newnham were to work together, "may we not hope their zeal will to some extent infect others and rouse the lukewarm to greater earnestness?"[5] She was further encouraged by a letter from a Newnham Council member who stressed that it was absolutely essential that there should be no suggestion of special examination requirements for women. In his view, the Sidgwicks were almost isolated in their stand against the Previous, and though they were likely to try to oppose identity of conditions they would not succeed.[6]

The Newnham Council received the Associates' resolution "with pleasure", and in their turn resolved that a committee be appointed to confer with Girton Council and resident members of the Senate "as to the time when a favourable opportunity will occur to make application to the Senate to admit women to membership of the University and to degrees".[7] With no recorded disagreement, it was assumed that there was a case for admitting women to University membership; the point at issue was, again, timing. Although there were no

signs that the University was in an especially favourable mood'
Sidgwick, though still very hesitant, accepted that the women's
case demanded consideration. His opinion was confirmed at
a meeting of resident members on 7th December, where it
was agreed that the University Council should be memorialised
with a request that they appoint a Syndicate to report upon
what conditions and with what restrictions, if any, women
should be admitted to degrees in the University of Cambridge.
How consciously this Memorial was designed to separate the
issues of membership and degrees is not known, but its most
remarkable feature was that it began from the assumption that
women *should* be admitted to degrees and simply left the
Syndicate to work out the mechanics of the operation. Even
more surprising was that in the space of about six weeks, the
Memorial received over 2,000 signatures of support. If this
was a true measure of the number of Cambridge men who felt
that women ought, at the very minimum interpretation of the
request, to be awarded the title of the degree for which they
had successfully passed the examinations, the events of the
following eighteen months are most perplexing. For in signing
the Memorial, 2,000 men had accepted that women should be
allowed to take at least some Cambridge degree, and were
simply concerned to see how this should be arranged. When
it came to a vote, a year and a half later, at least three-quarters
of these men had changed their minds.

A group of resident members formed themselves into a
committee to promote the admission of women to degrees and
invited representatives of the two women's colleges to join
them. Marian Kennedy of Newnham and Emily Davies were
appointed as Secretaries. Miss Davies kept rather quiet in the
ensuing controversy; it was clearly bad tactics on this occasion
for Girton to stand apart from Newnham and insist on their
own conditions for admission to degrees. Nor were Emily
Davies' views on the Previous especially popular with her
colleagues in Girton, though having taken the examination it
was no doubt irksome for Girton girls to be classed in the same
way as those from Newnham. On the other hand, the substitution of the Higher Locals for the Previous was not well
thought of by the main body of Newnham people, who,

despite their loyalty to Sidgwick, felt the issue only confused the case which the women were making for degrees.

But in the early months of 1896, the women's cause was riding high; it seemed only a matter of time before they would be awarded their degrees. One thousand two hundred and thirty-four past students of Girton and Newnham had petitioned the Senate and imposing Memorials were received from other interested groups. At first, the reasons for giving women their degrees were not very clearly presented; from the response to the Memorial of 7th December, the case seemed to be well understood. But as the first rumblings of opposition were heard, women began to consider the details of their platform. Their approach was far shrewder than it had been ten years previously; they were no longer so naive as to believe that, even to University men, an appeal to fair play and a reference to abstract justice would win them their case. The men's main fear seemed to centre on the possibility of women interfering with men's university education, and so the topic of women's place in the University was avoided. Instead the women chose to press the commercial advantages of having a degree and began to gather case-histories of students who had been passed over because they possessed merely a Tripos "Certificate". But it soon became clear that opponents could manipulate the point to the women's disadvantage. Alfred Marshall produced an eight-page pamphlet on 3rd February, 1896,[8] in which he accepted that there were professional disadvantages involved in not having a degree title. As a remedy, he suggested that women be granted the degrees of E.B.A. (*Externa*) or A.B.A. *Associata*). These titles would not imply that women had undergone the same residence as men nor would it give them a claim to any membership of the University. In Marshall's view, the question of residence was paramount and no girl should be expected to comply with the same rules as men did in this matter. A man's first duty was to fulfil his family's hopes for him and he was unlikely to have to concern himself during his undergraduate life with the welfare of his parents and his relations. The Cambridge conditions of residence were, in his case, not onerous.

But the same rules when applied to women have very different effects. A girl on leaving school can do many things both for parents and for younger brothers and sisters, which a lad could not do, even if he stayed at home. While the lad is almost sure to have to earn his own living by work outside the household, the girl will in nine cases out of ten be responsible later on for the household management either as a wife or sister; and concentration of nearly all her energies on merely intellectual work for three or four years is far from being the unmixed gain to her that it is to young men. But with our present arrangements, however urgent the need for her presence at home, she must keep her terms steadily under penalty of losing recognition for her work. If she decides to go her own way, and let her family shift for themselves, she gets honours; but her true life is impoverished and not enriched by them. Those whose natures are the fullest and who would turn to best account for the world whatever opportunities were afforded to them, are just those who are most likely to be deterred from coming to Cambridge for fear of this strain between their desire for knowledge with honour and their affection for those at home.

Marshall had been brought to this conclusion by his experience in Bristol, and he recommended that the best method of higher education for women was for them to spend half their time on domestic duties and half on study. A full reading of the pamphlet leaves no room for doubt that Marshall wanted to keep women out of Cambridge at all costs. He may well have felt that in general the "better girl of the family", as he put it, would not want to study away from home. He accepted that her inferior sister might be spared, but still opposed the awarding of a proper degree to her. Marshall's point that girls above school-age had responsibility for the welfare of their families was based on outdated reasoning. It reflected the persistently-held belief that women's studies are of less importance than those of men and can therefore more readily be sacrificed, a belief which had been criticised by the Schools Inquiry Commission as early as 1867.* Even at that time, it

* See above, Chapter 3.

was beginning to be recognised that uneducated, unmarried girls were a heavy burden to their families and a source of anxiety to their brothers and fathers. It was an appreciation of this economic insecurity which had driven women to seek education in the first place and press for more job opportunities. As editor of the *Englishwoman's Year Book*, Miss L. M. Hubbard, may have been tempted to exaggerate her case a little, but when she wrote the *Preface* to the 1886 edition of the *Year Book*, she was no doubt correct when she spoke of great changes having occurred in recent years.

> Not only is the duty of earning a living now fully recognised as incumbent upon women as well as upon men, who do not inherit independence, but the dignity of work, whether undertaken by them for remuneration or no, is upheld and the social status of a single woman is no longer considered as, in itself, less honourable than that of a wife.

Ten years later, in a lecture at University College, Liverpool,[9] Mrs Sidgwick was more precise about the problem. Fifty per cent of girls in the classes from which Cambridge drew its students did not marry, a figure far in excess of that for the population in general. She continued,

> . . . parents who are unable to leave their daughters a sufficient fortune to secure them comfortable independence would be guilty of culpable negligence if they did not provide for placing them in a position to earn their own living.

Mrs Sidgwick also believed that due to the increase of manufactured food and clothing, the invention of the sewing machine and other labour-saving devices, girls had very little domestic work to do in their homes. Instead, their time was filled with trivial occupations which contributed little to the formation of sound characters. The need to study away from home was still as great as it had been when Girton and Newnham had been founded a quarter of a century earlier. As it was explained at the Conference of Women Workers in

1894,[10] the strain and friction of studying at home sapped the mental, moral and physical powers of concentration:

> An absolutely free time, say even two consecutive hours a day, which at least is a modest demand, is almost more impossible for most girls in ordinary middle-class homes, than it is for domestic servants.

Students derived great benefit from having a room of their own, where they could work without disturbance, with no claims from outside, "no calls of clashing duty", regular hours and meals provided for them. Emily Davies had well understood this when she sited her college in the country, away from Cambridge; she had wanted her students to be *unavailable*. When Henry Sidgwick was considering founding his house of residence for women students in Cambridge, his mother explained to him how so many women during the freshest part of their lives used all their powers of mind and body in the accomplishment of those small duties and services to their families which did not call forth their highest powers, so that when old age with its increased leisure and its many feeblenesses overtook them, they lacked the energy to make effective use of it.[11] Women at college were accused of selfishness, since they put their own needs and desires above those of their families; this was a criticism which Alfred Marshall levelled against them, but the more modern viewpoint was that this narrow concern for family was equally selfish. Women should interest themselves in the needs of the wider community, not just as Lady Bountifuls, carrying soup to the sick of the parish, but as social workers with minds disciplined and judgements sharpened by study. The experience of college life could contribute a weakening of prejudices and an enlargement of sympathies.

In general, Marshall's views on residence were not echoed by other critics of the women's colleges, nor were his views on the intellectual ability of women. Marshall was one of the very few serious commentators to put forward the view that women possessed a lower intellectual potential than men. They were good at examination, since they were naturally diligent, but they lacked the ability to go further. Presented in mild language and projecting an image of great reasonableness and concern for the welfare and best interests of women, Marshall's document proved the rallying point for the opposition. By the end of the month the anti-women lobby had their own committees and two Memorials. The battle had begun.

Mrs Sidgwick made an able reply to Marshall's pamphlet,[12] providing him with hard facts about unmarried women, the health of students who try to combine home commitments and study, and stressing the professional disadvantages of having a qualification, a Tripos Certificate, the value of which was not universally understood. She accepted that facilities for non-residential degrees were needed by men and women alike and reminded Marshall of what was already available. But college residence was a most valuable part of Cambridge education, mentally, morally and physically, and those women who could take advantage of it should not be denied it. As far as intellectual potential was concerned, Mrs Sidgwick challenged Marshall's claim that women were not capable of constructive work. What opportunities had women had for higher work?—there were no fellowships, prizes or academic posts available to them. She sternly warned Marshall that "the whole course of the movement for the academic education of women is strewn with the wrecks of hasty generalisations as to the limits of women's intellectual powers". None the less, Marshall's pamphlet was very damaging, for he could claim to have taught women for many years and to have been one of their original supporters.

Sniper fire was now beginning to be heard from various directions. The Bishop of Durham, B. F. Westcott, wrote to Henry Sidgwick saying that he could hardly think that Cambridge women students could be at a disadvantage without a degree and that they ought to be strong enough to bear it if they were. "Sensible people in England cannot have this Hindu superstition as to the degree letters."[13] Mr S. J. D. Shaw wrote to the *Manchester Guardian* saying that if the 659 women who had gained Honours since 1881 had not been able to make the value of their Cambridge education felt in the world, this education was a failure and the University could "hardly be expected to lay aside old prejudices and reorganise its social status to help persons who are so little able to make use of their privileges".[14] On the other hand, support came from some curious quarters. The British Medical Association in its *Journal* of 15th February, 1896 felt that women should not be refused the valuable hallmark of a degree, and they strongly criticised Marshall's suggestion that women could divide their time between home and study. Strain begins for students when there is a conflict of loyalties and mental training is impossible amid the distractions of home life. But the *Journal* was not speaking for all doctors. Some claimed that a Cambridge education was not suitable for women as they needed courses adapted to their special mental and moral features. Rivalry between the sexes caused only harm in the long run.

A cry for "special courses", often accompanied by the suggestion that a university for women be established, was sent up repeatedly by women's opponents. Not once, however, did they suggest the precise differences which should exist between courses for men and women, and as the women so often pointed out, in all the institutions of higher education open to them there were a vast number of courses which women could follow. If they followed those at Cambridge, it was because they suited their purposes. But though the argument about courses for women was devoid of any theoretical basis, some confusion may have existed in the minds of casual observers who saw the women at Newnham taking the Higher Locals instead of the Previous—Higher Locals must therefore be specially adapted to "women's needs". Another popular and often repeated opinion was that men should not be responsible for women's education, a somewhat hypocritical suggestion since men claimed the right to exercise responsibility for woman in all other spheres of activity. Also popular were schemes for a women's university where, in the distant future, women Professors might run women's courses in an institute of academic excellence all of their own. So confused were the motives of many writers on the subject that they often did not even envisage the scheme in the hands of women. The women's colleges in Oxford, Cambridge and London were to unite under their own Charter and while continuing to follow the syllabus, teaching and examinations of their original university, would award their own degrees. This idea had first been put forward by G. F. Browne in 1888,[15] and further expanded in an article in the *Nineteenth Century* in May 1893, where the new foundation was to be named "The Imperial University" in honour of Queen Victoria's long reign. It is not clear how this plan was to solve the problem of the assumed unsuitability for women of courses of higher education originally designed for men, and it is to be noted that the teaching of women was to remain in the hands of men. But one point was assured: by founding a separate degree-conferring body for women, the threat of their interference in men's education was removed.

Other men were less ambivalent about the responsibility of each sex for its own education; the women's university was to be completely isolated from Oxford and Cambridge and staffed by women teachers. This suggestion was the more dangerous as it was consistent. Henry Sidgwick's attitude towards it was that women's education was still in a state where experiment was desirable and a women's university could be considered in this light. But it was too soon to expect women to be able to provide their own academic staff and at no time could the existence of a women's university be a valid excuse for refusing education to those girls who wanted to attend Oxford or Cambridge. A women's university could no doubt, by that time, teach its students to succeed in examinations, but there would remain an élite who were interested in knowledge for its own sake and who wished to gain an understanding of the methods by which it was being advanced in a variety of subjects. Such an education could only be given in an institution where the active prosecution of original research and thought was being kept up and, for the time being at least, this meant Oxford or Cambridge.[16]

In the press and private letters, competition between women and men was a recurrent theme. Mrs Sidgwick was personally advised to "seek and follow as only a woman can" by a gentleman who signed himself "Member of the Senate". In page after page of thickly blotted ink and scrawling writing, he accused womankind of Satanic ambition and pride and an ungodly, unnatural competition with man, to whom the all-wise Creator had allotted her as helpmate.[17] This letter was the work of a crank, but the question of competition was no longer just one of offending manly pride. There was a real fear that women would compete with men for jobs. Many men were hoisted by the petards of their own prejudices. They demanded respect as a family's bread-winner; as a result, women's wages were lower than men's and women pushed men out of jobs. The professions were very vulnerable to an attack from women. If, as men had so often insisted, women had special "feminine" talents, medicine was a very obvious profession in which they could display them. Women were taking over school-teaching and the instruction of young boys.[18] It was feared they would soon follow women in Europe who were "forcing their way not only into the pulpit but into the Bar, where their intrusion into criminal cases can hardly fail to be injurious to justice".* They had made certain encroachments on public offices at local government level, and there can have been few members of the academic staff at Cambridge who regarded as permanent a situation in which outstanding women could be passed over for University appointments and the rewards of Fellowships. Undergraduates were concerned with the bogey of over-crowded professions because of the rapid expansion of tertiary education, and, when some Senior Members turned to the undergraduates to support their opposition to women, this fear proved a fertile soil into which to plant their ideas.

The opposition called a meeting, under the Chairmanship of A. Austen Leigh, the Provost of King's, at the Masonic Hall on 22nd February, 1896, to oppose the B.A. degree for women and "co-education" in Cambridge. The Master of Selwyn objected to any step which would tend to a more complete assimilation of the education of men and women in Cambridge, the outcome of which "would not be education but degradation". Professor Clifford Allbutt "calculated" that in ten years

* From an "Old Oxford Professor" now in Canada to *The Times* 10.5.1897. The letter continued, "they are now trying to force their way into the militia and the police. The other day, a score of them asserted their right to be present at a great prize fight and rivalled the male spectators in brutality."

there would be a thousand women students in Cambridge.*
Such an influx would inevitably lower the standard of
University teaching, for women on the whole were intellectually
inferior to men. Marshall put forward again his proposal for
some degree title for women which would not imply membership of the University. He opposed any steps which would tend
to make Cambridge a "mixed" University, since it could not
be shown that any mixed University had ever attained "high
rank". The meeting agreed that the best general solution to
the "women question" was the establishment of a women's
university.[19]

A public expression of this opposition was not felt to be
urgent; it seemed possible that the women could be defeated
by other means than an exhausting battle of counter-
memorials and flysheets.† The Grace proposing that a
Syndicate be established to consider the women's case had
been published on 17th February and was to be voted on on
12th March. The form of the Grace had been taken from the
Memorial drawn up by Sidgwick and it by-passed the question
of whether women ought to have degrees and concerned itself
with how they would be awarded. A second Grace defined the
membership of the Syndicate. These terms of reference had
already been attacked in a flysheet the previous month, and
in the week before the vote further flysheets appeared condemning the membership of the Syndicate because it contained
too many declared partisans, and only two men who had
graduated after 1876. The Committee for promoting the
admission of women to degrees immediately saw in this a
threat, not simply to the second Grace on the composition of
the Syndicate, but also to the first one which established its
existence, and they circularised their supporters warning them
of this danger.

The opposition group then made their charge against the
membership of the Syndicate more explicit. "It is felt that two
of the Members of the proposed Syndicate, honoured by all

* Seventy years later there were still less than 1,000 women
undergraduates in Cambridge.

† The name given in Cambridge to the written expressions of
opinion which are circulated during University controversies.

Cambridge men on account of their splendid services to the University, are specially disqualified for the exercise of judicial functions in this matter by their close connection with a College which is somewhat in the position of a suitor in the case which will come before the Syndicate." The two members referred to were clearly Sidgwick and Dr Peile. The objection was unprecedented and hurtful, especially to Sidgwick, who was as much devoted to the well-being of the University as to the welfare of Newnham. The supporters hastened to remind people that the Syndicate's function was deliberative, not judicial, and that it was customary to select men who had special knowledge of the questions under consideration. Whatever their hopes, the opposition must have been voicing some genuine fears about the composition of the Syndicate, for when the two Graces were put to the vote, the first was passed, but the second defeated by a narrow majority, 186 votes to 171. A summary of opinion at this point would seem to be that a large number of Cambridge men wanted women to have the University degree, but that some of them at least were afraid that the proposed Syndicate was so partisan that the conditions for admission to degrees would be made too easy. It is also clear that declared opponents of the women were facing the possibility of defeat and that they would have to embark on a more positive campaign of opposition. The tactics of interfering with the Syndicate were dropped and a second body was appointed in May without opposition. Instead, two Memorials were circulated; *Memorial A* earnestly deprecated "the admission of women to membership of the University or to any of the Degrees which are conferred on members of the University"; signatories of *Memorial B* were "prepared to support a proposal for conferring some title which does not imply membership of the University on women, who having satisfied the requirements of the University, have already passed or shall hereafter pass a Tripos Examination". By October these had received 2,437 signatures.

During the summer vacation there was not much public discussion on the Degree issue, but before the University went down, two flysheets were directed against the women which must have worried and annoyed them.[20] The first was from

H. R. Tottenham of St John's, who felt that those who had drawn up the two Memorials did not represent a group of people who, like himself, wanted women removed entirely from the University. This group was never large; but the threat of total rejection must have been continuous anxiety for the women for although they had been in Cambridge approximately thirty-five years, their formal links with the University were very slender. The second flysheet was simply exasperating. The Provost of King's, Austen Leigh, elaborated on Marshall's theme of residence. He did not oppose residence for women, he simply dismissed it as a poor imitation of the real thing which would never qualify them for a true Cambridge degree.

> The value attached to the B.A. degree depends to a large extent on the fact that for three years our undergraduates have undergone a severe ordeal of character and conduct. They have been in a position of freedom and responsibility. Their share in the common life of a large and miscellaneous body of men has tested and developed their capacity for self-control and self-reliance. They have gradually trained themselves for the duties and opportunities of later life. There is little of this in the life of a Girton or Newnham student. It may be liberty compared to her home life; but it is a very faint copy of the wider opportunities and severe trials which an undergraduate must face.

The moral code of the Victorian middle-class accepted that men had "uncontrollable passions". The male, however, was not to be penalised for this weakness; it was the female's duty to surround herself with chaperones, hide her body in cumbersome clothes and avoid every indiscretion in order to protect the male from temptation. The authorities at Newnham and Girton had gone to extremes to see that their students gave no cause for comment, circumscribing them with petty rules so that they would conform to the strictest interpretation of the current code of social behaviour. Now they were to be penalised for the caution which they had adopted, not so much to discipline the girls, but to protect them from the indiscipline of the young men. Austen Leigh must have been well aware just *how* many Poll men used their "position of freedom and responsibility", and that for most undergraduates the three glorious years of college life were not so much a preparation for life as an escape from it.

Arthur Berry and W. N. Shaw, the energetic Secretaries to the Degree Syndicate, began preparing the ground for the Syndicate's deliberations early in October. Despite their limited terms of reference, they felt obliged to consider the position of women in the University generally, and why women should be awarded degrees. For information on the first point, they circularised all the lecturers on the General Board List asking:

1. Are your lectures open to women? Are any special conditions attached to their admission?
2. Are women admitted to ordinary Laboratory courses? To the Laboratory for advanced research?
3. Are the above permissions to attend Laboratories for lectures restricted to the women of Girton and Newnham?
4. Have any inconveniences or advantages resulted from their presence? Are such effects different from what they would have been if the additional numbers had been men?
5. Have you found it advisable to alter in any way the subject-matter or method of your teaching in consequence of the attendance of women students?[21]

The replies to these questions came in rather slowly; they were carefully analysed and many were printed in the final report. The answers to questions four and five are rather comic when read today, but they represent feelings strongly held at the time.

History "No inconvenience; perhaps some advantages, as the class of women who take up history is relatively better than the class of men who take the same subject on the whole."

"Inconveniences have certainly resulted as far as men are concerned; the women coming more punctually and generally together, have occupied the best seats."

"No inconvenience, except an extra pressure on the

lecturer's time due to the fact that so large a percentage of them do papers in connexion with lectures, compared with men."

In Classics, Biology and Geology there were complaints that the subject matter of lectures had to be modified for mixed audiences and in the laboratories "certain drawbacks arise from the chivalrous feeling that women must sit first, come first and see first". The same habits of the women produce different reactions in the men teachers; some found their enthusiasm an embarrassment, others welcomed it; some found their presence improved the undergraduates' manners, others found they aroused inconvenient notions of chivalry.

A lady is more easily affected if fault is found with her work and if unexpected difficulties arise. Men also are shy of exposing themselves by making mistakes in their answers if ladies are present.

A few lecturers, particularly in the science subjects, complained that the women needed greater attention since they lacked a good basic training—a complaint which was no doubt justified. There is only one comment on the inferiority of women's intellects and that is under the Moral Sciences section. The hand is unmistakably that of Alfred Marshall.

As regards lectures, I consider my first duty is to Members of the University and consequently endeavour to lecture as though men only were present. When lecturing to women alone, I have adopted a different manner of treating my subject which I believe to be better adapted for them. Their presence in the class prevents men from speaking freely either in answering or asking questions; it therefore makes the lectures more mechanical and similar in effect to the reading part of a book aloud than they otherwise would be.

As regards the informal instruction and advice given 'at home', I do not admit women to my ordinary 'at home', . . . but make occasional special appointments for them.

I adopt this course partly because of the difficulty of getting men and women to open their minds freely in one another's presence, and partly because I find the questions asked by women generally relate to lectures or book work and/or else to practical problems such as poor relief. Whilst men who have attended fewer lectures and read fewer books and are perhaps likely to obtain less marks in examinations, are more apt to ask questions showing mental initiative and giving promise of original work in the future.

Although Marshall did not think much of feminine intellects, the evidence from the lecturers was drawn up in statistical form and the balance was tipped slightly in favour of the women. The Syndicate also asked all those who had sent in Memorials to elaborate on their arguments. They received from the women teachers at Newnham and Girton their views on the disadvantages of non-membership of the University. Certificated students of Newnham and Girton were restricted in their use of the University Library as if they had not gone through the University course. Women students were excluded from almost all scholarships and prizes in the University. These were of academic and financial value and might encourage a student and enable her to pursue her studies free from financial worries. Indeed there was no encouragement or recognition for certificated students doing advanced study and research and the women lecturers suffered academic isolation since they were barred from University teaching and membership. The uncertainty regarding admission to lectures was a continual worry—there had been specific cases where women had been turned away from laboratories. Most of all, the replies stressed the professional disadvantage of having no easily recognisable degree title. B. A. Clough and K. Jex-Blake, Secretaries of the Joint Newnham and Girton Committee wrote,

We find that, since women leave college without proceeding to a degree, a very general impression exists outside the University that the course of study they have pursued is inferior to that pursued by men. Apart from the question of material injury, it is certain that the prevalence of this opinion causes an amount of discouragement and inconvenience which in our judgement is not insignificant and constitutes a real hardship. Further, the education of the younger generation of girls is affected; for parents and teachers are led to underestimate the value of University training and are not encouraged to look to the University as the central educational authority.

Headmistresses wrote in to say that Boards of Governors, especially in small country towns, knew little or nothing about degree qualifications and could not understand the value of a Tripos Certificate. The head of a scholastic agency described how in the smaller schools and private schools, which formed together the majority of girls educational establishments, there was no doubt that graduates had an advantage. It had once been explained to her that "the letters B.A. or M.A. looked so much better on the Prospectus". Other women described their difficulties when going to teach or study on the Continent, in America and in the Colonies. In a private letter to Mrs Sidgwick, Elizabeth Garrett Anderson explained that though she had wanted her daughter to read for the Natural Science Tripos, she had had to recommend that she attended London University where she would actually gain a degree, which would thus exempt her from the first medical examinations. Several cases were described of parents who, though recognising the value of a Cambridge education, sent their daughters to universities which awarded a degree, or insisted that they took a London University degree as well as Tripos examinations while at Cambridge, a practice which placed a great strain on the girls. In her reply to the Syndicate's inquiries, Mrs Sidgwick, as Principal of Newnham, made it clear that Tripos certificates were a great inconvenience, though she felt the nature of the evidence involved made it difficult to prove specific instances of discrimination against the certificate in favour of a degree from some other university. She concluded her lengthy letter,

And though Cambridge women would be in a better

position with the Degree, I believe that the position of a Newnham or Girton student with a good Tripos certificate is, from the point of view of obtaining employment as a teacher, on the whole not inferior to that of the graduates of other Universities at present. But it is doubtful whether without fuller recognition from the University, this position can be maintained against the competition of all the other Universities—except at present Oxford—in Great Britain. What I desire is to maintain and strengthen the connection of Cambridge with the education of women, believing it to have been hitherto to the University at least unharmful and to women an unmixed gain.[22]

Though not unaware themselves of the difficulties involved in assessing this evidence on professional disability through lack of a degree, the syndicate were inclined to accept it. Unfortunately, when Mrs Sidgwick's letter was made public, the first sentence of the paragraph quoted above was taken out of context by the women's opponents, to illustrate that women had no professional need for a degree.

Quite early in their deliberations, at their meeting on 24th November, the Syndicate voted by eight votes to two that women should not be admitted as undergraduate members of the University but that they might be given the title of the B.A. degree. The Syndicate then went on to define the conditions under which women would be admitted to degrees, and the heads of Newnham and Girton were questioned on the delicate issue of the preliminary examination. In particular, the Syndicate wanted to know if the women themselves attached any importance to the greater freedom which they were currently allowed before taking a Tripos, i.e. that they were able to present a Higher Local Certificate in lieu of the Previous Examination. For Mrs Sidgwick this was an opportunity to ride the Newnham hobby horse and she had to discard at least one outspoken draft before finally addressing the Syndicate. Because the Higher Locals could be substituted for the Previous, schools had the opportunity to put more emphasis on Modern Languages, which was especially valuable for those coming to Cambridge to study science, for much of the literature came from the Continent. Mrs Sidgwick believed school teachers liked to prepare their pupils for the Higher Locals since it ensured a wider knowledge and culture than the smattering of Classics and very elementary Mathematics required for the Previous. She found great difficulty in framing her opinion on the general desire to continue this freedom of choice. Some women, she knew, thought that the course for women should be in all respects identical with that for men "for identity's sake", and others felt that all girls who went to university should learn Latin and Greek, but it was difficult to get an unbiassed opinion on the matter. In her view, if women could be assured that having a different preliminary examination would not prejudice the case for degrees, then they would in general prefer to continue with their present freedom. Miss Jex-Blake at Girton* deprecated the alternative to the Previous since it contributed to the ambiguity of the Tripos Certificate and created an artificial distinction between men and women in the matter of education which was prejudicial to the interest of the latter. It had always been the policy of Girton to enter girls for the Previous examination and in her opinion, most large schools had adapted themselves to its requirements. Sidgwick chose not to deliver, through his wife, another tirade on the poverty of the Previous. From the very beginning of the new campaign he had been confident that his views on this examination would triumph and he had even encouraged Emily Davies to make public the differences between them on this point. Even following the unprecedented rejection of his nomination to the Syndicate, Sidgwick was still a great influence in the University. The women, however, had to some extent outgrown the philosophy of their guru, and were able to form their own opinions. Eleven out of twenty members of the Newnham staff consulted by the Syndicate did not support the alternative to the Previous Examination and a further two thought the issue unimportant.

In their evidence to the Syndicate, the anti-women faction confined itself to an elaboration of its plans for joint action with Oxford and Trinity College, Dublin to found a women's

* The full text of the Girton reply has not come to light.

university. If Cambridge conceded the degree to women, the result would be a large and sudden increase in the numbers of women going to Cambridge, with a falling off in the numbers of women going to Oxford, and a converse tendency amongst the men "since there cannot possibly be any doubt that the admission of women would be distasteful to Undergraduates. At a new 'Women's University', the energies of women students might find ample field for action and their special needs might be fully considered."[23] Even in the early drafts of their report, the Syndicate felt the issue of a women's university outside its terms of reference. The final form was much stronger and stated, "the Syndicate are not in favour of such a proposal". Later drafts of the report are less inhibited than the early ones, since a decisive rift had appeared between the Syndicate's members in February 1897. The split, as F. W. Maitland reported to Sidgwick, was totally unprecedented; five members had decided to dissociate themselves from the report and had claimed the right to produce their own. These five published a minority report[24] which proposed that women be granted the title of "*Magistra in Littera* (M.Litt.) or *Magistra in Scientia* (M.Sc.), or some other title of a degree, not being the title of a Degree in the University".* The majority report, signed by nine members of the Syndicate, including the Vice-Chancellor, was published in the *University Reporter* on 1st March and its most important conclusion was that women should be awarded the titles of their degrees, first the B.A. and then, two years later, the M.A. They were to continue to have an alternative to the Previous Examination. However, no provision was to be made for the official admission of women to lectures and laboratories, nor was there to be any extension of privileges in the matter of prizes or the University Library.[25] In calmer times, these omissions would surely have been protested by the women as the weak spot in the whole arrangement, for it left the University simply in the position of an examining body in relation to its women students. But it was not the time for such a nice point; opinion had turned strongly

* The M.Litt. and M.Sc. were not then degrees of Cambridge University.

against the women and their supporters and they were fighting with their backs to the wall.

The Committee which had organised Memorials A and B took its stand on the point that the Syndicate proposals gave the women so little of what they had originally asked for, that there was bound to be a renewed request for full membership—"the avowed object of the recent agitation". This was a telling point and little credence was given to the pledges from the women and their supporters that they would be satisfied with degree titles only. They frankly admitted that in the previous year they had believed that the general feeling in the University was in their favour, and had been led therefore to ask for further recognition of women students. They had never intended to ask for more than the University was willing freely to grant; now they were glad to accept what had been offered. The Secretaries of the Joint Newnham and Girton Committee wrote to the Syndicate saying that the measures proposed would, if passed, satisfy the practical needs of the large majority of those whom they represented, but they were perfectly aware that they could not speak for the militant minority, still less for future generations of women students. Resident Cambridge men were afraid of the possibility of renewed agitation which would disrupt the work of the University; in the press, the argument was given a more general treatment. The Syndicate's proposals were described as "the thin end of the wedge", giving women a vantage point from which to make further demands and finally to take over the University. As the *Pall Mall Gazette* put it:

(It is a) half measure that could never stay as it is and would undoubtedly lead in the end to full feminine membership. It is just like the Suffrage question, we may observe; give a few propertied women votes and the whole deluge will follow sooner or later. 31st March, 1897.

The Times and the *Morning Post* joined in. Women were concealing their real motives in accepting the proposals, but they knew they were gaining a lever to force their way into the governing body, and would thus be able to convert Cambridge into a mixed university. The point was further rubbed home when a Mrs Alice Stopford Green wrote a lengthy letter to *The Times* (19th May, 1897) describing the women's statement that they would be satisfied with degree titles as "transparent dishonesty". Titles would necessarily lead to membership in the long run and women were perfectly aware of it. If this confirmed their worst fears, some men woke up to the fact that it was not the current proposals which were the "thin end of the wedge", but the Graces of 1881, which first gave women the right to take the Tripos and had given them a platform of disability from which to campaign. A letter in the same issue of *The Times* from a "Perplexed M.A." may have appealed to the uncommitted, for he believed that the proposed new system would put women with titular degrees in the same position as the great majority of men with regular degrees who were disenfranchised because they did not keep their names on the University Register. Yet he was missing the point, since the men could always (at a price) get themselves registered, while the women could not. The great weakness in the out-pourings of the anti-women press was that they never gave any reasons why they believed that women should be prevented from sharing in the responsibilities and benefits of the University. They were simply held to be self-evident. The supporters of women were not slow to elucidate their opponents' motives.

Women are admitted to the Honours Examination; they answer the same questions on the same terms as men, and the only difference is, that they too often for the liking of the men, pass higher than they do. *Warrington Guardian* 22nd April, 1897.

It is clear from the vote that men intend to keep all the distinctions, the authority and the emoluments of the University in their own hands. It is clear, also, that the majority of them are determined still to deny to women the help which the concession of the title of a degree might give them in earning their own living as teachers. *Birmingham Post* 22nd May, 1897.

The provincial press was especially scathing about the self-centredness of Cambridge. An East Anglian paper[26] complained that the proposals had aroused a "ridiculous amount of feeling"; The *Lincolnshire Echo*[27] felt it "had a right to expect something better from a great seat of learning. The spectacle of a powerful University forgetting its logic in a fit of prejudice, selfishness and timidity is not a particularly edifying one for the country at large". The *Daily Graphic* in a piece headed "Medieval Cambridge", claimed that the fierce struggle raging there over the question of degrees for women showed clearly the mental isolation which resulted from secluded study.

> Had Cambridge been a centre of modern industry, as well as a seat of learning, such a debate as is now proceeding would have seemed impossible. The question at issue seems so simple, that the man who has to get on with his work and earn his living under the conditions of modern life is filled with wonder at the amount of controversy that can be distilled out of it. 19th May, 1897.

The *Daily News* tossed the ball back into the Cambridge court with its comment,

> The Senate . . . will decide the great and important question whether women who have qualified in the same manner as men shall be allowed to take the same degree. An impartial philosopher or an unprejudiced man of the world would naturally say that to ask such a question was to answer it. 17th May, 1897.

But in Cambridge, the answer did not seem so simple. Flysheets continued to obscure the obvious and when the issue was sent for consideration by the whole body of the Senate, the debate was to last for three whole days.

The marathon discussion of the majority report took place Saturday, 13th March, 1897, Monday, 15th March and Tuesday, 16th March, in the Arts School and a special report of the speeches was published on 26th March. Apart from a superb piece of oratory from Professor F. W. Maitland in favour of the women, which was too clever to do the cause any good, few speeches are worthy of mention. From the first, supporters of the report took the line of gratitude and quiet moderation. The Syndicate had offered them the titles of degrees for which they were very grateful and they tried to reassure their opponents that University life would continue unchanged as it had for the past sixteen years, since women were first officially admitted to examinations. There would be no revolution—simply, instead of a Tripos Certificate, a woman would now be awarded a degree diploma. As the opponents of the women's case grew increasingly irrational and emotional, supporters moved further and further on to the defensive and failed to make their case. Every old argument against women's education in Cambridge was thrown at them and Sidgwick's pledge that if this proposal was carried, he himself would take no part in any future movement of the advancement of women in Cambridge could not satisfy those who saw the granting of degree titles as the prelude to further advances.

The debate did not end with the Arts School discussion; nearly two months remained to the date of the vote, during which time each side tried to convince the great anonymous body of Cambridge M.A.s of the justice of their cause. The newspapers reported each thrust and counter-thrust in a fashion reminiscent of war-reporting. The University was in a state of uproar and many men opposed the women for no other reason than that their "agitation" had disturbed academic tranquility. *The Times* reported that private friendships had been severely strained and that there was a degree of hostility "previously unknown" in the attitude of men towards the claims of women.[28] As a writer in the *Westminster Gazette* described it,

> Cambridge has been working itself into a fever heat over a not entirely novel question of degrees for women. Why so much heat should have been so suddenly engendered, it is not easy to discover. The question of the position of women in the University has been before the Cambridge world now for more than twenty years. It has been discussed up and

down with all the ingenuity that academic training can develop but hitherto with comparatively little passion. Yet the present issue, which seems one of the simplest raised in the course of the controversy, has divided Cambridge into two camps and stirred up an amount of feeling that has no parallel in the memory of the oldest resident.[29]

A spectrum of excuses was offered for keeping the women out of the University. Some men felt it would be a grave misuse of the funds which benefactors over the centuries had given the University if they were applied to the education of women. An occasional writer felt he could make his point by ridicule and drew pen-portraits of red-nosed, bespectacled Cambridge girls who never married and who had no conversation other than mathematics.[30] On the other hand, it was insinuated that women crowded up to Cambridge, not for the benefits of a higher education, but because of the proximity of two thousand young men.[31] Those who did acquire some knowledge during their three years' study had wasted their time, for, according to one "University Man", "to darn a stocking well and sew on buttons and all such other attainments in domestic economy, would be found more useful and contribute more to the general well-being than an ability to discuss the binomial theorem or the differential calculus".[32] A few men even claimed 'Higher Authority' for their campaign to keep women from graduating. Describing the women's request as "intrinsically vicious", James Mayo thundered," a University course is an incident in and a part of certain professions (and of those only) which are and by appointment of Divine Providence, must always be, exclusively virile".[33]

A week before the vote, the women lost a group of their supporters who withdrew on the curious grounds that although they still supported the women's right to have the titles of their degrees, the proposal could only be passed in the teeth of a great deal of opposition, and they felt they should not oppose the opposition. No doubt, they were probably concerned that the women, if successful, would have to face a great deal of hostility and even exclusion from lectures. Their action does suggest, however, that even at that late date it was believed that the vote would be close. The tactics of some Senior Members suggest that they were still very much afraid that the women would win.

Though no names can be named, the accusation that some Senior Members of the University incited the undergraduates to oppose the women was repeatedly made by responsible members of the Senate. Most of the accusations appeared after the defeat, but the warning given by Maitland to Sidgwick on 19th March, 1897* suggests that there was truth in the allegation that some malicious forces were at work. Today, it is good politics to suggest that the feelings of the under-graduates should be taken into account in any controversy: it was a totally alien concept then. Yet men who would normally have been horrified at the idea of consulting under-graduate opinion used its vocal opposition as a weapon in their fight against the women. A group of resident members led by Adam Sedgwick, great nephew of the Geology Professor of the same name, wrote to the *Standard* in May arguing that if the undergraduates repudiated the idea of a mixed university, the Senior Members ought to follow suit. An "Onlooker" replied, expressing surprise that notice should be taken of undergraduate opinion, which had only turned against women very late in the day.

I think, Sir, that many a Cambridge resident is sorry to have to believe that the passions of those young men have been unscrupulously stirred by agitators . . . of maturer growth.

The undergraduates were young and though usually most chivalrous to women students, easily roused. They were indulging in a lapse of manners and sense which would embarrass them in later years.

But sympathy and sorrow would be wasted on any older persons who have not scrupled to inflame the passions of

* "What I fear most is an attempt to raise the undergraduates i.e. to get from the man emphatic declaration I am pretty sure that the attempt will be made." U.L. Mss.

their juniors, knowing well that a fire, though never kindled for 5 and 20 peaceful years, is still ready to break out when the spark is lit.[34]

The undergraduates conducted their own ballots on the issue and over two thousand of them petitioned the Senate through the Vice-Chancellor, to keep women out of the University—a step which had not been taken since 1771, when persons *in statu pupillari* had asked to be relieved of the need to testify to the Thirty-Nine Articles on the grounds that they had not the time to study them thoroughly. On 11th May, the rules of the Union Society were suspended to allow a debate on the motion "this House strongly condemns the recommendations of the Women's Degree Syndicate" to be open to all junior members of the University. The motion was carried by 1,083 votes to 138 and its message reinforced by thirty "devoted undergraduates who bound themselves by a mighty oath not to take their degrees in June if such an insult to a male University was perpetrated".[35] The conclusion drawn from all this show of feeling, was that if women were given privilege at Cambridge, all the men would exit to Oxford, and in the opinion of contemporary observers it was this fear that decided the vote. The *Pall Mall Gazette*, no friend of the women's cause, reported with great seriousness,

> The boat race disasters of Cambridge are largely due to the circumstance that the Eton eight has developed a preference for Oxford. If the fashion is enlarged until it includes family and scholarship, where will the University be then, poor thing?[36]

An anxious father, who described himself as a Queen's Counsellor and a supporter of "any reasonable scheme for redressing the alleged wrongs of women", wrote:

> I am a Cambridge man myself. My relations in the past and in the present have been and are all Cambridge men. My surviving sons—one and all of them—I sent to Cambridge, to my own college. We are a Cambridge family to the back-

bone. And so I hoped that it would continue to be. But
now I am assured that if this scheme of the Syndicate is
passed into law, the *nati natorum* will most certainly go to
Oxford, and not to Cambridge![37]

The *Manchester Guardian*, usually quite warm in the women's
favour, remarked that it was not the time to encourage any
novel or *outre* step which might frighten away the average
undergraduate; Cambridge had been slightly falling behind in
popularity as the records, particularly in rowing, showed.[38]
As the rowdy meetings and the facetious articles in their
magazines revealed,[39] many undergraduates were thoroughly
enjoying the sight of their elders roused to great passion by the
women's case and were happy to contribute to the fun. But a
few were more thoughtful in their opposition. Alan McLean
lobbied the future Prime Minister, A. J. Balfour,*[40] explaining
some of the inconveniences which arose in mixed classes. He
studied Natural Sciences and was adamant that certain
important parts of the courses were left out, as they could not
be discussed in the presence of ladies. In the Physical
Laboratory, he was obliged to wait endlessly for the assistance
of the demonstrator, for each time his turn came round a
woman would come forward and she would have to be deferred
to. At demonstrations and lectures women students sat in the
front seats and had the first and best views of the specimens.
After all, he explained in exasperation, undergraduates are
Gentlemen! And no doubt the women behaved like "ladies"
and expected to be deferred to. His grievance was probably
quite genuine. If progress was to be made in co-education,
women would have to be prepared to adopt new manners and
attitudes; this was not, unfortunately, always appreciated and
it was usually men who had to make the concessions.

The vote on the Grace to admit women to degree titles, was
fixed for Friday, 21st May, and as *The Times* correspondent
kindly reminded the *non-placets*,† special trains of the Great
Northern Line would leave King's Cross for Cambridge at

* Brother of Mrs Sidgwick.

† At a public vote in the Senate House, M.A.'s vote *placet* for
the Graces or *non-placet* against.

12.15 p.m. and return at 3.50 p.m. and 9.0 p.m. The station being on the very outskirts of town, *non-placet* M.A.s were met by excited undergraduates in fliers (one-horse hackney carriages) and conducted at break-neck speed along Regent Street, through the market place to the Senate House. The scene there was one of general festivity; banners were strung out from Caius College and an effigy of a woman student in blue bloomers, riding a bicycle, was suspended from the windows above Macmillan's bookshop (now Bowes and Bowes). It had been reported that Caius students had raised £50 for the purchase of flour, fireworks and rotten eggs, so that they could give the M.A.s an "ovation".[41] Since the majority of those for whom this welcome was arranged were present to vote against the women, it seems clear that the undergraduates were happy to seize any excuse for a lark and were not themselves particularly concerned with the matter under consideration. An anonymous writer left a vivid description of the scene in front of the Senate House that afternoon.

The arrangements for taking the votes was excellent; the scene will never be forgotten; the excitement of the undergraduates who assembled in great numbers, the spectators at every window and on the tops of houses and St Mary's Church, and fireworks in the Senate House Yard, all formed a most memorable evidence of the general interest.

A vigorous cock crow emanating from the roof of Caius College and done with marvellous fidelity, was the signal for the commencement of operations. Forthwith, the occupants of the front rooms at Caius began to hang out their banners on the outer walls and a roar of laughter went up as there slowly descended from the upper window the lay figure of a woman with aggressively red hair dressed in cap and gown . . . Up till about 2 p.m. nothing worse than confetti and flour had been thrown. The dons, after voting, stood in solemn and serried array, within the Senate House Yard, waiting for the verdict. Someone threw a cracker over the palings and this was the signal for the commencement of a general bombardment. Cooped up like sheep in a pen, the devoted dons, some thousands in number, were pelted with fireworks of every description, while the smoke rose in clouds above their heads. The noise of the explosions and the cheers and the counter-cheers were deafening. There was no help for it. The M.A.s were in for a lively time and they got it. Some of them picked up the empty cases and threw them at their tormentors, but the majority had to stand a terrible fire and look as dignified as they could.

When the vote was announced, 1,713 against the Graces, 662 in favour, pandemonium broke loose.[42]

The women had been soundly defeated and not merely by the out-voters. Of the resident members, that is those working at the University or living in the city, 320 were against and 149 in favour. In only one college, Emmanuel, did those in favour of degree titles for women, exceed those against (12–7).

The undergraduates began their celebrations by storming down to Newnham with the news. A student there remembers listening from the roof of one of the Newnham buildings, to the roar from the town which increased in volume as the attacking force gradually approached, to be finally held up by the closed College gates, with the dons assembled beneath the archway.[43] When their gentlemanly instincts were appealed to they left the women alone and returned to the Market Place for a night of wild celebration.

The night's festivities were recorded in an extra-special edition of the *Cambridge Weekly News* entitled "The Triumph of Man".[44] A huge bonfire was started in the Market Square, the students raiding shops for doors, shutters and fencing with which to feed it. They even took a brewer's dray. Firecrackers were tied together in bundles and flung haphazardly into the crowd and through open windows into the rooms of the houses round the square. A proctor and his two bulldogs came up and were immediately mobbed. They were rescued by the police, who escorted "the representatives of University law and order" to the safe asylum of Christ's College. According to the report, the police took a very sensible view of the whole demonstration and it was owing to their unfailing good humour and the way in which they kept their tempers at critical moments that serious disorder did not occur. The fire-brigade were called at midnight to put out the bonfire and when some of the under-graduates resented this interference, the hoses were turned on them. The *News* added that a fund was being raised by 'Varsity men to cover the damage done during the day and night, the sum mentioned being £100.* It was also being subscribed as a mark of appreciation for the conduct of the police. The undergraduates' behaviour was generally excused as "high spirits" and at least two other papers, the *Daily Mail* and the *Illustrated Sporting and Dramatic News*, brought out a special, pictorial supplements on the day's events. The rest of the press made sober comments on the results according to their lights; the *Westminster Gazette*, which had supported the women throughout, published a letter from a "Cambridge M.A." describing the paper as the most lying, unfair and unscrupulous rag of the age.[45] Several of the opposition papers raised the suggestion that the existing privileges would now be withdrawn from women in Cambridge. This was hotly denied by University men, who claimed that such a notion was ungenerous and alien to the spirit of fairness which the University had always manifested to Newnham and Girton.[46] It was indeed strange, in view of the violence of feeling which had been aroused during the two years of debate, that the defeat had no repercussions for the status of women in Cambridge. The women, after all, were still there and still presented a potential source of disruption. Two explanations can be offered for this paradox: many who had voted against the women were inconsistent in their prejudices—they were not prepared to deny women an education, just to deny them the hallmark of that education which might have brought them into competition with men; and secondly, teaching women at Cambridge had for many years been a lucrative way in which to supplement a college stipend, and gave work to a "large body of competent, but only partially employed, teachers of the higher branches of learning".[47]

* One Danish student from Emmanuel, who had broken a window during the gathering at Newnham, wrote a long letter of apology to Mrs Sidgwick and sought to pay for the damage. He concluded by requesting that he be informed if there were any Scandinavian ladies in residence.

Emily Davies wrote that she was not greatly discouraged by the vote. She had never really been able to support the Syndicate's proposals. For the Sidgwicks, the blow was probably more personal and hurtful, but they kept a brave face on their defeat. A student who was up at the time said that they learnt from the leaders of the campaign with what courage and good temper it is possible to fight a hard and losing battle.[48] In her addresses to the Newnham students in 1897 and 1898, Mrs Sidgwick drew many useful lessons from the defeat, though she could not conceal her distress at the amount of prejudice and ignorance which had been displayed by some members of the University. The publicity meant that the value of Tripos Certificates might be better understood, if not the whole of the women's case. Clearly, the University felt that women's colleges were still an experiment and Mrs Sidgwick warned the students that any failure of work, health or manners would be held against them. For the girls themselves, the result of this defeat was, that for the next twenty years, their college life continued to be minutely ordered and at a time when some of the stricter social conventions were beginning to be relaxed, this proved very irksome. But for the women's colleges themselves in their relationship with the University, the situation is best described in the words used in the college biographies—"no change".

9

A TEMPORARY WAVE OF REACTION?

IN 1919 GIRTON COLLEGE celebrated the fiftieth anniversary of its foundation. The years since 1897 had seen no major eruption of the women's claim to University membership. There had been a certain mellowing of attitudes with the passage of time, the women's colleges were now a generally accepted part of the Cambridge scene and though rivalry between them still persisted it was of the friendly variety, with only dim memories of the old ideological divisions remaining. Henry Sidgwick had died in 1900 at the age of sixty-two; Emily Davies was living in retirement in Hampstead, sprightly in mind, but too infirm to attend the Jubilee celebrations o the college she had founded.* The pioneering attitudes had been left behind and though the women's authorities continued to be minutely careful over the behaviour of their students, it was generally recognised, even by their most determined opponents, that women were in Cambridge to stay and would always have some degree of relationship with the ancient university. But the nature of that relationship remained undecided and attempts to define it in the years of post-war reconstruction again stirred passions across the nation, even at that time of national emergency.

From the turn of the century to the outbreak of the First World War, almost nothing was done by the University that might be interpreted as furthering the women's claim to membership. Certain regulations governing the Previous Examination were extended to women in 1898[1] and in 1914 it was accepted that women could be granted certificates of research[2] for work beyond degree level. Professor Mayo complained of the move but felt it was too late to object to

* She died on 13th July, 1921, aged 92.

the women's presence. The women, too, realised that the clock could not be put back and were less timid in their espousal of causes beyond the field of education than they had been in the early days of the movement.[3] Many Cambridge women now worked for the suffrage movement without fearing to harm the cause of women's education. A definite improvement had occurred in the position of the middle-class woman since the days, mid-century, when she had been the property of some man. It is a matter of debate to what this change in the quality of life must be attributed, but a major factor must have been the improvements in female education, which had given women the insight and authority from which to challenge conventional notions of their "natural" inferiority. By 1914, there were fourteen universities and university colleges in England and Wales offering women higher education and full and equal recognition with men. The total number of full-time students at these institutions (i.e. excluding Oxford and Cambridge) was 11,230, of whom 2,900 were women.*[4] In 1893 Miss Alice Cooke (an old Newnham student) had been the first woman appointed to a University teaching post; in the year preceding the war, there were about 120 women in such posts.[5]

If other universities were more generous in their attitude to women, why then did women continue to clamour for places at the women's colleges at Oxford and Cambridge? There were strong academic grounds for their preference, for the old universities still trained and employed the finest men teachers to whom the women students could hope to have access. However, there were (and still are) more glamorous reasons for the popularity of Oxford and Cambridge, despite the disclaimers of the women's leaders. Residence away from home for several months of the year and the companionship and relative freedom that this entailed and even the possibility of romance, all played their part in attracting girls to Oxford and Cambridge. When asked in a radio interview the reason why women came up to Cambridge, Lynda Grier, one time Principal of Lady Margaret Hall, Oxford, replied that despite

* Most London Medical Schools were also closed to women.

the absence of a degree, the work was of degree standard and besides, there was "fun, freedom and friendliness".[6] A Newnhamite who was at college from 1899–1902 described in another interview the strict control exerted over the behaviour of the women students by the college authorities. Newnham students were forbidden to speak to men in the street—but despite the vigilance, romance did blossom. Nor were the women students as dully dressed as the authorities might hope: the fashion was frills, lace and ribbons on their blouses and an old French tutor asked how he could be expected to teach with that before his eyes.[7]

Women students of this period did not produce the same brilliant results as their predecessors, much to the distress of the college authorities who knew that though women of the calibre of Agenta Ramsay and Philippa Fawcett were often dismissed as freaks, average performance from their students was on the other hand taken as a sign of women's inferior intellect. In 1904 Mrs Sidgwick spoke sternly to Newnham students about her anxiety at the growth of distractions which were drawing women away from their proper work. One of the benefits for which the early students had been most grateful was that at college they were free from the petty interruptions of home life and could concentrate on their studies. Now some students were saying it was easier to work away from college where everything was "hurry and fuss".[8] Recent examination results bore out Mrs Sidgwick's view of the prevalent lack of concentration but she could not expect the same pioneering response from these girls, who could only dimly appreciate the struggles and sacrifices which previous generations had made and from which they were now benefiting. Such apparent indifference on the part of the young for the hard-won victories of the old is a familiar source of friction between the generations, for it is hard for those who have gone before to remember that life is a continuum and the young in their turn will have battles to fight: but it is also the mark of a victory so firmly won as to be commonplace. Yet were the students right to feel themselves secure at Cambridge? The policy of the women's colleges was to work quietly and steadily in the pursuit of academic excellence and

The Newnham College staff, 1896. *Standing, l to r*: E. R. Saunders, H. G. Klaassen, K. Stephen, L. Sheldon, M. E. Rickett, B. A. Clough, A. Gardner; *sitting*: A. B. Collier, E. M. Sharpley, I. Freund, M. Greenwood, Mrs Sidgwick, M. J. Tuke, H. Gladstone, P. G. Fawcett.

The scene outside the Senate House, 1897

1948: degrees for women.

1972: King's College accepts women students.

to take in their stride the day when membership would, they felt, inevitably be granted to them. Indeed this was the pattern at Oxford; full membership was granted there in 1919 with scarcely any disturbance. But for the women at Cambridge the years of patient waiting were not to be so easily rewarded. The movement for granting women membership of the old universities started towards the end of the war and in Oxford moved smoothly forward to a successful conclusion; in Cambridge it ran into opposition as fierce and bitter as anything the women had previously experienced and ended once again in an uneasy truce.

The First World War marks a clear dividing line in the history of most human affairs. It was particularly significant for the affairs of women. For it was the period in which they were given the opportunity to demonstrate their real capabilities in fields which had previously been exclusively masculine. By all accounts they did this with a vigour and success which even the most prejudiced observer could not deny. The contribution made by Cambridge-educated women was specially noted in the celebrations which marked the Girton jubilee in 1919. The guest of honour was Rt Hon. H. A. L. Fisher, President of the Board of Education, who declared in his address that the work performed by women during the European war would have greatly suffered from the absence of the leadership and the training of women who had received a fine liberal education in the atmosphere of the ancient University.[9] The newspapers in their reports of the celebrations took up the theme, listing the war work done by Cambridge women and adding strong comments on the unreasonableness of the University in refusing its women students degrees or University membership.[10]

If the University felt any reflected glory in the praise heaped on its women students, it had little cause to do so, since the only concession it had made to the war work of women was to allow them in 1916 to sit the examinations for the first and second M.B., to which they had previously been denied admission. Following a resolution passed by both the women's colleges, a letter was addressed to the Vice-Chancellor which he put before the Special Board of Medicine in April 1916.

The letter stated that the women who wanted the advantage of a Cambridge science course as well as qualifying for medicine, had to work under serious disadvantages since they had to take the medical examinations of other examining bodies and this often meant delay and extra expense. If the women could take the first and second M.B. while at Cambridge they could then proceed without further delay to take the final M.B. in any examining body which accepted Cambridge qualifications. The Special Board agreed to their admission and expressed the view that the women students would cause no inconvenience; indeed women had been present at medical lectures for some years and since 1911 they had been admitted to lectures and dissections in the School of Anatomy. In the discussion which followed the publication of the report, Doctor James Mayo,[11] and Professors W. R. Sorley and William Ridgeway all emphasised that admission to medical examinations should not be interpreted in any way as a step towards admission to degrees. Professors Ridgeway and Sorley saw the new permission as a war emergency measure.[12]

The discussion had revealed that the attitude of the women's oldest opponents at least had not mellowed with time and circumstance, and the women therefore naturally looked with more hope to the return of the younger dons from the war. Yet it was by no means certain that the young men would prove any more tolerant of women's claims than their elders. It had been the attitude of the younger men and even the undergraduates which had swayed opinion against the women in 1897 and now, twenty years on, these same opponents turned again to the younger men to stop the women's advance.[13]

In April 1918 a Memorial was circulated to resident and non-resident members of the Senate in which twenty-four members explained their opinion that the time had come to consider afresh the position of women students.[14] Reference was made to the recent war work of women, the services they had rendered to the nation and to the Act of Parliament enfranchising women over twenty-eight which had received the Royal Assent on 6th February that year. They felt that the time had passed for half measures and that women should be admitted to full membership without any restriction of members. They based this conviction not only on the new position of women in the country but also on the record of the women's colleges, Girton and Newnham, and they were especially anxious that the "distinguished staffs of these colleges should not be kept any longer in a position of inferiority". The women students should not be in Cambridge simply on sufferance and without receiving the full recognition of their studies. The Memorialists begged that "as soon as the general state of affairs allows the University to give full consideration to the matter, the Council of the Senate should be asked to nominate a Syndicate to report on the measures necessary for effecting this object".[15]

The opposition was quick to show its hand and chose to concentrate on the issue of timing, even though the Memorialists had specifically asked the University to choose an appropriate time. In May 1918, R. F. Scott, the Master of John's, circulated a paper in which he deprecated the "obtrusion of highly controversial questions which have been dormant for many years in the University and which are in no sense urgent at this stage of the war when the younger members of the University who are most closely interested in a satisfactory solution are almost all absent". The issue was to be raised when they returned: the "satisfactory solution" which he recommended in advance was that an official body representing the women's colleges in Cambridge should obtain powers under a Charter of Affiliation with the University to confer degrees on women students.[16] And so arose again the bogey of women's degrees and a women's university.

Not all the younger dons were grateful for the care taken to preserve their ancient heritage. The Economic Historian C. R. Fay wrote to the *Cambridge Review* in June 1918, brushing aside the suggestion that the subject was controversial and therefore should be left until life returned to normal. He argued that the war could not continue to be used as an excuse for apathy; on the contrary, those left at home ought to try to solve the controversies and thus prepare the way for unhindered progress in civil life when that life began again. He strongly resented the suggestion that the seniors of the University were safeguarding the traditions for the younger generation by doing nothing. Fay had put his finger on the kernel of the whole problem of post-war reconstruction in all areas of British life, economic, social and political. The *status quo* could not be maintained: it had gone for ever and all attempts to re-establish it would prove fruitless. It was a hard lesson for the country in general to learn, and Cambridge was so shocked by its disappearance that some of its members sought refuge in a dream of a previous century—in this case a dream of a university untroubled by the challenging voices of female students. But two points in the new order were to frustrate this fond hope.

Jobs were scarce in the post-war years. The end of the war brought a contraction of industry, the effect of which was felt on the economic life of the whole nation. Women war workers were dismissed in their thousands, public opinion swung strongly against those who tried to go on working and it was accepted by the women themselves that they should make way for the demobilised soldiers.[17] At the same time, war deaths and inflation had further exacerbated the problem of unsupported women.* The war had revealed to women their capacity for work and many of these had now to keep themselves. The Association of Head Mistresses in conference in Birmingham in August 1919 spoke of the growing demand for higher education for women, since girls were now regretting the eagerness with which they had taken up clerical work during the war without gaining any qualifications.[18] As an article in *Country Life* put it, "they have realised how greatly their chances of happiness and success in working life must be enhanced by an education which can open up vistas beyond those of shorthand and typing. And their fathers and mothers have realised this too".[19] This growing appreciation by parents of the value of education for their daughters was also directly related to the second factor which was forcing Cambridge to come to terms with the post-war situation. One legacy of the war was a rise of over 100 % in the cost of living. Cambridge, like many of the women it wanted to forget, was dependent on savings, endowments and fixed income whose values were

---

* 63% of the female population in England and Wales were over twenty years old in 1920, and only 38% of them were married.

halved in the inflation. In 1918 the newer, State-aided universities formed a deputation to ask the Government for an increase in public subsidies: Oxford and Cambridge accepted an invitation to join in the request, though they had previously, as universities, received no State aid.* The Government asked the universities to submit applications based on their financial needs and when Oxford and Cambridge each asked for considerable sums, it was felt that grants could not be made without enquiring into their resources and expenditure and that this would inevitably involve questions of university government. Such were the universities' financial straits that they agreed, though reluctantly, to what many felt was an intrusion on their privacy and independence. Interim awards were made to both Oxford and Cambridge but with this injection of public money and the prospect of regular State aid, their internal organisation became legitimate ground for public debate. The general public could no longer be told to "mind its own business" on university affairs and it was generally expected that public pressure would first be felt and successfully applied in the area of female equality. As the *Manchester Guardian* declared, "at Oxford and Cambridge the old illiberal exclusiveness, alien to the country as a whole, still lingers in many minds. But now that these two universities are appealing to the nation for aid from its taxes, it would not be unreasonable for the nation's stewards to ask that a share in the benefits of any contributions it may make should be equally open to the future citizens and taxpayers of either sex".[20] Women over twenty-eight were now enfranchised, and M.P.s were nervous of their possible behaviour, fearing they would vote *en masse* and perhaps form a women's party. Women's opinions were anxiously canvassed and heeded and it seemed certain that if Oxford and Cambridge declined to admit women to membership of their own volition, then Parliament would force it on them.

So women, for the time being at least, seemed in a strong position. When compulsory Greek in the Cambridge Previous

* Small amounts had been given to certain departments e.g. medicine, agriculture and teacher training.

Examination was abolished in 1918* this was taken as a success for women, some of whom, under Sidgwick's guidance, had long been associated with the anti-Greek faction. The local press claimed the exclusion of Greek was partly due to the pressure from the "lady students", † and was a measure of their strength. It was true that women were still refused their degree at the old universities, but "the obvious and likely policy" for the Cambridge authorities was "to yield gracefully and quickly" leaving "poor Oxford, still handicapped by compulsory Greek, yet further in the lurch".[21] Fortunately Oxford preferred to give the case of its women students priority over reform of the dead languages. The pattern at Oxford in regard to the University's relations with its women students had been very similar to that followed in Cambridge. A proposal to admit women to the B.A. was brought before Congregation in 1896 and after causing much controversy in Oxford and in the country it was rejected before reaching Convocation.‡ Cambridge rejected a similar proposal the following year. In 1909 Lord Curzon (then Chancellor) examined the position of women students at Oxford in his memorandum on University reform and the Hebdomadal Council§ pledged itself to bring the question of degrees for women before Congregation.[22] This it did in March 1913 and the discussion of the women's case was well advanced by the end of the academic year, only to be interrupted by the outbreak of war. Disappointing though this seemed it was held, in retrospect, to have been an advantage since not only did it allow time for quiet consideration and solution of controversial points, but also for account to be taken of the post-war changes in the status of women. For them, the war

* See Appendix A.

† This seems unlikely. See Appendix A.

‡ At Oxford, all important University business was first submitted to Congregation, i.e. the body of resident members, for their approval before it was passed on to Convocation, the body of resident and non-resident members.

§ The Hebdomadal Council is the Executive Body of the University and approximately equivalent to the Council of the Senate in Cambridge.

had been "a wonderful period of progress"[23] and Oxford, waking to a new reality, intended to recognise this. On 25th June, 1917, the statute allowing for the matriculation of women students was provisionally approved by the Hebdomadal Council, but there was some considerable doubt about the legality of such a step. A detailed case was drawn up and placed before Counsel in March 1919 who gave it as their opinion that the University had the right to matriculate women and admit them to degrees, but that the wisest step would be to obtain express Parliamentary sanction for the move. However this became unnecessary when in the same year the Sex Disqualification (Removal) Act was passed containing a clause which expressly permitted universities to matriculate women without further legislation.[24] A Statute was drawn up in Michaelmas 1919 and after considerable redrafting was presented to Congregation for approval. The preamble of the Statute allowed for the matriculation and admission to University degrees of women students and had to be accepted or rejected without amendment. The main body of the Statute, which was open to debate, dealt largely with residence qualifications. All degrees, except that of Divinity, which at the time was the exclusive preserve of those in Holy Orders, were opened and no special regulations were imposed on women. They were admitted to the University government, i.e. Congregation and Convocation, Faculties and Boards of Faculties, all Boards and Delegacies and as examiners in any extamination.

The newspapers of the day noted with mild surprise the absence of any opposition to the proposals, which were passed without a division in the Hilary term of 1920.[25] Women undergraduates were shortly to be seen wearing gowns and specially designed caps and in June 1920, Miss Eleanor Francis Jourdain, Principal of St Hugh's College, and Miss Mildred K. Pope of Somerville College, both Doctors of the Sorbonne, were appointed to University lectureships.[26] As it became clear that storm clouds were gathering in Cambridge over the issue of admitting women, some effort was made in the press to explain the ease with which the matter had been settled at Oxford. It was pointed out that arrangements in

Oxford had been such that University men had had much more official involvement in organising the teaching and examination of women than Cambridge men.[27] Oxford women had for some time been members of certain Boards dealing with Local Examinations and teacher training, whereas Cambridge women were totally excluded from such responsibilities. Beyond this, Oxford was simply coming to terms with the new status of women. Yet the newspapers could not fail to remark on the "abiding wonder"—the order in which the vote and the degree had been granted. The country had long since agreed that women should be awarded degrees; such was the practice of all universities except Oxford and Cambridge, "the two whose answers counted for most". Men were often certain that the degree should be granted, though the prospect of giving women the vote was anathema to them. As Lord Curzon put it, "there is all the difference in the world between giving women an opportunity of increasing and improving their natural powers, and granting to them a share in political sovereignty".[28] Yet the vote had come first. By 1920 it was possible for a woman educated at the old universities to put M.P. after her name, though not M.A. It was this "manifestly ridiculous" situation which Oxford was now taking steps to rectify. But the papers were wrong in regarding as separate the issue of degrees and votes, at least as far as Oxford and Cambridge were concerned. At the old universities, graduation and government were inseparable. Oxford had realised that since all the "adult" women of the country might vote on issues affecting men, it was no longer sensible to exclude women from the government of the University. To have done so would have been to have put more faith in the under-educated masses than in their own highly trained women. The enigma then was not the step forward which Oxford made, but the frantic efforts Cambridge was making to stand still or even to walk backwards.

The explanation of this may simply be one of timing. At Oxford some measure of reform had been considered before the war and plans for the admission of women were well in hand by its end. The statute went through at a time when its opponents must have regarded its success as inevitable and believed that resistance would only result in compulsion from a Parliament which was nervous of the women's strength. In Cambridge, pre-war schemes of reform had never got off the ground and when the time came to draw up proposals, the climate of opinion was somewhat different. Gratitude towards the women for their war work was turning sour and as the Cambridge controversy dragged on into the '20's, M.P.s grew less concerned with the opinions of their women constituents. Resistance stiffened as the fear of Parliamentary interference faded and the capitulation of Oxford became a point in favour of Cambridge's stand to remain a single-sex University, rather than a source of criticism.

Cambridge women had been actively considering the issue of membership since the Memorial of the Easter term of 1918. The Newnham Associates first discussed again the possibility of admission at their general meeting on 2nd November, 1918, and were clearly concerned about the question of "how" rather than "if".[29] A Committee was appointed to consider the position and its report, which was issued in March 1919, reflected this attitude of confidence.[30] It did, however, warn that strong opposition existed still, composed of the old opponents of women's degrees and of those who, though not opposed to the expansion of women's work at Cambridge, wanted them to work for a co-university in which degrees and examinations should be common to both sexes, while the government and control of each sex would be separate. The Committee suggested that the reason for opposing women's membership, which would give them a vote in the Senate, was that it was generally held that women would use this vote solidly in their own interest rather than in the interest of the University. When this view was challenged, opponents pointed out that members of the women's suffraget movement had set aside party loyalties in the promotion of the women's cause and Cambridge women would similarly combine to promote their own interests in the Senate. The Committee also warned that the opponents of women's degrees, if they could not be certain of victory, would combine with the waverers in a vote for titular degrees, "the granting of which would be rather an embarrassment than otherwise to the women's cause". Feeling against the titular degrees was strong; Cambridge women with, no doubt, an eye to developments at Oxford, had gone beyond the stage where they could accept something which one of them described as an "insult" and "a set-back to our cause".[31]

The formal reopening of the issue of women's membership is not clearly documented. However, it is known that a meeting was called on 4th March, 1919, in the Guildhall for those in favour of admitting women, and the Council of the Senate reported on 26th May, 1919, that they had received two Memorials concerning the admission of women to degrees. These they reprinted without giving details of the numbers of signatures received and they proved to be the papers which had been in circulation the previous year, the first calling for the full admission of women and the second for the alternative solution of a university for women. The Council submitted a Grace to the Senate for discussion in the Michaelmas term:

> That a Syndicate be appointed to consider whether women students should be admitted to membership of the University, and if so with what limitations, if any; alternatively to consider, if women students are not admitted to membership, by what means the University could co-operate with the Women's Colleges or other bodies in the conferment of degrees on women students.[32]

At a meeting of the Newnham Associates in Easter term, 1919, several members spoke in favour of pursuing an "active" policy when the issue came before the Senate the following term. This was agreed upon, though not unanimously, for some members believed that no move should come from the women's side.[33] The college authorities had "in view of the changed conditions brought about by the war and by the opening of political life to women, and in view of the urgency of the question concerning the position of women in the University" established a joint Girton and Newnham committee to consider a "common policy in matters of concern to both Colleges".[34] Over the years, the educational policies of the colleges had grown very similar. Now that Greek had gone from the Previous, an earlier bone of contention had been buried; the Poll degree was soon to disappear too in its old form,* and though the issue of "Poll women" was again brought up by women's opponents, the point was scarcely worth arguing, since the college authorities knew only too well that they could not accommodate the many candidates with high Honours potential who applied for admission, and there was certainly no space for Poll women.

In the Michaelmas term of 1919 the discussion began in earnest. In general the newspapers found it difficult to say anything in favour of the existing Cambridge policy. *The Times* began to hedge a little and produced an article in which it declared that though it was logical and perhaps desirable to admit women to membership, they would not any longer be able to escape from certain fees and rules of discipline to which the men's colleges were subjected.[35] The women could not expect to gain admission if they hoped to be treated less severely in these matters. The women, of course, had absolutely no intention of evading their responsibilities and a oint Girton-Newnham letter was quickly despatched to *The Times* saying that the women's colleges "would gladly contribute the necessary fees, capitation tax and other payments to which they may become liable, if recognised as colleges or public hostels of the University" and would be "subject to the Statutes and Ordinances of the University which regulated discipline both as regards the wearing of academical dress and generally".[36]

As part of their campaign, run this time with the aid of a paid secretary and organiser, the women drew up a list of their existing disabilities.[37] Little use was made of the peculiar difficulties which Cambridge women faced in gaining employment with only a degree certificate; by now its meaning must have become well understood and accepted, though some difficulties remained. Since few people were prepared to deny women the right to education, even if they rather regretted their having it, prominence was given to the academic disadvantages within the University. Specifically, it was pointed out that women students still only attended lectures

* See Appendix B.

by courtesy of the lecturer concerned and not by right. There was no security, and this privilege might be withdrawn by one or more lecturers whose classrooms were already bursting with undergraduates. Generally, parents made less money available for the education of girls than for their brothers, yet women students were eligible for only five of the 145 scholarships, studentships and prizes of the University. Women research students, because of their lack of official status, could not be appointed as demonstrators like their male counterparts and so lost the chance of valuable experience and often of much needed income. Another financial disability which women students faced was that they were excluded from Government grants made to those intending to teach, since these were only tenable at universities or colleges forming part of a university— and the Cambridge women's colleges lacked this status. Old students, often women of wide administrative ability and teaching experience, were excluded from all University discussions and votes on educational matters which were often of vital concern to secondary education. The isolated position of the staffs of Girton and Newnham was deeply felt. These women were recognised as being of high academic ability by their male colleagues, yet were excluded from all discussion and decisions on syllabuses and the setting and marking of examinations, not only for their own students but also for children in secondary schools. From this position of sub-ordination they had to teach the products of these schools and to prepare them for Tripos examinations, the details of which were agreed in their absence. Finally, all Cambridge women, of whatever standing, shared the same disability as regards the use of the University Library, though this was most hardly felt by the staffs of the women's colleges who, whatever their degree of scholarship, could only use one of the world's finest libraries on the same conditions as members of the general public.

The Grace* appointing the Syndicate to consider the women's case was discussed at some length on Thursday, 30th October, 1919. There was little real opposition to the appoint-

* Above p. 9.13.

ment, though some speakers would have liked the terms of reference altered. Most speeches were a rehearsal of the arguments which were to be heard many times in the following years and despite the reports of conflict which appeared in the press,[38] the Grace was passed without a division on 6th December, 1919.[39]

The Syndicate which delivered its report in May 1920 had been unable to come to agreement.[40] Six members[41] recommended that women should be admitted to full membership, with certain limitations, as set out in Report A. Six others[42] recommended in Report B the establishment of a women's university, consisting in the first place of Girton and Newnham, the intention being to maintain existing facilities for study and examination at present available to women in Cambridge but so as not to hamper the independent development of the new university. The recommendations of Report A were expressed in a brief paragraph without any exposition of the reasoning behind them. Women were to be admitted to full membership of the University including its government. They could be matriculated from "Public Hostels"*—in the first instance Girton and Newnham—and were to be specifically excluded from men's colleges. In this way it was felt that women would achieve equality of status in the University, while the University gained the power to control their members. Exactly how this should be done was not spelt out in the proposals: apparently the signatories of Report A relied on the Public Hostel Ordinances to do this.† Thus the University was to have "effective control over the number of women students admitted and over the conditions of their residence", but no specific limit on numbers appeared in the appended draft statute.

* That is, an institution at a stage prior to that of a fully-fledged College.

† Ordinances are the detailed rules which give effect to Statutes. They can be modified by the University without reference to Parliament, the necessary procedure for altering Statutes. The Public Hostel Ordinances gave the University wide powers to interfere in the regulation of the institute concerned. However, the only Public Hostel in existence at the time was Selwyn and no limit had been placed on its numbers.

This was unfortunate on two counts: limitation of the number of women was a major issue in the ensuing debate and the apparent absence of specific controls on numbers made it easy for the opponents to play on the fears of the uncommitted. At the same time it illustrated that the signatories of A were not whole-hearted in their support of equality of opportunity for women; opponents were quick to point this out and to suggest that by discriminating against women in this way, they were creating a cause for future agitation. This was the argument used with equal cunning in 1897 when the Syndicate proposed giving women degree titles, and it seemed it was an argument which could always be used with success while the women's supporters were not prepared to go the whole way in granting them equality. What the signatories of Report A were saying was that they agreed *in principle* that women should have less opportunity than men for education in Cambridge and that such a principle should be embalmed in a Statute. For it was well known that *in practice* there was little chance, for economic reasons, of the women's colleges expanding more than a very little and that if the money could be found to start new women's colleges, the University could very easily refuse to recognise them.

In marked contrast to Report A, Report B was five pages long. Its signatories had kept three questions before themselves during their cogitations—the interests of the present University; the interests of the women connected with it; and higher education throughout the country. *Prima facie*, admitting women to membership of the University was the simplest solution to their demand for equality; but this was a naive view, for even the signatories of Report A had introduced limitations on the normal privileges of membership which discriminated against women from the outset, and such abatement of privileges was a fruitful source of future controversy. There were to be no non-collegiate facilities* for

* Under a Statute of 1869 it became possible for a student not resident in a college to matriculate at the University. The aim of this provision was to reduce the expense to the student of residence in Cambridge. In practice, such students belonged to Houses, the most famous of which was Fitzwilliam House, since incorporated as

women, though it could not be denied that women required them as much as men. Women were to be excluded from appointments and scholarships which carried with them fellowships at men's colleges and again agitation could be anticipated. This was a dangerous method of argument, for it pointed out opportunities which were being denied to women: yet its strength rested in the fact that few men accepted that women should in practice be given complete equality of opportunity, and that the threat of further agitation and upheaval would make more impression on men's minds than doubts raised as to the justice of the situation.

The signatories then switched to the opposite tack. The safeguards incorporated in Report A they claimed were in any case illusory, for colleges were largely autonomous and there was therefore nothing to stop men's colleges from appointing women as fellows and lecturers. They pointed out that the spiritual and material wealth of the University rested largely with the colleges "and a powerful body of new members of the University are likely to demand a share in these riches. For the moment they (the women) may be content with having stormed the walls of the University but in time they will be heard knocking loudly at the gates of the colleges." Any college could develop on co-educational lines and "in this matter, the social as well as the educational future of the University would be at the mercy of the caprice of any particular college". What the writers of Report B did not mention was that this had always been the case and that if the system of autonomous college government was to continue in the way so beloved and glorified by Cambridge men, it always would be the case. Report A had done as much as it was possible to do under the circumstances of college autonomy; it refused matriculation to any women coming from anything other than a recognised *women's* institution. The public expression of anxiety about women in men's colleges was novel to the controversy* but

---

a college. The numbers of non-collegiate students were always controlled by the University. At Oxford there had long been similar facilities for women.

* The first public mention of the issue appears to have been made in a letter to the *Cambridge Review* by "M.A." 7.11.1919.

was clearly a point of discussion which the signatories of Report B felt should be given prominence.

The report then moved on to the educational aspects of the problem. If admitted to membership along the lines proposed by Report A, women would be on General Boards of Studies, and could receive appointments as Professors, lecturers and examiners. This, according to Report B, would have disastrous results educationally, since such women would "use their influence in favour of women's abilities which are for routine rather than original work".

When it falls to her as a member of a Board of Studies to decide on a schedule of work or as an examiner to assess the value of answers, there will be a certain tendency for the "women's vote" to be given in favour of accuracy and routine work at the expense of originality or high qualities of scholarship. The "women's vote" may in many cases be the deciding factor and influence men's education in an unfortunate direction.

No evidence was adduced to support this interpretation of "women's behaviour"; no thought was given to how such unsatisfactory and partial women could come to be appointed (necessarily by a group of men) as lecturers or examiners, nor was any indication given as to why "originality and scholarship" was always to be preferred to "accuracy and routine work". Convinced as they were of the special characteristics of the female intellect, the writers of Report B brought forward the old theory which had been dormant for twenty years—the theory that the education which is best suited to men is not best suited to women. Nor was it certain that the mixture of women with undergraduates had been so beneficial in Cambridge University life in the past that it ought to be further developed. And drawing two final and contradictory arguments out of their rag-bag, they concluded that the "experiment" of having men and women share the same education had not been carried on long enough—long enough for what they did not say. In any case one university in Britain should remain for men only—so that despite their belief that the experiment had not been carried on for long enough, not long enough was long enough and it should stop.

The proposal put forward in Report B was that a new university should be founded for women only, the nucleus of which would be Girton and Newnham. They would make use of the teaching and examinations of Cambridge but could alter the examinations to their own designs. That University teaching would be open to them seemed at first sight a generous proposition, though the true meaning of this became clear later on; as far as examinations were concerned, since the secondary education of women had improved to a point where women could enter Cambridge on at least the same educational level as men, no concessions had been asked for in preliminary examinations and there had never at any time been any request for alterations in any degree course or examination. The promoters of Report B admitted that the women would reject their proposals of a separate university on the grounds that a degree awarded by women to women would be of little value, but in laying their report before the Senate, they asked them to ignore this and to accept their proposals. For if Report A were to fail, it was likely that strong and determined efforts would be made to get Parliament to interfere on behalf of the women, and then the University would be in a much stronger position to defend itself if it had a plan in hand. In other words, the report's main purpose was to create a situation in which the women would appear ungrateful and in a bad light, since the University was offering them such a helping hand to found their own kingdom. Subsequent events confirm this interpretation of the report as insincere, and when it came to the vote, it was recognised as such by all but the most bitter of women's opponents.

In an Appendix to the Syndicate's reports, Will Spens, although a signatory to Report B, elaborated on his compromise "federal" scheme. This was designed to secure full membership of the University for the women, at the same time as the independence of the education and disciplining of both sexes. The Senate would consist of two Houses, one for men, the other for women, sometimes meeting separately and sometimes together. The women would have a fixed representation on the Council, Boards and Syndicates, except that they should have their own Syndicate to deal with discipline. Graces concerning both men and women would be submitted first to the men's House and after having passed there with or without amendment, would be submitted to the women's House which could also pass or amend it. In the event of a disagreement between the two Houses the matter would be decided by a two-thirds majority of members of both Houses sitting together. In detail, the scheme was distinctly disadvantageous to women, because Graces thrown out by the men's House would never reach them and in the case of a disagreement between the two Houses, the men would outnumber the women by approximately ten to one.

Following publication of the reports, the Council of Girton and the Governing Body of Newnham passed identical resolutions welcoming Report A as being of the greatest service to the education of women.[43] They were, not surprisingly, "strongly of the opinion" that the interests of women's education would not be forwarded by the Report B proposals and in the event of Report B's passing the Senate, the two colleges would take no steps to implement it. The old students of both colleges also came forward with their support for Report A, expressing their earnest hope that it would be accepted by the Senate, since it offered them the same privileges as undergraduates. These they felt they had earned during the fifty years of close association with the University, an association which they valued so highly that they hoped to see it confirmed by admission to full membership. From such a standpoint, they were therefore utterly opposed to Report B which excluded them from any real relationship with the University and also to the federal scheme, since the latter in creating a separate House for men and women implied a difference between the interests of men and women in so far as they were persons seeking learning, a "difference which they [the students of Girton and Newnham] believed to be non-existent". They did not wish for admission to men's colleges nor for the appointment of a woman to any University post unless she was considered to be the most fit person to occupy that post.[44]

The Royal Commission* on Oxford and Cambridge had begun its investigation of University affairs in November 1919 and the question was raised in the Cambridge women's colleges of their joining together to ask the Royal Commission to recommend a Government grant. The Oxford colleges had already made such an application and it was felt the Cambridge colleges should take the opportunity to do the same.[45] In a memorandum to the Commissioners in July 1920, Girton and Newnham included a description of the position of women in Cambridge, emphasising the difficulties and isolation under which the staffs of the two colleges worked. These, they pointed out, in view of the opportunities of academic careers for women in other universities, could only lead to a decline in the standards at Cambridge. The Commissioners, however, felt unable to deal with the question of the University's relationship with its women students, since the matter was under consideration by the Senate.[46] This approach to the Commission was perhaps ill-advised and timed, since outside interference in the University's affairs was resented by many Cambridge men, irrespective of their attitude to women's membership, and it confirmed the view of the signatories of Report B that women lacked respect for the sanctity of University autonomy. The Commissioners' reply must also have strengthened the belief that if the University could be seen to be making some effort to solve the "women problem", the Commissioners would not interfere.

The public discussion of the reports was interrupted by the summer vacation, though the fact that there was not the total ceasefire which had characterised previous controversies no doubt reflected the difficulties of taking long holidays in post-war Europe. The question of numbers remained prominent and it seemed that the anti-Report-A faction had gained the upper hand by showing that the report contained no real check on the numbers of women who, they claimed, would inevitably "flood" Cambridge. However, in their anxiety to demonstrate the effectiveness of their own plan in limiting numbers, they merely confirmed the hollowness of their claim

* See above p. 9.8.

to be "benefitting" women. As they explained in a flysheet on 1st October, 1920, if women belonged to a separate university, the control of their numbers could be easily effected, since Cambridge University would retain full powers to regulate the admission of women to its lectures, laboratories and libraries. The supporters of Report A were quick to expose the duplicity of their opponents[47] who had pledged in one of the proposed Graces to implement Report B that "the Senate desires to continue to students of the new [women's] University, the privileges as regards instruction and examination now enjoyed by Girton and Newnham as well as access to libraries, museums and laboratories". As now interpreted by its supporters, security of access to teaching, the most fundamental and, under the existing circumstances, the most pressing educational privilege which the women at Cambridge required, would not be safeguarded. With this admission of its real intent, Report B lost the support of all but the most prejudiced of women's opponents. But it had served a purpose in exposing certain weaknesses in Report A. On the one hand any plan to limit the numbers of women within the University would be a contradiction of the professed aim of giving women equality with the men students, and a fruitful source of further controversy; on the other, it was generally agreed that the numbers of women should be limited, and yet Report A did not seem to guarantee this.

Report B had also brought into the limelight the issue of women in men's colleges. This was regarded *ipso facto* as highly unsuitable, and understandably so in the prevailing moral climate. Yet at the same time as it was accepted as uncontestably and obviously unthinkable to have students of both sexes as members of one college, the exponents of this argument chose to suggest that the women and their supporters were contemplating co-residence. The women and their friends protested that they too regarded such a move as unthinkable and not something they desired in the least (though the more progressive among them appreciated that their opinion was conditioned by circumstances rather than being an enduring principle). As a reporter "from the women's colleges" wrote indignantly in the *Queen*,[48] "in matters of

hygiene alone, our own colleges are far more conveniently and comfortably built", and it was pointed out that in the universities which freely admitted women, separate accommodation had always been arranged for them and they had never wanted anything else. The opponents answered smugly that they did not think that pressure for admission would necessarily come from the women themselves, though of course the women's leaders could not pledge themselves for the actions of their successors, but some misguided men's college, encouraged by the official University policy of matriculating women, might easily be "temporarily swayed by theory or policy to elect women into its fellowships or find it necessary on economic grounds to admit women students".[49] Now the men's colleges had probably always had the power to admit women to membership, and at the very least they had had it since the Sex Disqualification Act of 1919, so that the possibility of an impoverished college, unable to find men students, turning to women to fill the places was not a new one. It was held to be self-evident that the women should not share the men's accommodation—and there were sound reasons for that—nor share in the rich endowments for educational purposes from which the old colleges benefited. No reason was offered for the latter exclusion, and the women and their supporters would have found it extremely difficult to explain why a college should not offer places to women if it could not fill them with men. In Cambridge, then as now, the education provided by the whole University environment was considered as only secondary to the education received in the communal life of a college, and it was firmly held by most Cambridge men that such an education could not take place in a mixed college. This was not surprising in view of the prevailing masculine arrogance and ignorance regarding the intellectual capabilities of the opposite sex, the social code which required a girl to conceal her brainpower and behave like a butterfly, and the moral code which required both sexes to regard the unchaperoned company of the other as improper.*
One flysheet openly expressed this view and explained its

---

* For modern thinking on this point, see below, Chapter 11.

signatories' reasons for not supporting Report A. Remembering how reluctant people are even today to countenance co-education, it is not surprising to find sincerely and strongly held views against it in the 1920's. On 2nd December, 1920, E. D. Adrian and H. A. Holland* issued a flysheet opposing Report A since it did not deal satisfactorily with the issue of numbers. University co-education was undesirable because of its effect on work, particularly scientific work. It was wrong to suggest, as some people did, that Cambridge was already a "mixed" University, since the women amounted to only about ten per cent of the undergraduate population. If their numbers rose to equal that of the undergraduates, the effect on the atmosphere of the University would be "deleterious".

The signatories of Report A had written that Cambridge was far too precious a national possession to be reserved in the twentieth century for a single sex. But by its very nature what was so precious about Cambridge could not be shared. This was its college system which "offers the free intercourse of men of congenial minds with a clash of diverse intellectual opinion and some association with older men who have intellectual ideals if not achievement to their credit". The admixture of a large number of women would "by altering the habits of undergraduate life, impair the heritage of the men". Women had little to offer, since intercourse between the sexes would, for the most part, be of a trivial nature and would "diminish the time spent by students either in work or in more valuable intercourse with others of the same sex". They felt that the best solution to the present problem was to give women the titles of their degrees, in return for control by the University of their numbers, and they looked forward "to a time when the prosperity of the country [would] make possible the maintenance of one or more self-governing women's Universities geographically separated from any men's University". They were not, however, completely convinced of the triviality of women's company, for without giving women graduates in general votes in the Senate, they hoped to secure

* Married 1929 Marjorie Tappan, Girton, one of the first women to receive a University appointment in 1926.

the services of "distinguished women teachers" for the University. "We should welcome powers specially to elect particular women to membership of the Senate and would advocate the exercise of those powers in the case of the lecturers of Newnham and Girton." These recommendations had little to do with the arguments which preceded them, since it was not explained why some co-education could be tolerated, but not much.* But unwelcome though the flysheet must have been to those working in the women's cause, it did at least have the merit of being a direct and open statement which, though it rested on matters of opinion rather than of fact, was far more tangible and open to discussion than the veiled hints of the other opponents. The women's authorities must have found it difficult to expound the virtues of a full undergraduate life shared by both men and women, since they had always gone to such lengths to keep their students isolated, at least from social intercourse with the men. They did however point out that the pursuit of knowledge was neither an exclusively masculine nor a feminine affair and that girls who came to Cambridge were not of the frivolous type who would waste a man's time.[50] It would not hurt the men to meet decent women and there was no real need for men and women to be such strange animals to each other. As a Newnham woman was reported as saying coyly to an *Evening News* representative, "a man might just as well know a woman is neither an angel nor the other thing".[51]

The women were really caught in the same cleft stick over their contribution to coporate life as they had been by Alfred Marshall twenty-five years previously. If they demonstrated how little their girls were allowed to mix with the under-graduates, they were told they were not really living the true University life and could therefore not claim University membership; on the other hand, if they admitted that the two sexes did have valuable intellectual and social intercourse, they were accused of distracting the men and wasting time. The popular press found the topic a fruitful source of entertaining

* The Adrian/Holland fly was later described by D. S. Robertson and G. I. Taylor as "an unselfish crusade to teach women what they ought to want".

copy, and produced several colourful pieces by interviewing real or imaginary "old dons" on the subject.[52] In an interview given to the *Evening Standard* one "Old Don" professed himself horror stricken at the thought of giving women further privileges:

It all began in '87. Miss Ramsay was Senior Classic and a year or so later Miss Fawcett passed above the Senior Wrangler. That was startling, I agree. But the women have done nothing like it since. Nothing except worm in here and start a lot of dances. Before the war, the undergraduates would have nothing to do with them. They were fresh from school, you see, of that sound, honest age when boys have a healthy contempt for their sisters. Before a lecture you would see a close clot of girls round the door of the hall waiting for it to open; behind them a gang of Indians—for they were hard swotters too. Then, a long way off, you saw the ordinary undergraduates who didn't want anything to do with either crowd. But now they go out for their elevens with the girls; go off to lunch with them. There are *thé dansants* and ever-lasting dances at the Liberal Club and the Masonic Hall. You wouldn't believe it was the same place. And last term the Union—the Union mind you—actually passed a resolution in favour of admitting the women. It is these ex-servicemen, they got fond of dancing in the Army, didn't they? We are being filled out again this term with the normal pre-war sort of fresher—schoolboy. It will be interesting to see what view they take. There may be some hope there.[53]

Asked why he objected to the women having degrees since they attended lectures etc., he replied, "Ah, you don't know these Girton and Newnham girls. They are very pushing—very!"

The women's authorities did not grant new permissions lightly but some account had to be taken of the new relationship which had sprung up between men and women during the war. Following a request from the students for a reconsideration of the chaperonage rules, the Newnham College Council ruled in May 1919 that it was no longer necessary to be accompanied when going with a man into a tea-shop but that "it was not desirable that students should go unchaperoned with men on the river, except that a student may go with a brother or a fiancé".[54] However, there were some determined forces in the ranks of the women students which caused the authorities much doubt and deliberation for they were more often governed by anxiety for the women's good name than by prudishness. In the following year the river rules were relaxed and "parties without chaperones may with the leave of the Tutor go on the river in punts or boats but not in canoes. Such parties may only take place before dinner (8 p.m. Sundays) and more than one student must be present except that a student may go alone with her brother or her fiancé. No such parties may include more than one punt or boat and no parties may take place on Thursday".*[55] The *Daily Mail* reported how these "New Liberty" rules were alarming the old guard.[56] Several dancing societies had been formed and licensed by the Proctors and these licences were accepted by the authorities of the women's colleges. Girl students were reportedly allowed to entertain undergraduates in their own rooms providing another girl was present and the conversation was not a tête à tête (or a "you and me" as someone translated it). Men and women could meet for tea in tea-shops and an undergraduate could entertain his sister in his rooms in the presence of other men, a practice which had previously been strictly forbidden.

Such pieces as the *Evening Standard*'s "Old Don" interview probably harmed the women's cause very little. But attempts were made to bring up more serious allegations against their behaviour. A few students had been sent down from Newnham over the previous years, generally for academic incompetence but occasionally because they infringed college rules. Specifically the offences had been that of riding through Cambridge on the carrier of a man's motor cycle on a Sunday morning, coming in late and climbing over the gate and going to the

---

* Newnham women tell me that this was because of the half-day closing on Thursdays of Cambridge shops!

theatre with undergraduates. These last two offences had occurred before the war. No case of serious misconduct had ever occurred, but such was the anxiety of the college authorities to avoid giving any offence that a girl who had shown herself "unreliable" was sometimes sent away before the end of the Easter term, so that she should not be exposed to the temptations of the May Week festivities. There were, however, some other cases completely beyond the control of the College which brought discredit on its good name. These involved two ex-Newnham students who some years after going down lived as married people with men who had been Cambridge undergraduates without any religious or civil ceremony. They were described as belonging to the "socialist and pacifist groups" and this took place during the war. Both pairs subsequently married.

Unfortunately these stories were jumbled together and exaggerated until a rumour emerged of "serious misconduct" having occurred between Newnham students and undergraduates in Cambridge. Careless and sensational journalism added to the difficulties, as for example, when the *Daily Mail* at the end of its harmless gossipy piece on the "New Liberty" rules added, "rumours have been circulating that this new liberty has been abused to the ruin of good manners, but the rumours are, for the most part, quite unjustified".[57] Unjustified rumours they remained and were not used by any of those responsibly involved in the admissions debate to discredit the women, but they caused considerable pain to the women's authorities,[58] and especially to the then Principal of Newnham, Miss B. A. Clough, the foundress's niece.

"Evidence" of the unwelcome influence of women was also adduced from the situation at Oxford. A Cambridge man, W. F. Pelton, wrote to the *Spectator* telling of "persistent rumours" from Oxford that they were now regretting their action in admitting women to membership. Women were a nuisance and tended to crowd out the men,

> . . . and there is yet another consideration, due to the presence, not of those ambitious and industrious females, but to that of the pass-woman who is devoid of any such

ambition.* These are reputed to be quite content with one or two morning's lectures, which having been attended, leave them perfectly free to fritter away the greater part of the golden afternoon in the playing fields in company with men whose thirst for knowledge is just as easily assuaged. The inevitable result of this seductive intercourse must be ɐ lowering of the standard of University life, and this retrograde process is already being accelerated by a large increase in the number of dances organised on every conceivable excuse, whereby the poll man may beguile the dreadful tedium of the intervening hours between hall and bed time not less pleasantly than did his father or his grandfather.[59]

Pelton's attack sounds more like a criticism of the Poll degree than of women at the ancient universities. Because of the shortage of space, the existence of "Poll-women" was not a real issue in the Cambridge debate and the criticisms of women at Oxford were strongly repudiated in a letter from a group of Oxford dons to *The Times* on 7th December, 1920.

The "Old Don's" comment about girls being "very pushing" was also repeated in a more serious form by members of the Senate. Dr E. C. Pearce, the Master of Corpus, was quoted as saying "women cannot be admitted on equal terms simply because they are not content with equality. They mean to rule and usually do in the end".[60] Professors Ridgeway and Sorley were the chief exponents of this particular theory. In Professor Sorley's view, the women were not out for education but for power and in evidence of this, he pointed to the rejection of titular degrees and a women's University which had been made in a circular sent to all old Newnham and Girton students by their Joint Committee. No votes in the Senate and lack of influence in examinations had also been quite openly mentioned in the list of disabilities put out by the women's side.[61] Professor Ridgeway went further and

* 24 women graduated with Pass degrees in Oxford in 1920. The total number of women students in Oxford that year, representing three years' intake, was 574. (*Oxford University Gazette*, 1920. Calendar for the Association for the Promotion of Education of Women in Oxford.)

specified the ways in which women undermined the higher education of men, which, he declared, was far more important than the higher education of women. According to Ridgeway, when certain proposals made for the new English Tripos did not suit the teachers of Newnham and Girton, they did all in their power to defeat them, even calling in the assistance of outsiders.[62] Again women had an unfair advantage over men in examinations when they could use personal charms to influence the examiners. He knew of an instance where a girl with second class marks had been awarded a first, forcing up two "undoubtedly second class men" with her, thus lowering the standard of the Tripos. She subsequently married one of her examiners.[63] Professor Ridgeway's specific accusations were not well received, but it is true that one of the most frequently repeated claims of the controversy was that women, if they were given membership and therefore voting rights in the Senate, would use their power there and on Faculties and Boards to alter the University's educational patterns for their own benefit and to the detriment of men's education. Some opponents of the Ridgeway and Sorley persuasion believed they would do this from a deliberate desire to control and dominate; others believed it would be the inevitable result of a pressure group seeking its own best interests. Yet apart from the debatable story of the English Tripos and the scarcely credible one of the woman student charming her examiner, not one other single piece of evidence was brought forward to support this claim of women's likely behaviour. Perhaps those with long memories remembered how Sidgwick had used the women students of Newnham as the vehicle for some of his ideas on educational reform of the University; but if their memories had been generous, they would also have remembered that the foremost and most influential woman to work for the establishment of women in Cambridge, Emily Davies, had taken it as the first article of her educational creed that her women students should follow the University's courses exactly as they were laid down for men.

There was little the women could do to counter the vague but insidious suggestion that they wanted to alter men's education, but to reiterate that they did not. There was a very large range of courses available in Cambridge and if none of these suited a girl, she was under no compulsion to attempt one, but could choose from the courses at other universities and colleges. On the issue of power, R. T. Wright, the husband of Mary Kennedy, one of the first five Newnham students and a lifelong supporter of women's education, suggested that power was only a bad thing when in the hands of an enemy. There was no evidence that women would work against the University—they were men's allies in the field of education and Cambridge should therefore want them strong.[64] Another writer drew attention to the appeals which had been made during the controversy to "University tradition". In his view, one of the most important parts of Cambridge tradition in the 1920's was that it possessed the two most famous women's colleges in the world. Their past success had been mainly dependent on University goodwill and as long as they had been able to compete with the Oxford women's colleges on equal terms they had prospered. But if Cambridge continued to discriminate against women it was doubtful if they would be able to hold their own.[65]

The formal discussion of Report A which took place in the Senate House on 14th and 15th October[66] was little more than a repetition of the points already made in flysheets. Will Spens tried to demonstrate from the proportion of firsts in recent Tripos results that women were not suited to the Cambridge system of education and examinations, especially in Science. From this he argued that the women would try to alter the men's courses to their own benefit if given the chance and should therefore be given a university of their own in which to make experiments. The line of argument was weak; statistics of Tripos results could be manipulated to support a wide range of theories and even if Spens's interpretation was valid, he could hardly argue that the value of university education could be measured simply by the number of first class students it produced. There were exchanges on the issue of numbers which seemed to leave the supporters of Report A somewhat exposed. Professor Sorley, who repeated his belief that women were only out for power, claimed that under the Public Hostel Ordinances there was no limit on the number of persons admitted nor on the buildings erected. Dr R. Parry replied that the Public Hostels were specifically created under Ordinances, thus allowing a flexibility of regulation which would be lacking if they were created under Statute. A limitation on numbers could therefore be imposed. But Professor Sorley was quick to show that a restriction would be placed on women which did not also apply to men. Supporters of Report A rested their case on the grounds of justice and expediency and despite the length of the discussion no new arguments emerged from either side. Few voices were raised in positive support of Report B, but there was considerable opposition to Report A. The reports were to be voted on separately and the more controversial Report A was taken first.

In the months preceding the vote, the women energetically lobbied members of the Senate in support of their case. This was a massive, time-consuming and expensive task relying largely on individual effort, though this time the Joint Committee employed an old Newnham student, Miss Agnes Conway, to co-ordinate the campaign. The interest of members friendly to the cause had to be held and they had to be persuaded to go up to Cambridge on the appointed day to register their votes, a trip which was often troublesome and expensive. Old students were sent lists of possible supporters in their own region and wrote personal letters urging them to vote; in London, supporters were classified by profession— doctors, schoolmasters, university teachers, clergy, civil servants etc.—and lobbied that way. The press in general supported the proposals of Report A but *The Times*, though professing itself favourable towards the women, in the opinion of the campaigners failed them on several occasions.[67] Important letters countering the arguments of opponents were said to have been held up or not published, though an especially valuable letter did appear on the day before the vote signed by a large number of Oxford dons, totally rejecting the suggestion that the women newly admitted to membership there had disturbed the University in any way. During the whole debate eighteen flysheets appeared, thirteen in favour of the women and five against, including amongst the former, a flysheet signed by sixty-one graduates of Cambridge, all professors and lecturers at universities other than Oxford and Cambridge, who spoke from their personal experience of institutions in which men and women were educated in conditions of equality. As the voting results were to show, the Senior Common Rooms of individual colleges held strong feelings on "the women". Trinity Hall was probably the most favourable and the Master and every resident Fellow there signed a letter which was sent to all graduate members of the college urging the women's case on the grounds not only of justice but as a source of real benefit to the University.

The undergraduates reversed their decision of May 1920 when they had supported the admission of women to membership by 365 votes to 266, in another debate at the Union at the end of November. This new vote against the women of 423 to 337 was said to have been largely influenced by the speech of Professor Sorley in which he again played on the theme of women's desire for power.[68] According to the popular press, the undergraduates were annoyed to find the Senate vote fixed for Wednesday, 8th December, two days after most of them had gone down. The Senate had done this in an effort to avoid the riotous behaviour which had accompanied the voting in 1897; "hence the grievance of the undergraduates who realise that the chance of pelting a professor comes only once in a lifetime and has been snatched from them".[69] A last minute poll taken from all the undergraduates revealed that 2,329 were against the proposal of Report A out of a total vote of 3,213 (approximately 5,000 undergraduates were in residence). Trinity Hall and Emmanuel showed the strongest support for women, St Catherine's, Downing and Clare were firmly against.[70] The women's supporters claimed that the opinion of the undergraduates was of no great relevance to the debate. Only the most extreme opponents hoped to remove women from Cambridge entirely, and both reports and the suggested compromise schemes did not really effect the position of women as students but as graduates.[71] The numbers of women would be controlled by the University and the catch-phrase was "a woman with a degree would take up no more room than one without a degree'. The opponents countered this by reiterating their belief that women would interfere in men's education for their own ends if given membership of the Senate and that the control of numbers was by no means as certain as the supporters of Report A liked to make out. Women would compete with the men for the licensed lodgings which were proving so difficult to secure in Cambridge at that time.[72] However, it is clear that in 1920, unlike 1897, the undergraduate had little influence on the outcome, perhaps because he was no longer able to threaten dons with an exodus to Oxford if women were admitted to Cambridge.

As the voting day drew close, the newspapers were less confident in their predictions. The *Daily Mail*[73] felt the clergy were likely to vote against the women, but a Newnham woman closely involved in the campaign shrewdly anticipated their support, since so many of them had daughters either at Cambridge or at other colleges. The parson was now regarded as a complete convert to feminism and it was vital that he should vote.[74] "If we are beaten," she declared, "it will be by high railway fares—the parson is a poor man". Nearer the mark was the suggestion that the doctors opposed the women's advance, giving as a reason the overcrowding in the laboratories and lecture rooms.*[75] Their opinion however was not shared by the *British Medical Journal* which came out strongly in the women's favour as it had done in the 1897 controversy, believing women should be admitted to the University "as a matter of highest educational and national policy".[76] An important letter which was published in *The Times* two days[77] before the vote, from Ernest Rutherford, Cavendish Professor of Physics, and William J. Pope, Professor of Chemistry, dealt authoritatively with this issue of overcrowding; in the two laboratories "over which they had the honour to preside" space was admittedly very short. But the solution of this problem was not the exclusion of certain students, but the

* There was a strong move amongst the men at University College Hospital, London to get rid of the girl students and the same reasons were given. The girl medics claimed that the men resented their successes in examinations and in winning those prizes for which they were allowed to compete. *Daily Express* 13.10.1920.

expansion of the laboratories with the aid of outside benefactions. They welcomed the appearance of women in their laboratories, since residence in Cambridge was meant to prepare young people to take their proper place in the outside world and this world, to an ever increasing extent, was one in which men and women were called on to work together in harmony. It was clear that women could often make a substantial contribution to the advancement of knowledge and "at the present stage of world affairs, we can afford less than ever before to neglect the training and cultivation of all the young intelligence available". By admitting women to degrees and a share in University government, Cambridge could hope to keep in touch with the reality of modern life. They took up the point that reforms made in the previous century, such as the admission of non-conformists, the marriage of Fellows and the provision of teaching and research facilities in science which had opened the door to a wider University membership, had always proved a valuable stimulus to the social and academic life of the University.[78] It was claimed that women had no right to share in the benefaction which had been given specifically for men's education.[79] This same objection had been raised over the admission of Dissenters to membership in the previous century, but in retrospect it could be seen that the University had benefited greatly by their admission. It had been suggested to the Dissenters that they found their own university, yet even when they could gain degrees at other institutions they persisted in their efforts at Cambridge. The case of the Dissenters and the women were parallel; ultimately they would succeed as the Dissenters had done and in the long run the University would benefit.

But such an analogy was not appreciated; as the Master of Trinity, J. J. Thompson, wrote to *The Times:* "I am not impressed . . . after all, there are greater differences between men and women than there are between Non-Conformists and Churchmen and I think that even a Liberal may be consistent if he thinks that while there are no grounds whatever for any differentiation between the secular education of Dissenters and Churchmen there are sound ones for doing so between men and women".[80]

When the votes came to be counted on 8th December, it was seen that the Grace approving Report A had been defeated by 192 votes, 712 being given in favour and 904 **against**. The press was somewhat taken aback; spokesmen for the women pointed out that many of the non-resident supporters had been unable to get away mid-week, hinting that the *non-placets* had nothing better to do with their time than come up to Cambridge to oppose them.[81] The *Daily Herald* in a piece entitled "Cantabsurdity" said the defeat was the result of ancient prejudices which had not much life left in them and drew for their readers a pen portrait of the narrow and embittered Cambridge male:

> The sour man graduate (drawing) his fluttering gown closer round his lean legs as he flits, shadow-like, among historic shades mumbling brazen shibboleths and nodding a wooden head. Well the women will survive and these men are only a survival.[82]

Other papers too shrugged off the defeat as "a temporary wave of reaction" and felt that the decision was bound to be reversed. Meanwhile, Oxford would continue to grow as the major centre for women's education in England and the migration there of Girton and Newnham was confidently predicted.[83] Parents of girls who were in Cambridge taking the Previous Examination prior to admission grumbled at the attitude which the University had taken. One father was quoted as saying indignantly, "people don't seem to realise that women are not accepted for Pass degrees like the men. They have a higher, not a lower standard, for they are compelled to work for Honours. When they get them, there is nothing to show". Many of the parents said they wished they had entered their daughters for Oxford.[84] The defeat of Report A was a signal for some men to pour out abuse on the women, and vice versa—and it was possible to glimpse for a while the real strength of the bitterness which lay beneath the façade of tightly controlled middle-class manners.[85] From Yorkshire came the lone voice of an impoverished clergyman who had spent £2.10.0 on a third-class return ticket to

Cambridge, and who asked in future for a postal vote.*[86]

Yet had the newspapers followed the details of the debate more carefully, they would have realised that many men not prejudiced against the women's cause were unhappy about the provisions of Report A. They were too far-reaching, too out of step with the unspoken Cambridge motto of *festina lente*. It may be asked why Oxford had swallowed similar proposals without a murmur. The timing of the ground-work of the reform is perhaps the key to the problem and during the months in which Cambridge lagged behind Oxford, many men had convinced themselves of the harm which would result if women had a voice in the education of men. Dr Parry, the Vice-Master of Trinity, commented to the *Daily News*, "there is a spirit of reaction abroad against women, but it will pass· If the vote had been taken two years ago, the women's cause would have triumphed".[87] The threat of a large "woman's vote" seemed real at Cambridge because of the power of the M.A. vote. In Oxford the larger voice was that of the residents and as yet few women had University appointments. Constant repetition of the view that women would interfere and harm men's education did the rest. Contemporary opinion held science men in general and the medical profession in particular to blame for the defeat of Report A. Medics, it was believed, had a closer understanding of the physiological and psychological differences between the sexes, though it was never explained how they then arrived at the conclusion that for equal academic work, men and women should be unequally rewarded. The invocation of their professional wisdom was probably no more than a cloak to hide a more instinctive reaction against any progress on the part of women. According to the *Times Educational Supplement* the reaction was prompted by fear—"Medical men in all savage races fear women, but it is remarkable that this particular superstition should survive amongst their descendants at Cambridge"[88]—but it seems more likely that their motive was, simply, self-preservation. If the medical profession was opened to women, it might well

* A wish which was not granted. Voting on University matters had always to be done in person, though voting for the University M.P. was conducted by post.

become a female preserve, as school teaching now was, especially in the treatment of children and the elderly and perhaps all other females too. Men who had long used the argument of women's special aptitude to bring up children and tend the sick as a method of keeping them at home, now felt themselves sitting on a time-bomb which threatened to destroy their own careers.

However, the evidence of scientific and medical opposition is not so straightforward. Among the most vocal opponents of women, Pearce was a classicist, Sorley a philosopher, Scott had followed his Mathematical Tripos with Law and then some historical writing, and Ridgeway was a classicist and archaeologist; of the two scientists on the Syndicate of 1920, one signed Report A and the other Report B. Two of Cambridge's most famous scientific men, Rutherford and Pope, had championed the women; the Medical Board of 1916 had welcomed women students.

On the other hand, although there is no list of medical opponents relating directly to the vote of 1920, when similar proposals were brought forward in the following year, an opposition flysheet circulating in London contained nineteen medical names out of the first thirty-two on the list.[89] An analysis of the vote of 8th December, 1920, reveals no association between first degree and voting behaviour*, yet contemporary opinion† is so strong on this point that it can perhaps be assumed the doctors played a significant part in developing a consensus against women.

The women took their defeat philosophically. Public opinion was largely in their favour and the Royal Commission on Oxford and Cambridge which was still sitting, could be expected to support their cause. In the fashion of the newspapers, they believed the defeat was only "temporary"; there was no question of retreating to their colleges and waiting

---

* For a brief analysis of the voting figures, see Appendix C.

† And even hindsight. Lord McNair Q.C. (A. D. McNair) who was a champion of the women's cause in the 1920's (above p. 10.8) retains today a strong impression of the opposition amongst scientific and medical men at the time. The latter long continued their discrimination against women trying to enter the profession.

patiently for another twenty-five years and a "suitable opportunity" to present itself before asking for degrees again. All the other universities in the British Isles accepted women students, awarded them degrees, research opportunities and teaching posts, and the Cambridge women were quietly determined that their beloved University should recognise them and perhaps recapture its position as leader in the advancement of women's education which it had held half a century previously.

IO

A MEN'S UNIVERSITY: ROUND FOUR

THE AFTERMATH OF the 1920 defeat in no way resembled 1897, when the women's cause had been dropped immediately. The Royal Commission, which was looking into the University's affairs following its request for financial support, was regarded as a great threat by the women's opponents and they were most anxious to forestall the Commission's intervention in the "women" question. Almost before the voting was over on 8th December, 1920, reports were appearing of a compromise plan based either on the federal scheme or on the rejected proposal of 1897 to give women titles of degrees without membership. Report B was formally brought forward on 12th February, 1921, but its defeat was a foregone conclusion. A flysheet appeared on 1st February signed by fifty-two members of the Senate proposing to *non-placet* the Grace and they included several of the original authors of Report B. The reason given for this was that the proposal for an independent women's university would never be implemented by the women even if passed by the Senate and it was therefore better to work for a more realistic solution to the problem. Instead they proposed that women's degrees should be conferred on women who had fulfilled the degree requirement, so long as they did not become members of the University and the University could control their numbers. If this was their "realistic solution", they were clearly underestimating the tenacity with which the women would pursue their claim to full membership; on the other hand, as events proved, the signatories of the flysheet seemed to have the measure of the University's feelings in the matter.

Report B was rejected by 146 votes to 50, but it was generally acknowledged that the matter could not be allowed to rest there. Two Memorials were received by the Council of the

Senate proposing that women should be given the titles of degrees. They were published in the *Reporter* of 8th March, 1921,[1] although they had been in circulation since the beginning of February. The first, which collected the larger number of signatures, proposed to give women the titles of their degrees while limiting the numbers who would receive teaching from the University. To those who felt such a concession was just a preliminary to agitation for more, they emphasised the fact that "there is a widespread feeling in the country that the existing situation involves an injustice and there is no chance of a quiescence of the controversy until this is removed. Once the proposed concession has been made, it will be clear that any further agitation will be concerned with the question whether women graduates are to participate in the control of men's education, and with the question of maintaining a ratio between the numbers of men and women accepted for tuition". However, in its specific recommendations the Memorial did appear to suggest that there could be some consultation between women teachers and Boards of Studies and talked of "privileges" to be given to women. The second Memorial which was largely the work of R. F. Scott, the Master of John's, was much simpler and sought only to give women the titles of their degrees and to limit their numbers.

Both the *Cambridge Review* and the *Cambridge Chronicle*[2] reported the new schemes, especially that of the Master o John's, in glowing terms, believing they dealt generously "with the only real grievance" of the women: that of having no degree letters after their names. Yet the issue of degree titles had scarcely been mentioned in the debate of the previous term; the isolation of women teachers and the insecurity of University teaching for women had been the major issues. The women perhaps took courage from an analysis of the December voting figures which appeared in the same issue of the *Cambridge Review*. Among active University residents there had been a majority of 19 in favour of Report A (214–191) and a majority of 25–15 among the Professors who had voted. But opinions differed on the significance of the resident vote. For some, the resident was a narrow don buried in a somnolent and academic atmosphere, and for others a man living in the centre of an active educational world; the non-resident was characterised as a country parson, ill-informed and sentimental, or he was a man of the world with practical experience and knowledge of affairs.[3] So not everyone interpreted the resident voting figures in the women's favour and since the University insisted that it was best governed by the section of its graduates who had the time and money to care about its affairs, there was no point in arguing about the resident vote *per se*. But the analysis did give the lie to the commonly held belief that the non-residents never altered the vote as cast by residents, and it strengthened the position of those University men who were hoping to see the Royal Commission produce a scheme for University reform which would weaken the power of the out-voter.

On examining the new Memorials which it had received, the Council of the Senate came to the conclusion that some compromise scheme might be worked out so long as it embodied two major principles: that men's education should be left in the hands of men and that, whatever their new privileges, the number of women students who would enjoy them would be strictly limited. The Council therefore suggested that the Vice-Chancellor, Dr P. Giles, Master of Emmanuel, should convene an informal meeting of the supporters of Report A and others who had declared themselves in favour of a compromise. Out of this March meeting[4] emerged a scheme which would admit women to matriculation and degrees, all University prizes, academic posts and membership of Boards and Syndicates and give them representation without a vote on the Council of the Senate. Their numbers were to be limited to 500 and it was also provided that a woman Professor would not be, *ex-officio*, Head of a Department. A Representative Board of Women was to be set up to deal with discipline and other unspecified matters. The women's colleges were consulted on the proposals and though they placed on record that the settlement did not meet all their wishes, they agreed not to approach the Royal Commission if the proposals passed the Senate by the end of Easter term 1921. It was this promise not to invoke the dreaded "outside interference" which had prompted the Council of the Senate, on its own admission, to depart from the usual procedure of appointing a Syndicate to report to it, and instead to draft for immediate discussion and submission to the Senate alternative Statutes embodying the compromise scheme just discussed and another awarding women titular degrees as put forward in Dr Scott's Memorandum of 14th February.* On 3rd May, the Council of the Senate issued the draft Statutes embodying the two main schemes for dealing with the women question. The first, known as the "compromise" proposals from the Vice-Chancellor's meeting in March, included a clause making it impossible for anyone to matriculate from other than a single-sex college and was accompanied by a Memorial from 177 members supporting it, of whom 115 had voted *placet* on 8th December, 1920; 50 had voted *non-placet* and 22 had not voted. The second scheme conferred the titles of degrees on duly qualified women, the detailed provisions of which would be discussed after the vote.[5]

The compromise proposals were quickly challenged in a flysheet which rejected the new scheme as relinquishing the control of men's education by men.[6] The new proposals were scarcely distinguishable from those of Report A defeated the previous December and the opponents, outraged at the contempt with which a decision of the Senate was being treated, declared war. Few people took any pleasure in the renewal of hostilities. The *Church Times* expressed the hope that non-resident voters would be spared the expense of again casting their votes, adding wistfully, that since both sides of the dispute seemed bent on compromise, was it possible that they could settle the matter between themselves?[7] In May 1921 two letters of major importance appeared in the *Cambridge Review*. The first was an ultimatum from the secretary of the Committee of Members of the Senate who supported the admission of women to full membership. On behalf of the Committee, he warned that an approach would be made to the Royal Commission when they considered the position of women, unless a solution which the Committee could support had been previously adopted by the University. Though admittedly a

* Above p. 10.2.

compromise, an acceptable solution was that published as the result of the Vice-Chancellor's meeting in March. A letter from the heads of Girton and Newnham appeared in the same issue of the *Review*, in which they accepted the proposals of the Vice-Chancellor's meeting which "though not fully satisfactory, confer a substantial benefit". They too pledged themselves not to appeal to the Royal Commission if the compromise proposals had been accepted before the Commission had finished its work. This "veiled threat with a time limit" as it was described in the Senate House discussion in May, probably angered more men than it scared. It was held up as a typical example of the meddlesome and insensitive behaviour of women and further proof that they should not be given power in the University. Yet if the ultimatum did little to further the merits of the women's cause, it probably had some influence on those men who had little interest in the issues actually involved but who wanted the matter and the disruptive and acrimonious debate it entailed, settled one way or another. Now they were being clearly told that unless it was settled in one particular way, the agitation would continue.

The discussion on the schemes was taken on 12th May and it was clear from the outset that strong objection was taken to the way in which the proposals had been brought forward.[8] It was held to be unconstitutional or, at the very least, unprecedented. Certainly it was an unusual step for the Council of the Senate to reopen a question which had been voted on the previous December and in terms which seemed to many scarcely distinguishable from those which had been rejected. In addition they had taken over from a duly appointed Syndicate the business of reporting on the issue and then had called for their own report to be discussed only nine days after its publication. W. L. Mollison, the Master of Clare, ascribed their "undue haste" to a panic-like fear of the Royal Commission. Some speakers seemed inclined to call the women's bluff and let them go to the Commissioners. The government grant might be withdrawn, but they would prefer to be free "even if poor". Will Spens, a signatory of Report B and author of the federal scheme, was now anxious for some agreement to be reached and saw the threat of outside interference as quite genuine. Speakers from both sides attacked the provisions of the schemes; the first would confer power on women without responsibility; the second, for titular degrees, could not be final "and would not endure eighteen months".[9]

The high-handed approach which the Council of the Senate had taken in bringing forward the schemes continued to be strongly criticised in the following weeks. Little could be done about their *fait accompli* but strenuous efforts were made to alter the voting procedure which the Council had decided upon for the two Graces.[10] Votes cast for Grace I—which gave the women more or less everything they asked for except full membership—would be counted first, and if there was a majority in favour, the votes for Grace II, for titular degrees, would be destroyed uncounted. Supporters of Grace II were incensed at this "rigging" of procedure; their scheme might get a larger majority in its favour than Grace I, and yet be ignored. In their view, the order of voting ought to be reversed, the more moderate scheme being taken first. As the supporters explained:

> Under a Constitution which does not provide for the moving of amendments, a perfect method of ascertaining the precise preferences of every voter is impossible. This fact is familiar to members of the University and has frequently proved inconvenient before now.[11]

In the present case, the arrangements had been designed so that everyone would be able to record their preferences accurately, except for a possible group of voters who preferred Grace II to Grace I, but would accept I if II failed. Such a group had so far not made their presence felt and there was little reason to believe it had many members. The explanation was a subtle one and perfectly reasonable, but it failed to answer the objection as to the size of the majority. Opposition was maintained and on 4th June the voting procedure was only narrowly sanctioned by 115 votes to 111, having been *non-placeted* at the last minute by the Master of Clare and others.[12]

Voting day was fixed for 16th June, and the women's hopes

of a beneficial if not totally satisfactory settlement by the end of the term must have been high when they considered the way in which the ranks of their supporters had been so recently augmented by men with power and influence in the University who had previously fought against them, and the speed with which the new proposals had been brought forward, apparently knocking their opponents off balance. Now national events intervened to steal the prize which women believed was almost in their grasp, a national event which to most people was of far greater significance than the struggle of a handful of middle-class women to secure University equality. The miners had been on strike since 15th April and their dispute, un-supported by the other unions of the famous "Triple Alliance", dragged on throughout the summer until they were forced to return to work at reduced wages. In June the coal strike was severely hindering the functioning of the rail services and the Council, impressed by the difficulties facing non-residents in travelling to Cambridge (and, it was suggested, unnerved by the narrowness of the procedural vote) decided to postpone the decision on Graces I and II until 20th October, 1921. It is unlikely that the miners could have found much sympathy for the disappointed women of Cambridge in their comfortable homes and colleges, though undoubtedly many of the women felt great sympathy for the miners' cause. If the miners' fight was more obviously a bread-and-butter issue, both the miners and the women believed they were fighting for justice and recognition of their human dignity. But the postponement placed the women and their supporters in a rather awkward position since it was generally believed that the Royal Commission would have finished its deliberations by the Michaelmas term. They had pledged themselves not to approach the Royal Commission unless the compromise had been rejected. Now it seemed they would be left with no second line of defence.

Little effort was made to sustain the dispute during the summer term; indeed most arguments had been stated the previous year. The women's opponents needed new and bold tactics to defeat this cat with many lives and these were not revealed until 6th October, 1921, only a fortnight before the vote.[13] The familiar reasons for rejecting Grace I were rehearsed; the scheme involved the interference by women in the education of men; the University would be pressed to exceed the limit of 500 laid down in the Statute and the arrival of more women would add to the disturbance in libraries and lecture rooms; the new proposals scarcely differed from those decisively rejected the previous year and should not be inflicted again on the Senate and the true interests of women could best be served by giving them the titles of their degrees. Then they played their trump card. If Grace I was passed, it was by no means certain that it was legal, having regard to the Sex Disqualification (Removal) Act of 1919. Counsel had given its opinion that the Statutes relating to Grace I were framed so as to discriminate against women on the grounds of sex and would therefore be refused Royal Assent. The passing of Grace I therefore would settle nothing and lengthy litigation was bound to follow. The only legally acceptable course open, other than the admission of women to full membership—a course already rejected in December 1920— was their complete exclusion. The publication of the fly created a sensation and it seemed the supporters might be caught by this objection raised so late in the day. Fortunately, the issue of legality had been raised the previous year but not brought forward publicly, so the women's side were not totally unprepared to make an answer.[14] Due to the efforts of A. D. McNair, a flysheet was issued on 14th October over his name and those of Dr R. A. Wright, K.C. and Dr C. S. Kenny, retired Downing Professor of the Laws of England, stressing that the Act of 1919 was a permissive one, allowing the University, if it so wished, to admit women to privileges reserved for men without having to obtain a separate Act of Parliament to do so.* In their opinion, it did not give women the legal right to demand that such privileges be opened to them. As a correspondent to the *Telegraph* pointed out, the Oxford Statutes had set a precedent, for although they placed certain restrictions on women which did not apply to men, they had been accepted by the King in Council and had not since been

* The relevant part of the Act is quoted on p. 9.10.

challenged.[15] In a sense the signatories of the 6th October flysheet had rather given themselves away, since if Grace I was potentially illegal, Grace II by the same reasoning would also be illegal. However, points of law which seem clear to the layman rarely are so, and the lawyers continued to debate. No matter how correct or convincing was the legal opinion for the women, the controversy must have shaken the nerve of many timid voters whose chief wish was for some lasting solution, irrespective of what it was. If Grace I would lead to lengthy litigation as its opponents suggested, then they would oppose it. In effect, the "legal red herring" as it was called in the flysheet, cancelled the "veiled threat with a time limit" and the two sides faced the vote as a true test of opinion on the issue of admitting women to University privileges.

One of the curious features of the second round in the battle was the way in which some of women's old opponents changed sides. The secretary of the pro-women faction was now Sir Geoffrey Butler who, the previous year, had urged the rejection of Report A. Sir Geoffrey was now convinced that the provisions of Grace I differed substantially from those of the scheme rejected by the Senate in December 1920 and together with another convert F. J. M. Stratton—a Report B signatory—he put forward his reasons for his new outlook.[16] The new proposals met and overcame the serious objection which had been made to the previous scheme; under Grace I, women would be excluded from the Senate which had the ultimate control of men's education. The disciplining of men and women students would be kept separate and the number of women students specifically limited. No man's college would be able to admit a woman to its membership. From his discussions with the women's colleges, it had become clear that they would not accept any permanent settlement on the basis of titular degrees. The women had, however, pledged themselves not to approach the Royal Commission if Grace I was accepted. Parliamentary interference would inevitably come if the Grace was rejected and such interference seemed almost certain to favour the women. Sir Geoffrey was also attracted by a subtle difference which he saw between Grace I and Report A and which enabled him to maintain his view that what was best for men was not necessarily equally good for women. Grace I did not expressly preclude a differentiation in syllabus between men and women as Report A had done; the women must have wondered if their new ally was not perhaps a cuckoo in the nest!

The press were certainly out of sympathy with the efforts of some Cambridge men to resist the inevitable. The *Times Educational Supplement* described the struggle over women's status as "tiresome" since "in a busy world where a result is inevitable, the policy of dying in the last ditch is neither heroic nor useful"—especially when no great moral principle is at stake. Perhaps there was something to be said for educating men and women separately, but if so the time for saying it had passed by in the last century.[17] The *Daily Graphic* produced a stirring article championing the women, over a headline "Men's Fear of Jumper Government". Cambridge would be disgraced in the eyes of moderate opinion if Grace I was rejected.[18] The *Evening News* carried a contribution from Charlotte Cowdray, author of *Thwarted Women*, which has the familiar ring of the anti-male attitude adopted by the more militant feminists of today. Feminists of the previous generation, she claimed, had missed their way in their efforts to prove their equality with men. They had squandered the gifts of womanhood, performing activities already well performed by the opposite sex. There was no longer any need to compete with men: women should want to be emancipated as women. Women no longer needed to emulate men; women were superior and they should demonstrate this in the Cambridge situation by founding their own University.[19] Miss Cowdray's ideas could not have had a very warm reception at Girton and Newnham, who were more alive to the practical problems of emancipation—and they probably felt that Miss Cowdray too had missed her way.

Arrangements for the vote on 20th October were well in hand and the papers reported that hotel accommodation was being quickly taken up. G. Grant-Morris wrote a stiff letter to *The Times* in which he urged all those opponents of Grace I who were coming up to vote against it, to apply to him for vouchers which would entitle them to day return tickets from

Liverpool Street to Cambridge at one and one-third the single fare. He generously suggested that Sir Geoffrey Butler, Secretary of the *Placet* Committee, would furnish his supporters with similar vouchers.[20] *The Times* leader of 18th October strongly supported the women; the following day the *Morning Post* was outspoken in its condemnation of the "unnecessary revolution". Professors Rutherford and Pope repeated their eleventh-hour attempt to swing the vote in favour of the women by supporting Grace I as they had supported scheme A. They warned that unless it was passed, bitter time-wasting discussions would continue to disrupt University work.[21] The *Newcastle Daily Chronicle* reported optimistically that graduate Cambridge was coming round to the women's cause and quoted an old don who was voting for Grace I because it would steal the best women from Oxford. In any case the women were confident of success since, if defeated in the Senate, they could rest their case with the Royal Commission which fortunately was still sitting and which seemed certain "to be on the side of the angels".[22] Other papers, more wary of Cambridge eccentricity, were cautious in their predictions of the outcome of the poll. Some hinted hopefully that the undergraduates would add some colour to the proceedings this time.[23] On the eve of the poll, the Union debated the motion that the House did not consider that the granting of titular degrees without membership of the University met the legitimate aspirations of women students. The motion was defeated by 375–185 votes. Professor Sorley spoke again of the inadequacies of women's mental equipment and their desire to interfere with men's education. As the *Westminster Gazette* reporter commented wearily, "if delight in endless repetition be indeed an attribute of childhood, Cambridge has discovered the secret of perpetual youth".[24] The Cambridge under-graduate was seemingly still not prepared to admit that a pretty girl could have a brain and although Cambridge women were more often to be seen in the company of men, and the women's colleges at Cambridge had always seemed more closely related to the University than had the colleges at Oxford, Cambridge wished to reject women, while Oxford had let them in. It was suggested that perhaps the men found women more approachable when they *didn't* wear caps and gowns,[25] a reminder of the ever-present fear of competition which lay behind so many of the curious excuses which were given for not admitting women to degrees.*

Polling day was Thursday 20th, October. The vote and the procedure for counting was slow and it was not possible to announce a result till late evening. The undergraduates, however, were not deterred by the delay and from 8 p.m. onwards, they gathered outside the Senate House chanting "we won't have women", and with handfuls of coppers, bribed the local street children to shout the same. Women students in the vicinity were hissed and the crowd was described by reporters as "a howling mob" or "a group of high-spirited undergraduates" according to taste. At 8.35 p.m. dead silence fell, as a University official appeared on the Senate House steps to announce the result: for Grace I, 694 votes; against, 908, a majority against of 214; for Grace II, 1012 votes; against 370, a majority in favour of 642. The students cheered and cheered and then urged on, as it was reported, by a mysterious "grey haired clergyman" a large group of them broke away and raced the mile to Newnham. There they attacked the bronze Memorial Gates of the College[26] with a hand-cart, conveniently "borrowed" from the College and seriously damaged the lower panels. The proctors arrived rather late on the scene and were later accused of either encouraging the men or at the very least being totally ineffectual in their efforts to restrain them. It required a strong body of policemen to shift the students, who had moved to another door of the college and were trying to force an entry. Driven away again by the police, they moved back to town to continue their celebrations.[27] It was said that the undergraduates had influenced the vote of their elders, motivated by a desire to be "different from Oxford".[28] The motive is suitably trivial,

* Scarcely credible is the report of an interview given to the *Daily News* 20.10.21. by Sir Geoffrey Butler. "Men complain that women students wear picture hats and obscure the view of the men in the dissecting rooms, although we have pointed out to the science men that if women wear caps and gowns they would be rid of this inconvenience."

but it is difficult to see how this influence could have had any effect on a large scale. Most newspapers were quite bewildered by the defeat of Grace I and predicted that the matter could not rest there. Either through the recommendations of the Royal Commission or the activities of the women's supporters in Cambridge, the issue would come to another vote very shortly. As the *Daily Telegraph* put it caustically, "we shall not have long to wait before Cambridge falls in line with the rest of the civilised world".[29] The only paper which took any pleasure in the women's defeat was the *Morning Post* which explained the two main reasons for the rejection of Grace I. The women's leaders were greedy and selfish in sticking out for full membership and were clearly out for power. At any time in the last twenty years the women could have had the titles of their degrees and the rank and file would have benefited. Under Grace I, the women were asking for a voice in the control of Cambridge and the only reason why they should want such power was so as to be able to interfere with the government of the University in their own interests. Secondly, Grace I contained proposals for limiting the numbers of the women students, thus discriminating against the women and creating a future grievance and source of controversy. The passing of Grace II was welcomed as filling a legitimate need[30]—the *Post's* writer conveniently overlooking the point that under Grace II the numbers of the women could also be limited and its provisions were certain to be a source of future grievance and controversy. According to the *Post*, the clergy, doctors and resident dons had voted against the women. The *Mail* gave the clergy and resident dons in favour, the doctors and lawyers against;[31] many papers attempted to make sense of the defeat by trying to expose the anti-feminism of certain professions and lay the blame for defeat there.[32]

Since the women now intended to approach the Royal Commission, there was no immediate, formal comment from them on the passing of Grace II, but a letter appeared in the *Manchester Guardian* from five ex-Girton and Newnham students, urging women not to take the titles of their degrees if they could possibly manage without them. They took the strongest exception to the position of isolation in which the lecturers at Girton and Newnham had been left, women to whose teaching and dedication they owed so much.[33] The *Observer*, too, was shocked that Cambridge believed it could do without trained minds, simply because they belonged to females. The country could ill afford to lose the contributions to the advancement of knowledge which women were able to make, nor was it sensible to place obstacles in the way of the education of one half of the population.[34]

The wild behaviour of the undergraduates was not to be quickly forgotten. The University authorities were reported to be taking a stern view of the matter and it was said that six men had been sent down for their part in the disturbance. One paper hinted that there had been Senior Members of the University in the crowd outside Newnham.[35] Two separate funds were started quite spontaneously by the undergraduates to make good the damaged gates. After some consideration, the Newnham authorities agreed to accept the compensation and an apology from the undergraduate body. But the attack had gone further than a rag and not a little bad feeling remained. Some undergraduates resented the stern punishment meted out to their fellows, especially as most of them were only freshmen, just arrived at the University.[36] Perhaps their grievance was justified if there was any truth in the suggestion that Senior Members had been involved in the disturbance. To some undergraduates, the serious view which was taken of the affair was simply an example of pettiness on the part of the women. When the friend of a girl student wrote to *The Times* describing the stamping and bad manners to which some science men treated the girl students who joined them for lectures,[37] an M.A. replied irritably that this was simply chaffing which women should accept as did the men. "The fact is, that many of these ladies claim to share in all the opportunities of men and yet to maintain a special and privileged position as women."[38] A mother who inquired of her son and his friends in Cambridge why they objected to the women, received the answer that the women were so pushing, so regardless of other people and altogether too aggressive. The mother commented that the cure for their present unpopularity was in the women's hands, and involved more gracious manners and pleasing ways.[39]

Possibly the post-war undergraduates did have something to complain about. The girl of the age was much less gracious than her predecessors and growing impatient of the social conventions which required her to conceal her abilities. No doubt she was "pushing" and cannot be sympathised with if she objected to being "pushed" in return. It was (and remains) an exasperating situation, for there were two worlds and women were canny enough to try to get the best of both of them. Yet their victories were often only trivial ones, and a woman faced real difficulties on entering a man's world. If she remained "feminine", it was felt she was incapable of tackling a job in the way a man would—and by implication, she therefore did not do it so well; on the other hand if she did approach a situation in a "masculine" way, she was resented and disliked as someone unsexed and "unfeminine".[40]

An effort was made in the *Times Educational Supplement* to explain the violence of the undergraduates following the women's defeat and the general antagonism towards women students which appeared to be lacking in Oxford men. They suggested that it was a resurgence of feeling against some women who had held pacifist views during the war and against others in the University who had stayed in residence and refused to fight or support the war effort,[41] though their argument was not supported by any evidence. Another reason was suggested by K. Fletcher-Barrett who wrote, "sex antagonism is bound to spring up as long as women, many of whom are married, retain well-paid posts while so many ex-servicemen are workless and starving".[42] It would be hard to find another sentence embodying so many entrenched attitudes, but no doubt Mr Fletcher-Barrett was expressing the mood of the day. Women who had worked to make the ammunition used by the soldiers, who had lost their men on the battlefield or who had at home a husband so incapacitated he could not work, were now held responsible for the unemployment and hunger of the men. The blame was as misplaced as when in previous centuries misfortune had hit a community and the local witch was held responsible.

Great haste was made in altering the Statutes allowing for the conferment of degree titles on suitably qualified women. The Grace approving the change passed the Senate on 5th November and was sent for the approval of the King in Council. The Ordinances governing the degree titles had still to be discussed, but these were an internal University matter and would be considered after receipt of the Royal approval. Now it was time for the opponents of feminine equality of opportunity in Cambridge to hurry, fearing the intervention of the Commissioners, and their anxiety must have been heightened by the analysis of the voting figures which was published during the month. Of active Cambridge University teachers, 226 had voted for the compromise scheme which Girton and Newnham had agreed to accept and 137 against, giving a majority in favour of 89. This had been turned into a minority of 214 by out-voters. Only one fifth of those in possession of votes used them (about one half of the residents, and one sixth of the non-residents). Professor Ridgeway claimed that this resident majority was the result of intimidation against young dons by supporters of the women and demanded the introduction of a secret ballot.[43] To other Cambridge men the voting figures were further evidence that a change was needed in the balance of power between resident and non-resident voters.

The Royal Commission was still sitting and on the defeat of Grace I it was now certain that women would turn again to the Commissioners in the hope of receiving fair treatment. Mrs Fawcett, who had spent the previous years working for women's suffrage, was still, at the age of seventy-three, taking a very active interest in the affairs of the Cambridge women's colleges. She urged them to wait for the Royal Commission's report and if it should prove favourable to their case, to press Parliament to introduce legislation on their behalf. The Senate was moving in the right direction, but with the imperceptible speed of a glacier. The proposal now accepted was one rejected as revolutionary twenty-four years previously. At that rate of change, women could not hope to achieve their goal before the century was out if they had to rely on the Senate.[44] It was felt in other quarters, however, that an approach to the Royal

Commission would heighten existing bitterness and a long acrimonious and disruptive battle to secure the necessary Parliamentary legislation was bound to ensue. Women should be content with the titles of degrees and wait quietly for happier and more enlightened days.[45]

On 14th November, 1921, the women's colleges made their delayed approach to the Commissioners. Since their first approach in July 1920 there had been two rejections of their case and now there was the offer of titles of degrees. Such a qualification would be useful but far from satisfactory and the women expressed their fear that different examination regulations would be imposed on them from the men, leading to a suspicion that the women's examinations and degrees were inferior. Educational work in the women's colleges would remain hampered as before, due to the exclusion of their teaching staff from educational matters. The students still had no security of teaching in the University lecture rooms and laboratories, they could not enter for scholarships or prizes and teachers remained ineligible for Board of Education grants. In the women's view, such problems would inevitably lead to the decline of Cambridge compared with other universities. The women also took the opportunity in their address to the Commissioners to place on record their dissatisfaction with the details of Grace I, which they had agreed to accept only in the hope of reaching an early settlement by agreement. The features of the compromise scheme which they did not like were the exclusion of women from membership of the Senate and the proposal for a board of women elected by women, with wide though not strictly defined powers, which seemed to them like a step towards the creation of a separate department for women in the University. They were confident that it would soon have been recognised that there was neither need nor justification for such a separation, but they wished to make clear formal objection to the plan.[46]

A week later, a memorial was sent to the Commission on behalf of the Grace II Committee, referring to the memorial which the Commission had received from the women, which aimed to "reverse, rescind or otherwise render ineffective" the decisions of the Senate. In a paragraph which was hardly flattering to the Commissioners, who were dedicating so much of their time to a consideration of the University's affairs, an investigation sparked off by the University's request for a grant from public funds the Grace II Committee asked them to ignore the argument that the resident vote was in favour of Grace I. Many residents, they believed, had been coerced through fear of interference from "external authority", i.e. the Commission. "It undoubtedly led many residents to vote against their convictions as to the merits of the particular question, lest a worse thing should befall the University."[47]

In the speculation which preceded publication of the Commission's report it became clear that the women were not simply relying on the good sense of Parliament to implement the Commission's findings. With energy and, for some, by now considerable experience, they began lobbying their M.P.s to support membership of women to Cambridge University.[48] The novelty of having an M.P. of their own to approach was not lost on the Cambridge women. Two ex-Newnham students found it quite an adventure and many others must have shared their excitement and apprehension. S. R. Courtauld wrote to the Newnham Principal, Miss B. A. Clough, "you will be interested to hear the result of our mission to the M.P. of this division. Maggie Cohen and I went yesterday primed with all your arguments and feeling nervous. But almost before we had begun on them, he announced that full membership was the only logical stopping place and it was bound to come and that he would support it if it came up in the House. . . . We were quite taken aback by this easy victory. One is not used yet to the privileges of being a voter!"[49]

The Commission's report, when it came in March 1922 was something of a disappointment to all the parties concerned. The University, which had calculated it needed £100,000, was to receive an annual grant of £50,000. Nor was there much to comfort the women. The Commission's ambivalent attitude was summed up in a memorable sentence, "we desire strongly that Cambridge should remain mainly and pre-dominantly a 'men's University' though of a mixed type as it is already".[50] Notice was taken of the fact that Grace I, giving women a modified form of membership, had only been defeated by the non-resident vote; however the Committee of the Commission considering the problems of Cambridge* were "fairly equally divided" on recommending legislation to establish equality of the sexes in educational matters in Cambridge as a condition for granting the University public money. It was generally held that such a proposal would have involved too great an intrusion on University autonomy. They did however suggest that women be admitted to University membership, membership which, on account of the Commission's recommendations concerning University government would have given non-resident women little power, but they were not prepared to take steps to see that their recommendatiou was implemented. Another of the Commission's proposals was the reorganisation of Boards of Studies along Faculty lines to facilitate the growing centralisation of teaching. Under this new scheme a women could be appointed to a University teaching post and as such would be eligible for membership of the proposed House of Residents in which much of the authority previously shared by all graduates was to be vested in just the resident members. As regards women's representation on the Council, Boards, Syndicates etc., the Commission's policy was that "no special consideration be given to women as women, but it should be in the power of the University to elect a woman if it considered she would be a valuable member of any body", a statement strongly reminiscent of a memorial put out by the students of Girton and Newnham in reply to the misgivings expressed by the authors of Scheme B in 1920 as to the behaviour of women as examiners.† No woman elected to a Chair could become *ex-officio* Head of her Department. The women's colleges at both Oxford and Cambridge were to receive a grant of £4,000 annually for ten years to be used for certain specified purposes. At Cambridge, this money was to be managed by a Women's Education Board appointed by the University. The Cambridge

* This was a Commission on both Oxford and Cambridge and special Committees were formed to examine each University in detail.

†Abov p. 922.

women's colleges were to become Public Hostels and the number of women in residence was not to exceed five hundred. Thus the Commission suggested that the women be granted something very close to equality with the men and the University was to be formally involved with the women's colleges. The limitation on numbers, though at the time of no great practical significance, was unfair in principle. A man's chance of being educated at Cambridge was severely limited by his social and economic circumstances; a woman's chance was further reduced by about 90 %. Two members placed on record their objection to this restriction on women and reiterated the view that public money should not be given without a guarantee of equality of opportunity for women.*

"No public money without equality for women" may have been a minority view on the Commission, but it was popular with the press, who confidently predicted that Parliament would support the women. In the women's camp there was not whole-hearted support for a Parliamentary campaign. Some felt it best to wait for the implementation of the Commission's proposals on the reform of University government and then to attempt to get the membership issue through the new House of Residents, since an analysis of the previous voting figures had shown that the resident members of the University favoured the women's case. The bolder spirits prevailed; Cambridge attitudes were unpredictable and the surer and speedier way to reform was through Parliament. Speed was also regarded as of great importance, since it was felt the disadvantage of Cambridge women *vis-à-vis* Oxford was already impairing their educational efficiency.[51]

In June 1922, Mr Fisher, President of the Board of Education, received two deputations from the women's colleges and other organisations of women's interests, asking him to insert in the Bill which he was drafting to give effect to the recommendations

---

* These were William Graham and Miss B. A. Clough who placed on record their view that the grant should not be given unless women were admitted to full membership and without any limit on numbers. Miss Clough's membership of the Commission Committee is illustrative of the acceptance accorded to Cambridge women *outside* their University.

of the Royal Commission, a clause giving women the right to degrees and membership of Cambridge University on terms of equality with men.[52] The *Times Educational Supplement* sounded a note of warning: such a clause would constitute a breach of faith involving as it did a reversal of the recent Senate House decision. The inclusion of a provision to admit women to full membership and degrees would only lead to a resurgence of bitter strife and controversy in Cambridge to the detriment of academic advance.[53] The supporters of women among University men were now themselves in something of a quandary, since it was feared that the "women question" would interfere with the proposals to reform University government, which, in the view of many progressives, held out so much hope for the future. As Professor Rutherford put it when approached by the Mistress of Newnham to join the deputation to Mr Fisher, "the opposition quite recognise that it [the proposed House of Residents] is dangerous from their point of view and in the University's interest it is not desirable to precipitate a direct attack".[54] Professor Rutherford was not mistaken in his judgement; the two issues were lumped together by the opponents of change who banded themselves into the University Defence Society. The Society was formed out of the old Grace II Committee in November 1921, and its first task was to draft a Memorial to the Commissioners in opposition to the one sent from Girton and Newnham. The Society's aims were to defend and uphold the decision of the Senate of 20th October, 1921, refusing membership to women, to defend the autonomy of the University against hostile action, parliamentary or otherwise, and to defend the status and privileges of the non-resident Members of the Senate.[55] When the contents of the Commission's report became public, the Defence Society described the proposal for a House of Residents as the replacement of a Senate, "containing men of wide experience and knowledge by a bureaucratic oligarchy from whose decisions no effective appeal is possible".[56] The Defence Society urged its members to oppose these new measures of reform, as well as any attempt which might be made to give women degrees, thus reversing the decisions of 8th December, 1920 and 20th

October, 1921. It was not until the following February that some of the residents, alarmed by the activities of the Defence Society, established a Cambridge University Progressive Society "to consider questions of University policy and promote action on progressive lines".[57]

Meanwhile, the Statute giving the University power to confer by diploma the title of degrees on women students of a recognised institution had received the Royal Assent. The University now had absolute authority to draw up the regulations under which women would qualify for these titles. These were considered in the Michaelmas term 1922, but three reports were published before agreement was finally reached on them. The Ordinances Syndicate was led by a moderate supporter of the women's cause, P. Giles, the Master of Emmanuel, but he found little sympathy for the women among the other Committee members, who were drawn from the group which had passed Grace II.[58] The first report was published on 24th October, 1922.[59] Girton and Newnham were to be recognised as institutions for the higher education of women. The numbers of women receiving University instruction was to be limited to five hundred and they were to be allowed to read for Honours degrees only. Degree titles would also be granted retrospectively to those women who had graduated before 1923. Considerable dissatisfaction with these proposals was expressed at the Senate House discussion of 2nd November, 1922.[60] Fees and the allowance of the Ordinary to those who failed a Tripos had not been dealt with, nor women's right of access to lectures, laboratories and the Library, and the proposals were therefore returned for reconsideration.

A modified report was issued at the end of November dealing with several minor problems;[61] a woman "allowed the Ordinary" could receive a degree title and while no Honours degree existed in Agriculture and Archaeology, they could read for an Ordinary degree in these subjects. Women research students would be supernumerary to the regulation five hundred. But the Syndicate ducked the main issue of guaranteeing instruction to women, "since the whole Report goes on the assumption of the continuance of the present practice, we think it is undesirable to complicate the present Ordinances by a regulation, the exact terms of which would necessarily be controversial". If at some future date it became necessary to regulate instruction, it could easily be done by an amendment to the Statute. Nor did they feel they could regulate on the matter of access to the University Library, though they did urge that the permanent Library Syndicate examine the matter at an early date. The revised report was discussed on 7th December, 1922,[62] when the omission of a guarantee of teaching for women was strongly attacked. Speaker after speaker supported the women, referring to the moral obligation placed on the opponents by their Memorandum of 14th November, 1921 to the Royal Commission, in which they had argued that the women were not placed in a position of disadvantage because they attended lectures etc. only on the goodwill of the lecturers, since teaching could be guaranteed them under the new Statute. In the minds of many Members of the Senate, this "could" had now to become "would".

Later that month a clause was inserted in the proposed Ordinances admitting women students of Girton and Newnham to instruction in the University and in the University laboratories, except as otherwise determined by a lecturer with the permission of the Vice-Chancellor. Colleges still retained the right to regulate admission to their own lectures, but such lectures were of diminishing importance. The revised report was welcomed briefly by Dr Parry at the discussion on 8th February, 1923, but he repeated that the new Statutes and Ordinances could not in any sense be considered a settlement.[63] These Ordinances were finally passed at a Congregation held on 3rd March, 1923,[64] but there was little rejoicing in the women's camp.[65] Not much importance was attached to the titular degree since it only meant giving the University money for something which was of little value. There was considerable speculation as to how many women would take their degree. The women's leaders freely admitted that it would be of considerable use to women non-residents in the teaching profession; future students would probably take it as a matter of course, since it added only two pounds to their fees. But as it stood, the degree title was nothing more than a decoration for the lecturers at Girton and Newnham. If the Library Syndicate agreed to give Library rights to the holders of the titular M.A. then the picture would alter.[66] The Heads of Girton and Newnham wrote to *The Times* correcting the impression that the new Ordinances gave women nearly all they desired. The degree title would be of value to some and the guarantee of instruction was something for which they had long campaigned, but Cambridge remained the only University in which women teachers were excluded from University posts and all share in the organisation of teaching and where no woman was eligible for University membership.[67]

The new regulations made little difference to the campaign for equality which was now concentrated on Parliament, where it was hoped to persuade members to insert a clause admitting women to full membership under the terms of the Oxford and Cambridge Bill which was to give effect to the proposals of the Royal Commission. Even while the title of degree Ordinances were being considered, the arena of interest had shifted from the Senate House to the floor of the House of Commons. In January 1923, the Cambridge women were advised, through the good offices of sympathisers in the House, that the Cabinet were unlikely to insert a clause in the Oxford and Cambridge Bill insisting that women be admitted to membership before Cambridge could receive any public money, but a motion proposing this could be moved from the floor of the House and, on a free vote, it was thought likely to be carried.[68] Later in the year, a different picture was presented when the women had a meeting with Sir Ernest Pollock, M.P. for Warwick and a Privy Councillor. He told them that it was believed by M.P.s that any attempt to insert the desired clause in the Bill would be met with the strongest opposition from Cambridge.[69] The final blow came in July, when an amendment to instruct the Statutory Commissioners for Cambridge to include in their deliberations the recommendations of the Royal Commission with regard to the position of women, was defeated in the Commons by 150 votes to 124. It was supposed to be a free vote, but the Government spokesman had spoken strongly against the amendment and most members took cover behind the University autonomy argument and the view that with a reformed government, Cambridge could best be left to handle its own affairs. The truth of the matter, as seen by *Time and Tide*, was that while everyone paid it lip service, there was no strong group in Parliament which really cared for the higher education of women. The women's case was always of secondary importance and could be sacrificed in favour of other interests. No one was prepared to put women first and the Cambridge women owed their defeat "not so much to the strength of their enemies as to the supineness of their friends".[70]

In January 1924 the Statutory Commissioners for Cambridge were appointed "to alter the University Statutes in accordance with the recommendations of the Royal Commission taking into consideration any representation made to them".* This was a detailed job in which the University co-operated fully. In a Memorandum of 8th August 1924, the Commissioners outlined their proposals for the reorganisation of teaching at Cambridge giving women a recognised place in the new scheme; but at the same time dealing the death blow to any hopes which the women might still have entertained of the Commission's supporting their plea for membership.

> The Commission have dealt with the position of women in the organisation of teaching. As at present advised, they propose to leave to the University itself questions relating to the admission of women to a share in the government of the University.

The Commission published a draft of the Statutes for discussion on 3rd and 5th November 1925. The attention of most University men was focused on the establishment of the Regent House and the limit placed on the power of the non-resident. Statutes C and D, however, were of major importance to the women and represented for them a great stride forward towards full integration with the University. Statute C established Faculties, Departments and Schools, recognising the drift which had been taking place for some years towards the centralisation

* Miss B. Phillpotts of Girton College was appointed a Commissioner.

of teaching. Members of Faculties etc. were to include those Fellows of Colleges who gave lectures or instruction recognised by the appropriate Faculty, including the Fellows of Newnham and Girton. Under Statute D, dealing with the appointment of University Teaching Officers, women were to be eligible for all posts, though not, by virtue of any appointment, for membership of a man's college. The disability under which the staffs of the women's colleges had laboured so long had now been swept away, completely ignored by the men who only four years previously had raised the dreadful spectre of "women interfering with men's education". At the Senate House discussion in November 1925 and at a subsequent discussion in November 1926, the matter was not once mentioned.[71]

The Supplement to the Cambridge Historical Register for 1921–30 recorded eleven women out of the 183 new lectureships created under the 1926 Statutes.* It was reported that some undergraduates objected to being taught by women, but as the novelty of the situation wore off, the objections were forgotten. The attitude of individual male teachers to the presence, now by right, of women students in their lectures and laboratories remained a personal matter. At Cambridge, where idiosyncrasy is affectionately nurtured and tolerated, some lecturers made great play of seating the women separately and addressing themselves solely to the "gentlemen". Life was sometimes made uncomfortable for women in the laboratories, especially in anatomy where it was easy to embarrass them by coarse remarks, questions and practical jokes. Again the situation was a difficult one, since the social code placed a great restraint on language and behaviour when women were present and the male medical students suffered particularly in this respect. On the other hand, the relations between men and women students grew increasingly relaxed as chaperonage rules were tacitly dropped. Mixed dramatic societies flourished, even mixed hockey was played, and men and women were frequently to be seen in each others' colleges. Several pin-pricks remained—for example, women were still not eligible

* A few women had had their lectures "recognised" by individual Boards of Studies before 1926, but they did not have official appointments.

for the Board of Education grant for student teachers—but these chiefly affected the staffs of the women's colleges. Though their influence had been greatly increased, they still had no voice in the government of the University and could not vote in the Senate House on matters concerning the teaching which they were undertaking. On a more trivial level, the heads of Girton and Newnham and the staffs of these colleges attended University functions and ceremonials by courtesy only and were counted as "wives" at social gatherings. Writing in 1936, M. A. Hamilton in her book *Newnham, An Informal Biography*, described the position of women half-in and half-out of the University as "irksome" and the University's attitude as "ungenerous". The differences between the positions of men and women in Cambridge had by then become tedious to rehearse and impossible to justify. The arguments which had been so vehemently expressed in 1920 and 1921 were recognised as belonging to a different era and, never having contained much to appeal to reason, they now had little left in them that could provoke an emotional response. After a decent interval, following the changes of 1926, it seemed appropriate that the position of women should be reconsidered. But memories of past controversies inhibited all but the bravest souls and again it was the major social upheaval, brought about by a second war, which enabled women to take another step forward.

EPILOGUE. THE RAISING OF A PROCTOR'S HAT

DURING THE WAR, provisions made for war service and the shortened degree led to some difficulties in the women's colleges regarding the quota which had been imposed by the Ordinances of 1923. When the wartime two-year residence period was replaced by the peacetime three years, a sharp increase in the number of women in residence during the change-over was inevitable and it seemed likely that this would coincide with some special obligations on universities to accept ex-Service people. Yet the women's colleges were naturally reluctant to limit their intake in anticipation of peacetime conditions, the timing and nature of which were most uncertain. The matter was settled amicably by consultation with the University,[1] and it triggered off more general discussion about the numbers and position of women in Cambridge.

This stirring of opinion resulted in a Memorial, got up by R. B. Braithwaite and K. P. Harrison and bearing over 140 signatures. In September 1946 it was presented to the Council of the Senate who reported on it and placed their deliberations before the Regent House for discussion two months later.[2] The memorialists, who had prepared their case without the knowledge of the women's colleges, felt that it was time to reconsider the position of women in the University, twenty years after it had given them most privileges except that of actual membership. The composition of the Senate had changed considerably in the quarter of a century since the 1920's controversy and much of the power of that body had been transferred by the 1926 Statutes to the Regent House, the body of resident members with University or college posts. It seemed an appropriate time to raise the issue again. The memorialists felt strongly the anomaly of a situation where two women were Professors, twenty were University lecturers and two were Heads of Department; women served frequently on Faculty Boards and Syndicates, yet the same women could not discuss reports nor vote on matters affecting their own Departments. As they commented, "to deprive some of the teaching officers of ultimate responsibility appears to be contrary to the principle of self-government in the University of Cambridge". It was not denied, however, that some problems remained to be solved before women could be admitted to membership. The most important of these they felt was the issue of numbers—should the existing restrictions be continued and, if so, in what form? The memorialists concluded by requesting that a Syndicate be appointed to consider the whole question of admission and the regulations relating to it. The Council of the Senate were favourable to this proposal and though comments were invited, no objections were raised.

A Grace appointing the Syndicate to examine the women's case was approved in January 1947, and their report was ready by the end of the summer term.[3] It was proposed to admit women to membership on the same terms as men while the University retained a statutory right to limit their numbers. Girton and Newnham were to become colleges within the University and the University would have the power to recognise other institutions for women as "approved foundations". The members of the Syndicate were not in total agreement, but they accepted that the number of women undergraduates should not exceed one-fifth of the number of men undergraduates. Girton and Newnham were not to exceed three hundred undergraduate students apiece* and a specific limit would be placed on the numbers matriculated from any future "approved foundation". These specific quotas were to be imposed by Ordinance, that is, they could be altered by the University without reference to the Privy Council. The report was brought forward for discussion on 4th November, 1947, and it seemed that it would be passed without comment. One speaker, Professor B. Dickins, came

* This figure was in excess of that which the women's colleges agreed would be their normal complement.

forward however to oppose the motion. He seemed to think he would be one of a long lone of disputants, but he had the floor to himself and no one bothered to counter his plea against the proposed new status for women. In his view, the women did not have any grievances which needed righting, they would gain nothing by membership of the University and, if Oxford was any example, nor would the University. Cambridge would do better to stand firm with Harvard and Yale as all-male institutions. The dim echoes of what had once been a white-hot argument found no one else to support them, and the discussion was closed.[4]

The Grace admitting women to membership was voted on 6th December, 1947. Everything had gone so smoothly; yet the women remained nervous until it was all over. Myra Curtis described the vote in a piece for the Newnham College Roll *Letter* as "not without an element of drama".

At the last moment we were informed that it would be possible for some of us to attend in the Gallery of the Senate House to see "the fatal cap-lifting by the Proctor". Six of us were there. Others were in the body of the Senate House with husbands or friends who were members of the Regent House. Some Graces of minor importance were taken first, and as the word "Placet" promptly followed the reading of the Grace, the Proctors lifted their caps. Then our Grace was read: "That the recommendations of the Syndicate . . . appointed to consider the status of Women in the University be approved". A long pause followed during which we held our breath. Someone *might*—though no one thought he would—say "Non Placet" at this last moment. Then there would be a vote. But if any opponent was present he said no word. The pause ended. The word "Placet" was pronounced. The caps were lifted and replaced. A slight tremor passed over the assembly, like a wind over a cornfield, and the thing was over. In future our visits to the Senate House for the passing of Graces would be as of right and duty. The six hurried back to College where there was a small impromptu celebration.[5]

Letters of congratulation poured into the women's colleges. In a typical reply, the Cambridge women wrote, "the whole thing is most satisfactory, because it went through so quietly and with such general goodwill".[6] In a jubilant letter, Kenneth Harrison, a Fellow of King's and one of the two leading memorialists of September 1946, wrote that he had been disappointed in the vote. He had hoped "a few toads would have come out of their holes to croak opposition and given us the chance of harassing them by a thumping majority".[7] Certainly the passing of the Grace must have astonished young and old alike; the young, that they should be asked to agree to the removal of an anomaly which they hardly knew existed; the old, that an issue which had torn Cambridge apart on previous occasions should be accepted with no more disturbance than the raising of a Proctor's hat. The papers remarked on the absence of controversy—and in its absence found little to write about. Popular interest was centred on the academic dress which the undergraduate women would now wear.[8] Gowns were agreed upon and priced at three pounds; they were like the men's but without the slit sleeves, since it was felt that the women would not want to display bare arms when they wore short sleeved dresses under their gowns in summer. Mortar boards, the familiar stiff squares, were rationed and only available to graduates.[9] The gown was not the only new expense; the real degree would now cost a woman £24.5.0 where before the degree title had cost £10.0.0. As it was grimly remarked in *The Times*, "all spirals it would seem, even that of women's emancipation, are inflationary".[10]

There was only one small hitch in the smooth progress towards admission. The new Statutes received the Royal Assent in May 1948 but by some oversight they were undated and thus became immediately operative;[11] in other words, women students about to sit their final examinations had the right to graduate that June. The authorities had hoped that the new dispensation should be formally recognised by the presentation of an Honorary degree to the Queen (now the Queen Mother) in the Michaelmas term 1948. The women's colleges agreed to hold back, having assured themselves that those graduating in June 1948 would not be put to any extra cost on account of the delay. Queen Elizabeth received the degree of Doctor of Laws in October 1948, ensuring by her grace and charm that the new status of women was initiated in an atmosphere of cheerfulness and due ceremony. The choice of the Queen as the recipient of the first degree bestowed by Cambridge on a woman was a wise one. It might have seemed more appropriate to honour an academic woman who had devoted her life to the furtherance of women's education, but in honouring first the Queen, the whole affair was raised to a higher level of ceremony and respect, making it difficult for anyone to apply to the later queues of graduating women Adam Sedgwick's epithet, "chits and bloomers!"

Women had arrived in Cambridge—or had they? Was their position very much different after 1948 than it had been after 1926? The answer to this question depends very much on the emphasis given to the substance rather than the shadow of authority and influence. Since 1923, women had been assured of their place in the University and since 1926 were involved in the University's main functions of teaching, examining and research. As members of Faculties, Boards and Syndicates, they had access to information which had previously only been theirs through "leaks" and hearsay. Their new-found influence depended on individual personality and its use on individual predilection, since there was no such thing as a woman's view on educational matters. In the Faculty groups to which they belonged, their lack of a Senate House vote was probably of no great significance and their opinions were as often heard and heeded as anyone else's. However, their position was anomalous and there was no reasonable excuse for excluding them from sharing fully and responsibly in University government, a point well made by the memorialists of 1946. Under the new Statutes women became, on the same terms as men, eligible for membership of the Council of the Senate and for votes in the Regent House. One point of apparent injustice remained—the implication of the Statutes and Ordinances of 1948 was that in the Regent House women were to be a limited (and small) proportion of the men voting there, and in the University as a whole women

were not to approach parity of numbers with the men. The
motives behind the imposition of this restriction were not
necessarily as malign as they had been in earlier debates and
with the smaller body of voters, more experienced in the
actual administration of University and college affairs, it can
be believed that the restriction was made for the women's
benefit. The cunning argument of the 1920 Report B, that if
women could not be given complete equality of opportunity in
Cambridge they should be given nothing,* had lost its force,
since the women themselves had never made an issue over the
limitation of numbers under the Ordinances of 1923.† It
had been accepted in the '20's and '30's that men had a
greater right to the limited space in Cambridge lecture rooms
and laboratories than had women, and the practical difficulties
of expansion under the college system—and a certain satisfac-
tion in their exclusiveness—ensured that the women did not
press for any increase in numbers. Their pragmatism was
close to the spirit of Henry Sidgwick, who had always used
the concessions—and discrimination—of the University for the
benefit of women students; no doubt Emily Davies would have
continued to fight for the principle of equality of opportunity
as she had fought, over the Previous Examination and the
Poll Degree, for the principle of equality of examination.
One might wish to judge whether the women's authorities, in
this matter as in so many others, followed the better precedent,
but in the immediate post-war period, the overall limitation
on numbers did not present any practical difficulties and
instead shielded the women's colleges from demands for over-
rapid expansion. Indeed in the twenty-six years since the
Statute was passed, the proportion of women students *in statu
pupillari* has always been well below the maximum proportion
agreed upon in 1948, the final reproof to those who had cried
on each occasion that women had tried to obtain their
degrees, "Cambridge will be *flooded* with women!" There was
no flood, just an expansion in numbers which was matched by

* Above p. 9.18.

† The only exception to this on official record is that made by
William Graham, supported by B. A. Clough, as members of the
Royal Commission on Oxford and Cambridge. Above p. 10.20.

growth in the University as a whole. Greatly assisted by the advice and financial help given by some men's colleges (as well as the energetic support of the women's colleges and in especial of Myra Curtis), a third women's college, New Hall, was founded and became a recognised Institution in 1954. Its numbers were limited to a hundred. Hughes Hall, formerly Cambridge Training College for Women, was recognised in 1949 as an Institute of the University for the purpose of training women graduates for the teaching profession. Its quota was seventy.

As pressure for places grew, the difficulties of operating the tight quota system became increasingly restrictive for all the women's colleges. Newnham took the lead in 1960 in asking the Council of the Senate to consider the removal of the quota completely. Following the deliberations of a small committee it was agreed that the overall limitation of twenty per cent of the number of men, and the quota placed on individual colleges should be removed, but the University retained the power under Statute B 1.3 to limit the number of women students in the University, a power which it did not and still does not have in the case of men students.

As women entered their second century of association with Cambridge, they also reached a new watershed in their development as members of the University. The issue was again one of numbers. Under the Cambridge system, all undergraduates must belong to a college, whose responsibility it is to teach and house students. At the beginning of the 1970's, there were twenty colleges accepting men undergraduates and three accepting women. Whatever the merits of the system, a college is an expensive unit to establish and maintain and it seemed unlikely that money could be found to build, endow and staff another women's college. Existing colleges could not expand indefinitely, and, whilst there was official encouragement for an increase in opportunities for women in Cambridge, the fact remained that only about 12 % of undergraduates' places in Cambridge were available to women. One answer to the problem lay in the opening of men's colleges to women students. The idea of a "mixed" college was no longer as outrageous as it had been when used by women's opponents in the 1920's. Three mixed institutions for graduate students had recently been opened[12] and the practical difficulties no longer seemed insuperable. In 1972, three men's colleges, Churchill, Clare and Kings, admitted women undergraduates in their first year. Now, after three undergraduate years, women occupy about a third of the undergraduate places in these colleges and further undergraduate places for women are shortly to be made available following the generous offer of ten million pounds to found and endow a new mixed undergraduate college, made by Mr David Robinson of Newmarket.[13]

However, even taking into account the recent expansion of places available to women students, the proportion, in 1974/5, of undergraduate students at Cambridge who are women, is only about 17 %, that is, below the level which it was agreed in 1948 could well be accepted. Even worse is the position of women wishing to pursue a University career. With only three women's colleges of moderate wealth, their chances of a paid Fellowship are small. And since college Fellowships commonly provide a spring-board to University posts, the figures for women's appointments are correspondingly meagre. At Michaelmas Term 1974, less than 3 % of Professors were women, as were less than 7 % of Readers. Of all University appointments at Cambridge, only 7 % are held by women.[14]

Two recent reports[15] have suggested that women should occupy 25 % of undergraduate places in Cambridge by the beginning of the next decade or even reach the national average of female occupation of University places, which is currently 36 %. With these goals in mind, all or most of the expansion of University places in Cambridge should be set aside for women whose collegiate life would be catered for by the opening of further existing male colleges to women. By the middle of the next decade, perhaps eight or nine existing colleges could be offering places to students of both sexes. The need for single-sex institutions is still strongly felt and accepted by even the most enthusiastic supporters of co-residence. On the other hand, "a College wishing to create a satisfactory and genuinely co-educational community should seek to have a proportion of not less than 25–30 % women".[16]

Colleges admitting women undergraduates are also expected to appoint women Fellows, as Churchill, Clare and Kings have already done. It is hoped that this will "assist the early academic careers of women, and . . . may lead to an increase in the number of women holding University appointments in Cambridge".[17]

But the expansion of places for women in Cambridge is not without its difficulties. Supporters of expansion note from University Grants Commission statistics that whilst a large pool of highly qualified women University candidates exists, only a small proportion of them applies for entrance to Cambridge. Years of restricted entry and special entrance examinations outside the normal 'A' level syllabus has meant that many schools never consider encouraging a girl to apply to Cambridge. Paradoxical though it may seem, it is unlikely that suitably qualified women candidates will suddenly make themselves available; positive efforts must be made to attract them. This is particularly true in the case of Science students and highlights a point which disturbs both supporters and opponents of the expansion of places for women. The present distribution of students between Arts and Science is 55:45, but the University's aim is an Arts/Science ratio of 50:50.[18] Great vigilence will have to be exercised to ensure that an increase in women students does not add to the existing imbalance between Arts and Science. It is unjust, however, to see women as the bogy in this matter. The flight from Science and Technology is a phenomenon currently experienced by many universities and is largely due to the changing preferences of men students and should not, therefore, be used as an excuse for depriving women of a university education. This type of argumentation is unfortunately deep-rooted; as we have seen in earlier chapters, it was always assumed that men's preferences in educational matters should take precedence over women's. New life has now been given to all the old objections against equality of educational opportunity by the doubtful application of cost-benefit analysis. Considering education as an investment realisable in income terms, it is calculated that the return on a woman's education is lower than that on a man's and "sound" economics therefore demands that a greater investment should be made in men's education. This view is by no means exclusive to Cambridge, nor does it carry any official weight, but it certainly finds expression there. Unfortunately, such analysis does not take into account an educated women's potential economic worth if she were freed from her heavy obligations of child-rearing. If couples shared the responsibility not only of supporting their families financially but also of day to day care of children and home, the life earnings of the two sexes could not be so divergent. Cost-benefit analyses based on existing patterns of remunerations for different types of work tell us little about the value to the community of the work done and as such are a most unsuitable ground for future investment decisions.

Subjective objections against disturbing the status quo in Cambridge are, as always, more difficult to meet. To many people in Cambridge, argument tends to be centred on the sensitive problem of preserving the special character of colleges if they become co-residential, and if Cambridge people seem over-concerned with the practical difficulties involved in making changes, it can be said in their defence that they have the trouble and expense of making them.

Undoubtedly, the type of education given by Cambridge, to whom and at what cost, are matters which will greatly exercise the University in the forthcoming century. In all future developments, women will be part of the University, not an "issue" to be given separate attention. The dichotomy between "the University" on the one hand and the "women" on the other has passed away, thanks to the patience and persistence of four generations of Cambridge women and their male supporters. From their example, and the whole story of women's admission to Cambridge University, reformers and resisters of change have many lessons to learn.

THE PREVIOUS EXAMINATION
(Little-Go)

THE PREVIOUS EXAMINATION, the gateway through which all students aspiring to a degree at Cambridge had to pass, was established in 1822. Its original purpose was to test whether a man was capable of benefiting from a university education and as such was an examination of elementary knowledge in the two major subjects of study at Cambridge at the time, Classics and Mathematics, together with the tenets of the Established Church. Following the reforms of the public schools, the Previous Examination (Little-Go) was regarded as a test of a man's schooling and thus dictated the subjects of study for students aspiring to enter Cambridge. Since entry conditions for Oxford were similar and since the majority of students entering the universities were of no special academic merit (see Appendix B), Latin, with elementary Greek and Mathematics were taught in schools to the exclusion of other subjects. It was argued by reformers that the study of a second classical language was of little value, since the amount of Greek needed to pass the examination was small, giving the student little insight into Greek language and culture, and took time which might more usefully be spent in acquiring a modern language or pursuing a scientific study. In attacking Greek, reformers such as Sidgwick had as their principal aim the improvement of academic standards in the universities. Sidgwick also felt strongly that women coming up to university should not be obliged to take the Previous Examination, since he did not want girls' schools to fall into the same pattern of education as the universities dictated to the boys' schools. In this, he was opposed by Emily Davies who insisted on identity of examinations with the men. (See *supra* Chapter 4.)

Adjustments were made in the regulations governing the

Previous throughout the century; usually these related to allowing Local Examinations passes in Previous subjects in place of the actual Previous Examination and Honours students were encouraged to pass the examination early in the University career or even before entry. Alternatives to the European classical languages were allowed to oriental students, who could be examined in their own classical languages, providing they did not then proceed to a degree in Oriental languages.[1] Several attempts were made to drop compulsory Greek for European students and the acrimony of these debates were second only to the attempts to gain University membership for women. The first big debate, in which Sidgwick played a major part, took place in 1871–3 and the issue was raised again in 1891. On both occasions the removal of compulsory Greek was soundly defeated and led him to anticipate a "long period of slow decadence" during which the University, through failure to adapt, would gradually fall into disrepute.[2] The third major battle took place in 1905, after Sidgwick's death, and was almost as ferocious as the women's degree battle of 1897. The Grace abolishing Greek was defeated by 1,559 votes to 1,052[3] and an attempt made in the following year not to demand Greek from those going on to Science degrees also failed by 746 to 241 votes. However, the issue was not allowed to rest. In 1913 a Syndicate was appointed to enquire into the structure and value of the Previous. In its report of the following year, the Syndicate declared the Previous was unsatisfactory and unrelated to current secondary education.[4] Discussion of the report was held up during the war, despite attempts by supporters to have it brought forward. The reforms had no easy passage when they were discussed in 1918 and the report was sent back several times for amendment. But opinions had changed so much that the elimination of compulsory Greek aroused little opposition and together with other parts of the report designated as "uncontroversial", it was passed in December 1918 by a vote of 161–15,[5] forty-eight years after a Report of the Endowed Schools Commission had urged its abolition on the grounds that it prevented a satisfactory connection between the University and the non-classical schools.

Appendix A

The Previous Examination continued in name up to the 1960's, but most students had for some time offered G.C.E. passes in its place. Latin as an entrance qualification for Cambridge was abolished in 1960.[6]

THE ORDINARY DEGREE
(also known as the Poll or Pass degree)

UNTIL THE END of the Second World War, there were two avenues by which a student could reach a B.A. degree at Cambridge; an Honours (Tripos) course and an Ordinary degree course, success in the Previous or "little-go" examination being a prerequisite for both courses. (See Appendix A). The purpose of the Ordinary was to give students a general education; the syllabus included Classics, Mathematics, Divinity and Special Subjects. The Pass degree was the subject of frequent debate and alteration during the nineteenth century and early twentieth century, but it remained at a level which would not overexercise the minds of the many young "gentlemen" who regarded three years at one of the old universities as their birthright, and who yet made no pretence to intellectual merit.* It was also (and remains in name today) the method by which a student who failed in an Honours course could complete or be given his degree. From the outset, women were debarred from entering specifically for the Ordinary degree, though they could be allowed it on a Tripos examination in which they did not reach Honours standard. (The regulations governing this procedure were

---

* Of the degrees awarded in 1887, 48% were Pass degrees
1892, 48% were Pass degrees
1902, 47% were Pass degrees
1912, 45% were Pass degrees.

Source: Royal Commission Oxford and Cambridge Universities 1922 x Cmd. 1588.

These figures do not necessarily represent the number of men admitted to take a Pass degree since they include those men awarded a Pass on failing Honours and do not include those who went down with no degree. From 1851–1906, for every 100 men, on average 41 took Honours degrees, 34 Pass and 25 no degree.

complicated, but on the whole were not as generous as those governing men students.) This exclusion was accepted on educational grounds by some of the women's supporters who had a poor opinion of the Poll degree and who fought for its reform. (See the controversy between Henry Sidgwick–Emily Davies, Chapter 4.) The women's opponents also supported this exclusion in the belief that if the Ordinary was opened to women, Cambridge would be flooded with poll women "who would be the natural companions of the idle and dissolute Poll men, thus adding to the already difficult problem of discipline". Although few of the women's authorities felt the Ordinary had any value for their students, the strict egalitarians were irritated by the differentiation of treatment between men and women.

The Poll degree was examined, reported on, discussed and amended many times before its demise as a distinct avenue to the B.A. degree. In 1934[1] women were allowed to proceed to the Ordinary Degree on the same terms as men. This was done to iron out anomalies in the regulations and it was stated by the women's colleges that they did not intend to alter their admissions policy and admit women solely for the Pass degree. By this time, too, men's colleges rarely admitted a Poll man and an investigation in the years immediately preceding the War revealed that the numbers of Poll admissions had dropped to sixteen in 1936.[2] It was recognised by the Syndicate which reported in 1945[3] that the Ordinary was now used principally by men who had failed to reach an Honours standard in a Tripos as a means of gaining a B.A., and as such it required drastic revision. The scheme suggested by the Syndicate and accepted by the University was that all degree candidates should proceed in the first instance to an Honours degree, but if they failed to reach an Honours standard, they might be allowed to proceed to an Ordinary Degree which in many cases involves their taking the same, though perhaps fewer, papers than an Honours student in their final examination.[4] Candidates can also be awarded a pass degree on the results of their final Tripos examination. Women students on their admission to University membership in 1948 came under the same regulations.

Appendix C
Copy to come

NOTES ON RESEARCH MATERIAL

1.

Material from the Archives of Girton College is described as "G.A.". Similarly Newnham Archival material is referred to as "N.A.". I am most grateful to the Mistress and Fellows of Girton College and the Principal and Fellows of Newnham College for permission to quote from material in the Colleges' Archives.

2.

In general "flysheets" have been examined at Newnham, but copies are in many cases available in the University Library's "Cam" collection (especially those relating to the 1897 controversy) and were occasionally published in the University *Reporter*.

3.

Printed papers relating to University matters can be seen in the University Library, Anderson Room and have the general classification "Cam". Collections of private papers are also available in the Anderson Room and will be referred to as "U.L.M.ss.". I am grateful to the Syndics of the University Library for permission to quote from items in their manuscript and University history collections.

4.

The Sidgwick papers deposited in the Wren Library, Trinity College, Cambridge, are referred to with the prefix "Wren". I should like to thank the Master and Fellows of Trinity College, Cambridge, for permission to publish extracts from these.

5.

In the later chapters of the book, use is made of contemporary newspaper material. This has been drawn from books of press-clippings preserved in both the Girton and Newnham Archives. No guarantee can be given that all relevant reportage and comment has been examined, but the coverage given by the two scrap-books is balanced and its thoroughness can be adduced from the fact that the two books, kept by Colleges who did not always see eye to eye, contain in large measure identical material.

NOTES

CHAPTER 1

[1] See, for example,

B. Stephen, *Emily Davies and Girton College*, Constable, 1927.

B. Stephen, *Girton College, 1869–1932*, C.U.P., 1933.

B. Megson and J. Lindsay, *Girton College 1869–1959 An Informal History*, Heffers, 1960.

M. C. Bradbrook, *That Infidel Place*, Chatto and Windus, 1969 (Biographical works on students and others connected with Girton are listed in the back of this book).

A. Gardner, *A Short History of Newnham College*, Bowes and Bowes, 1921.

M. A. Hamilton, *Newnham, An Informal Biography*, Faber and Faber, 1936.

B. A. Clough, *Anne J. Clough*, Arnold, 1897.

E. Sidgwick, *Mrs Henry Sidgwick, a Memoir*, Sidgwick and Jackson, 1938. (For a recent example of a biography of a Newnham student, see V. Glendinning, *A Suppressed Cry*, Routledge and Kegan Paul, 1969).

[2] D. A. Winstanley, *Late Victorian Cambridge*, C.U.P., 1947.

[3] Winstanley, *op. cit.*, p. 142.

[4] S. Rothblatt, *The Revolution of the Dons*, Faber and Faber, 1968.

[5] Rothblatt, *op. cit.*, p. 232.

CHAPTER 2

[1] Report of the Annual Meeting of Convocation, 8th May, 1866, London University.

[2] Cynthia White, *Women's Magazines 1693–1968*, Michael Joseph, 1970.

[3] White, *op. cit.*

[4] *Abstract of British Historical Statistics*, B. Mitchell and P. Deane, Cambridge 1962. The excess of women over men in England and Wales in the 20 plus age group was 4·15% in 1841, 3·9% in 1851 and 4·7% in 1861. The figures for 1821 and 1831 are just under 4%. (The reservations made by the authors regarding the accuracy of early census statistics should be noted). The excess of women over men increased during the following hundred years; in 1951, the excess was approximately 8%. Yet in 1951, only 30% of women in the 20–34 age group were single, whereas the

Notes

figure for 1851 was 48%. In 1861, 46% of women in this age group were unmarried; in 1961, 22%.

5 J. Stewart, *Jane Harrison*, London, Merton Press, 1959.
The belief that an education would lessen a girl's chance for matrimony persisted into the twentieth century. See, for example, V. Brittain, *Testament of Youth*, p. 73. Gollancz, 1933.

6 Suggested by S. R. Wills in an unpublished M.A. thesis, *Social and Economic Aspects of Higher Education for Women 1884–1870*, London 1952, and reproduced here by permission of the author, Stella Wills Rosenat.

7 R. Glynne-Grylls, *Queen's College 1848–1948*, Routledge, 1948, and Margaret Tuke, *A History of Bedford College for Women*, Oxford, 1939.

8 There are many books which trace the beginnings of the women's emancipation movement, usually taking as their starting point Mary Wollstonecraft's *Vindication of the Rights of Women* which was published in 1792, and dealt with such matters as changes in the law relating to property and custody of children in marriage and of course the suffrage movement. These matters cannot be dealt with here; the reader is referred to the standard work on these topics, Ray Strachey, *The Cause*, Bell & Son, London 1928.

9 Even in these families, the demands of family life could suffocate a girl's attempts to gain an education. See, for example, Victoria Glendinning, *A Suppressed Cry, op. cit.*, for an account of a Quaker girl who spent a term at Newnham in 1885.

10 Louisa Garrett Anderson, *Elizabeth Garrett Anderson*, Faber and Faber, 1939.

11 From the papers of Mrs. C. D. Rackham, née Tabor, (Newnham 1895–8). Kindly shown to me by her niece, Miss Masy Tabor, and published with her permission.

12 John Griffiths to Emily Davies, 19.7.1862. G.A.

13 G. D. Liveing to Emily Davies, 22.7.1862. G.A.

14 Information passed to Emily Davies by J. D. Ackland, May, 1863. G.A.

15 Emily Davies to Mr Potts, 11.11.1862. G.A.

16 Emily Davies to Mr Potts, 15.1.1863. G.A.

17 G. D. Liveing to Tomkinson, 18.6.1863. G.A.

18 Emily Davies to Tomkinson, 30.11.1863. G.A.

19 This report, headed "Cambridge Local Examination" angered Robert Potts, who was Emily Davies' chief correspondent in Cambridge at that time, as he felt she had no right to use such a description. Potts was a Fellow of Trinity, boastful of his ability to help or hinder the women's case. Undoubtedly, he worked hard for the women, but his support was sometimes an embarrassment to Emily Davies. For example, he was identified with the Married Fellows question, and married Fellows were regarded by some people as "an abomination". Miss Davies had to restrain Potts from writing to the newspapers on the girls' examination question "for fear of mixing the two things together in the minds of hasty people". Letter 19.10.64. G.A.

20 Emily Davies examination report, December, 1863, reprinted in *Report*,

National Association for the Promotion of Social Sciences, April, 1864. Cam E.T. 141.

The phrase "test and attest" was later used to good effect by Josephine Butler and the ladies of the North of England Council when they petitioned the University for examinations for women beyond the level of schoolgirls. It is said that the succinctness of the phrase so favourably impressed several members of the Council of the Senate, that they threw their weight behind the women's petition. This scheme for an examination for women only was bitterly opposed by Emily Davies who saw the degree as the next stage for women after Locals, as it was for men. The North of England Council wanted the examination as a qualification for teacher[5]s and in this sense it was a very practical proposal in view of the immediate need to raise the qualifications of teachers and the absence of degree courses open to women. Yet it is ironical that they should have succeeded in their plan by the use of one of Emily Davies's own phrases.

[21] *Ibid.*
[22] Emily Davies to Mr Potts, 9.1.1864. G.A.
[23] J. D. Ackland to Emily Davies, 12.11.1863. G.A.
[24] Sedley Taylor papers. U.L. Mss 6093.210.

CHAPTER 3

[1] Report 1867–8 xxxviii. Chapter VI is devoted to girls' schools.
[2] Report of James Bryce, Commissioner for Lancashire *ibid.* Chapter VIII on the education of girls.
[3] Bryce, *ibid.*, p. 822.
[4] Bryce, *ibid.*, p. 837.
[5] "In framing schemes under the Act (Endowed Schools) provision shall be made, so far as conveniently may be, for extending the benefits of endowments equally to boys and girls." 32 and 33 Victoria, Chapter 56 section 12.
[6] Unfortunately, many University men were quite schizophrenic in their application of the term "education". For upper and middle-class boys, education ideally was a process of sensitising their minds and characters to all that was considered valuable in the arts of man. For girls and lower-class boys, it meant training in skills which would enable them best to contribute to the comfort of their fellow-men, without giving them tastes and ideas above their station.
[7] Emily Davies to Miss Richardson, 25.10.1866. Quoted in Stephen, *op. cit.*, p. 149.
[8] On the subject of university reform, see Rothblatt, *op. cit.*
[9] Not all of Elizabeth Garrett's supporters were so tactful. *The Times* 3rd May, 1862, from "A Fortunate Wife":

Notes

"I am decidedly favourable to the endeavour now being made to procure for female students the privilege of being admitted to the examinations in the University of London, and this not so much on account of the possible advantage to be derived from obtaining such privilege in the furtherance of their aims towards professional employment as upon the broad ground of 'fair play' and equal justice. For I consider it at once unjust, impolitic and illiberal on the part of men to close the gates of knowledge upon aspirants belonging to the weaker sex, and the more so since the objections taken to opening the intellectual professions to women are based, avowedly, on the assumption that a course of solid study would have the effect of rendering women less suitable to the requirements of the other sex and less conducive to their becoming good wives and useful helpmates ... it is well-known that a vast number of women are unable, and some few are indisposed, to marry—the former class from the increasing difficulty of finding husbands, the latter class from various motives, comprising among them a reluctance to contract indissoluble ties under the conditions confessedly unfavourable to the weaker party, especially as regards the unequal rights over property. Thus, a certain number of women will probably follow the laborious path of scientific study as a means of enlarging their now limited sphere of professional occupations. Can it be consistent with true manly feeling to preclude these women from pursuing a course which would seem to furnish facilities for escaping from the hard alternative either of contracting marriage on any terms or of leading dependent, perhaps necessitous, probably weary, useless lives?"

This outspoken letter was written by Harriet Grote, wife of George Grote, a Radical and supporter of women's efforts to enter the professions, who at the time was Vice-Chancellor of London University. Mrs Grote was a very colourful character, given to flamboyant clothes—Sydney Smith had once quipped that he at last understood the meaning of the word 'grotesque' when he caught sight of her in a pink turban. Mrs Grote's letter stressed the vital importance of education for women because of the problems facing those who remained unmarried, but it also fired a warning shot in the war which was to be waged over the legal position of women inside marriage. Women were not admitted to examinations in London University, founded to provide education for all classes and denominations without distinction, until 1878. For the whole story of her efforts to enter the medical profession, see *Elizabeth Garrett Anderson*, Jo Manton, Methuen, 1965.

10 Quoted in Ray Strachey, *The Cause*, Bell & Son, 1928.
11 Emily Davies to Barbara Bodichon, 6.4.1867. G.A.
12 Anne Austin to Miss Richardson, 31.3.1868. G.A.
13 James Bryce to Emily Davies, 4.6.1867. G.A.
14 James Bryce to Emily Davies, 26.11.1867. G.A.
15 James Bryce to Emily Davies, 4.6.1867. G.A.
16 James Bryce to Emily Davies, 12.6.1867. G.A.

[17] James Bryce to Emily Davies, 26.11.1867. G.A.
[18] Emily Davies to Barbara Bodichon, 9.12.1869. G.A.
[19] Emily Davies to James Bryce, 20.11.1867. G.A.
[20] Emily Davies to Mr Tomkinson, 6.1.1869. G.A.
[21] Emily Davies to Barbara Bodichon, 11.11.1871. G.A.
[22] James Bryce to Emily Davies, 12.6.1867. G.A.
[23] "Some Account of a Proposed New College for Women." Paper read at an N.A.P.S.S. meeting 1868. G.A.
[24] Emily Davies to Mr Tomkinson, 6.1.1869. G.A.
[25] *The Times*, 10.10.1868.

CHAPTER 4

[1] She regarded herself as a failure as a schoolteacher; not so her pupils and their parents. When she left Ambleside on account of ill-health, the residents declared in a testimonial, ". . . we desire to tender to you our heartfelt acknowledgement of the high qualities which you have devoted to the education of the young persons who have been committed to your care, of the value of the instructions you have bestowed on them and still more, of the influence you have effectively exerted upon their characters." 16th April, 1862. (Newnham Archives).

[2] Mrs Sidgwick to her son William (brother of Henry) at Oxford 5th November, 1866:

"Mrs Arthur Clough called upon me this afternoon and during our conversation she mentioned a scheme which Miss Clough is very anxious to carry out in order to promote a better sort of education amongst girls. Since large girls' schools are generally objected to, the idea has suggested itself to her that if several schools in any large town would unite for the purpose, it might be made worth the while of some well educated man from one of the Universities to attend periodically to lecture on a given subject to these united schools. At first she asked if any such man was available at Rugby, and when Arthur [Mrs Sidgwick's other son] negatived this, she asked if I would mention the subject to you, as you had already taken much interest in the matter of female education. Miss Clough is soon going down to Liverpool to make enquiries about the Schools there and she will herself be prepared to assist in the remuneration if any such plan could be carried out. Perhaps you will think about this and tell me what conclusion you have come to? From what Mrs Clough said, I gather that her sister-in-law is very earnest in the matter and if the plan is found to be practicable she will be very anxious to receive the services of a man who warmly entered into the subject. I suppose she is scarcely yet prepared to enter into details—she only wants to have an idea where she might find a Lecturer, if there is any chance of her suggestion being carried out." Wren 101[172].

[3] H. Sidgwick to Mrs Sidgwick, December, 1866. Wren 99[77].

Notes

[4] Mrs Sidgwick to Henry Sidgwick, 14th May, 1867. Wren 101[174].
[5] Henry Sidgwick to Mrs Sidgwick, May, 1897. Wren 99[83].
[6] Information given in an unpublished M.Ed. thesis, Manchester, 1968, Sheila C. Lemoine. Quoted with the author's permission.
[7] A memoir by Henry Jackson, 7.11.1900. Wren 43[55].
[8] Mrs Fawcett in *Cheltenham Ladies College Magazine*, Spring, 1894.
[9] H. Sidgwick to Mrs Sidgwick, 1870. Wren 99[147].
[10] H. Sidgwick to Mrs Sidgwick, 15.1.1871. Wren 99[150].
[11] H. Sidgwick to Mrs Sidgwick, June, 1871. Wren 99[157].
[12] *Emily Davies and Girton College, op. cit.*, p. 103.
[13] *Ibid.*, p. 255.

After ten years of uneasy co-existence, Emily Davies was still not sure where she had Sidgwick. She wrote to Miss Bernard, then Mistress of Girton, in 1879, "If we could get trustworthy information as to his ultimate objects, it might be a help in judging whether it would do at all for us to act in any sort of concert with him. As the matter at present stands, it seems best to steadily resist the oft-recurring attempts to draw us into partnership." (G.A.). When Sidgwick finally revealed his "ultimate objects", Miss Davies found them in direct contradiction to her own; his revolved round reform of the Cambridge syllabus, hers around equality for women.

[14] H. Sidgwick to F. Myers, 20.12.1871. Wren 100[222].
[15] Mary Paley Marshall, *What I Remember*, C.U.P., 1947.
[16] Mary Paley Marshall, *op. cit.*
[17] Mary Paley Marshall, *op. cit.*
[18] At the first meeting of the college committee it was planned to build a new house with a *view* to large numbers, though not actually providing rooms for more than twenty-five in the beginning. Plans for housing a hundred students in each year of the course were dismissed as unmanageable. (M. Bodichon to Emily Davies 9.12.1868). In October 1869 Emily Davies wrote, "we shall have only five to start with, but I think the Lecturers will feel that the quality makes up for the deficiency of numbers". G.A.
[19] C. L. Maynard, *Between College Terms*, quoted in Stephen *op. cit.*, p. 31.
[20] Emily Davies to E. C. Clark. 15.3.1873. G.A.
[21] *Ibid.*
[22] Professor Seeley to Emily Davies, August 1870. G.A.
[23] Quoted in *That Infidel Place*, p. 31, M. C. Bradbrook, Chatto & Windus, 1969.
[24] In June 1871, Sidgwick was pressed to start a scheme for the Education of Rural Young Women by Correspondence. Together with other members of the Cambridge Association for the Promotion of the Higher Education of Women, Sidgwick gave advice on reading, marked papers and answered problems for young women by correspondence. The scheme flourished for twenty years. Sidgwick wrote to Myers in May

H*

1872, "All mine (correspondents) are irregular and arbitrary in their ways, except one young strenuous, well-trained governess in London and the admirable and delightful Annie Thomas with whom I am really disposed to fall in love, for the perfect way she writes out the Theory of Foreign Exchanges. (This observation must not be repeated, even in jest. I have a Magnifi-cent Character, but in my present line of business, I must play no tricks with it)." Wren 100[106].

25 Henry Sidgwick to Oscar Browning, 7th June, 1871, quoted in *Henry Sidgwick, A Memoir*, A. A. and E. M. S. Macmillan, 1906.

26 See *That Infidel Place, op. cit.*, Chapter II, "Trials and Temperaments".

27 Emily Davies to Barbara Bodichon, 4.5.1881. G.A.

28 Emily Davies to Barbara Bodichon, 12.8.1881. G.A.

29 Emily Davies to Barbara Bodichon, 1881. G.A.

30 Comparing the papers set for the Previous examination and the higher locals, several experts have given it as their opinion that the latter were of a higher standard. (See S. Lemoine, unpublished M.A. thesis *op. cit.*). Nonetheless, in inter-college rivalry, Girton students felt they were superior because of their adherence to the Previous examination. Miss Davies herself felt most strongly about women students 'choosing the easy road' of the higher locals. As late as 1917, a student coming up to Newnham was told by her aunt, a don at Girton, that academic standards at Newnham were inferior. (Private information).

CHAPTER 5

1 Letters to Miss Wolstenholme in 1871(?) N.A.

2 Henry Sidgwick to Prior, undated. N.A.

3 *Girton College 1869–1969 An Informal History, op. cit.*

4 E. M. Lloyd, *Anna Lloyd 1837–1925*, The Layton Press, 1928.

5 Even as late as 1929, Girton students were warned not to do anything to make themselves conspicuous and to put on their hats if they cycled nearer Cambridge than Storey's Way, about one mile from the centre of Cambridge.

6 A.J.B.H. to Emily Davies, February/March 1880. G.A.

7 Cam. b. 500. 8[16].

8 Mr Fitch to Emily Davies, undated. G.A.

9 Emily Davies to Henry Sidgwick, end of March 1880. G.A.

10 Henry Sidgwick to Emily Davies, 22.3.1880. G.A.

11 Girton was run by a London-based committee, Miss Davies managing always to be the most influential figure, which did not include either the mistress of Girton nor any member of the teaching staff. This arrangement continued until after the turn of the century. Newnham was managed by Cambridge people, closely involved with the running of the college. However, in their correspondence Miss Davies and Sidgwick used the terms "Girton" and "Newnham" for these management bodies

and hid the very personal nature of their dispute behind the words "your people".

[12] Henry Sidgwick to Emily Davies, 28.3.1880. G.A.

[13] Emily Davies to Henry Sidgwick, end of March 1880. G.A.

[14] *Ibid.*

[15] Henry Sidgwick to Emily Davies, 6.4.1880. G.A.

[16] Emily Davies to Henry Sidgwick, 13.4.1880. G.A.

[17] *Ibid.*

[18] Emily Davies to Miss Bernard, 26.3.1880. G.A.

[19] *University Reporter*, 30th April, 1880.

[20] *Ibid.*

[21] *Reporter*, May 1880.

[22] *Reporter*, 12th June, 1880.

[23] An interesting Memorial came from the proposed Nottingham University College and is one of the earliest indications that Cambridge was dragging its feet in the matter of recognising its women students. Nottingham Corporation were spending £60,000 in erecting buildings for the proposed college and it was intended that the college should become affiliated to Cambridge University in order that its students could graduate at Cambridge after a shortened term of residence there, as allowed by statutes recently introduced on affiliated colleges. It was desired that men and women should participate equally in the educational advantages of the University College and in any advantages which Cambridge would confer on Nottingham students. They were therefore anxious that women should be permitted to fulfil the conditions of residence required for the B.A. degree and be permitted to enter for that degree at Cambridge.

[24] *Reporter*, 1st February, 1881.

[25] Emily Davies to John Peile, November 1880. G.A.

[26] John Peile to Emily Davies, 13.12.1880. G.A.

[27] James Stuart to Emily Davies, 19.21.881. G.A.

[28] H. Sidgwick to his sister, Mary Benson, 20.3.1881. Wren 100[55].

[29] Letter from a Newnham student to a friend, 18th February, 1892. N.A.

[30] H. Sidgwick to his sister, Mary Benson, 9.12.1881. Wren 100[56].

[31] R. C. Jebb to Henry Sidgwick, 25.2.1881, Wren c 94[56]. For more information on Richard Jebb see Mary Reed Bobbitt, *With Dearest Love to All, The Life and Letters of Lady Jebb*. Faber and Faber, 1960.

[32] G. O. Trevelyan, *c.* 1905. Wren Add MSS b 71[1].

[33] Writing in 1887, Emily Davies told her correspondent, "Dr Sidgwick strongly opposed the motion for degrees and tried to stop it at the outset. Failing in this, and the steam having been got up by others, he was able to utilise it for carrying his own views. The Syndicate proposed a scheme which embodied his views, not ours and for us, it was that or none. We were strongly advised to accept it, as a step [towards degrees]." Emily Davies to Henry Jackson, 27.7.1887. G.A.

Notes

CHAPTER 6

1 Emily Davies to Henry Sidgwick, 27th May, 1887. G.A.
2 Henry Sidgwick to Emily Davies, 11.6.1887. G.A.
3 R. D. Archer-Hind to Henry Sidgwick, June 1887. N.A.
4 A. J. Tillyard to Henry Sidgwick, June 1887. N.A.
5 T. J. Lawrence to Henry Sidgwick, 7.6.1887. N.A.
6 A. J. Tovey to Henry Sidgwick, June 1887. N.A.
7 A.S. and E.M.S. *op. cit.*, p. 394.
8 In 1875 during a trip to Canada and the U.S.A. he had written enthusiastically of how women in the New World had "thorough freedom in the management of their own concerns". (Alfred Marshall to his mother, 10th July, 1875 from the unpublished Mss collection in the Marshall Library, Cambridge). Regarding the choice of a wife, Marshall told his mother, "for steady support I would have the strength that has been formed by daring and success". (5th July, 1875). Thirteen years later, he is quoted as saying that woman was a subordinate being, and that if she ceased to be subordinate, there would no longer be any reason for man to involve himself in matrimony. Marriage was a sacrifice of masculine freedom, and would only be tolerated by males so long as it meant the devotion, body and soul, of the female to the male. (See B. Webb, *My Apprenticeship*, Longmans Greene & Co., 1926). His wife was devoted—and subordinate—to him, though she succeeded in acting as lecturer at Newnham for many years after her return to Cambridge. They had no children.
9 Alfred Marshall to Emily Davies, 11.11.1880. G.A.
10 W. Skeat to H. Sidgwick, June 1887. N.A.
11 Professor Creighton(?) to H. Sidgwick, June 1887. N.A.
12 M. Fawcett to Henry Sidgwick, 23.6.1887. N.A.
13 Emily Davies to Henry Jackson, 27.7.1887. G.A.
14 Henry Sidgwick to Emily Davies, 11.6.1887. G.A.
15 Emily Davies to Henry Sidgwick, June 1887. N.A.
16 Helen Gladstone to E. M. Sidgwick, 11.7.1887. N.A.
17 Henry Jackson to Emily Davies, 13–26.7.1887. G.A.
18 Emily Davies to Henry Jackson, 27.7.1887. G.A.
19 *Ibid.*
20 The Committee circularised members of the Senate seeking their support for the Memorial. Two of the replies they received were: "am strongly of opinion that the introduction of women into the University has much lessened its reputation and is much to be deplored", Francis Darwin, Christ's College, Landowner; "desire to express my disapproval of the proposal as tending further to emasculate the University and effeminate English women and as detrimental to the interests of both", James G. Ward, Barrister, former Fellow, Emmanuel College. G.A.
21 *Manchester Guardian*, 24th November, 1887.
22 Henry Sidgwick to Archer-Hind 3.12.1887. N.A.

Notes

[23] Report of the Arts School Discussion, *University Reporter*, 26th March, 1897. Speech by A. Austen-Leigh.

CHAPTER 7

[1] Strachey, *op. cit.*
[2] The Royal Commission on Secondary Education 1895, xliii.
[3] A.S. and E.M.S., *op. cit.*, p. 511.
[4] J. Manton, *Elizabeth Garrett Anderson*, Methuen 1966, p. 104.
[5] E. M. Sidgwick, *Health Statistics of Women at Cambridge and Oxford and their Sisters*, C.U.P. 1890.
[6] Sir Francis Galton to Henry Sidgwick, 25.8.1890. Wren Add Mss c 94[1].
[7] Rackham Papers. (See Chapter 2, Note 11).
[8] *Ibid.*
[9] From a collection of papers in the University Library, Cambridge kindly shown to me by J. C. T. Oates, Reader in Historical Bibliography, Cambridge University, and published by permission of the Syndics of the University Library.
[10] 15th October, 1894. Reply and drafts only available. Cam. E.T.181.
[11] E. E. Read Mumford, *Through Rose-Coloured Spectacles*, Edgar Backus, 1952.
[12] ed. W. G. Brooke, *Statement of the Proceedings from 1892–1895 in connection with the Movement for the Admission of Women to Trinity College, Dublin*, Dublin, 1895.

CHAPTER 8

[1] Emily Davies to Henry Jackson, 16.9.1895. G.A.
[2] Henry Jackson to Emily Davies, 20.10.1895. G.A.
[3] Associate Minutes. N.A.
[4] Marion Greenwood to Emily Davies, 2.11.1895. G.A.
[5] Emily Davies to William Bateson, 4.12.1895. G.A.
[6] R. D. Archer-Hind to Emily Davies, 19.11.1895. G.A.
[7] Council Minutes. N.A.
[8] A. Marshall *On Cambridge Degrees for Women*. 3.2.1896. Cam. H.41.
[9] E. M. Sidgwick *The University Education of Women*. Lecture given at University College, Liverpool, May, 1896. N.A.
[10] Miss Maitland, Somerville College, Oxford. *The Student Life of Women in Halls of Residence*. Paper given at the Conference of Women Workers 1894.
[11] Mrs Sidgwick to Henry Sidgwick, February, 1865. Wren 101[163].
[12] E. M. Sidgwick, 12.2.1896. N.A.
[13] Bishop Wescott to Henry Sidgwick, 19.12.1895. Wren Add Mss c. 95[193].
[14] *Manchester Guardian*, 7.2.1896.

[15] *Reporter*, 1888, p. 384.
[16] Henry Sidgwick to Helen Gladstone, 9.7.(1898?). Wren 105[22].
[17] A Bachelor's Spokesman to E. M. Sidgwick. N.A.
[18] Conference of Women Workers 1895. Discussion following E. M. Sidgwick's paper *The Prospect of the Teaching Profession for Women.*
[19] Masonic Hall Meeting. Taken from the *Cambridge Review*, 27.2.1896.
[20] H. R. Tottenham, 23.3.1896, and A. Austen-Leigh 4.6.1896. N.A.
[21] This and other material on the Syndicate's work is in N.A. Some of it is duplicated in Cam. H.41.
[22] Henry Sidgwick to Emily Davies, February 1896. G.A. Emily Davies to *The Times*, 22.2.1896.
[23] Report of the Women's Degree Syndicate. Cam. H.41. Appendix IX. Memorandum from Dr Gardiner, Dr Vines, and Professor Turner, 4.11.1896.
[24] *Ibid.* Signatories were: J. Armitage Robinson, J. W. Cartmell, James Montague Rhodes, Lewis Shore, C. Taylor.
[25] *Ibid.* Signatories were: Dr Montague Butler (Vice-Chancellor), Arthur Berry, A. W. W. Dale, Professor F. W. Maitland, R. D. Roberts, W. N. Shaw, Professor V. H. Stanton, A. N. Whitehead and the Master of Emmanuel.
[26] *East Anglia Daily Times*, 22.5.1897.
[27] *Lincolnshire Echo*, 22.5.1897.
[28] *The Times*, 20.5.1897.
[29] *Westminster Gazette*, 14,15.5.1897.
[30] J. F. Nisbet. *Learned Ladies. St. Paul's Gazette*, 17.4.1897.
[31] G. Clarence Brighton. *Women at Cambridge. Echo*, 10.5.1897.
[32] *Morning Post*, 21.5.1897.
[33] James Mayo, flysheet, 14.5.1897. Cam. H.41.
[34] *Standard*, 21.5.1897.
[35] *Daily News*, 21.5.1897.
[36] *Pall Mall Gazette*, 20.5.1897.
[37] *The Times*, 20.5.1897.
[38] *Manchester Guardian*, 22.5.1897.
[39] The *Cambridge Review* quoted from the *Weekly Post* of Birmingham, Indiana, the story of a Miss Mabel Ely, who had held up a tram-car with a revolver and made all the women passengers remove their dresses and stockings and throw them out of the windows. Then each was made to take off her bonnet and destroy it. On arrest, she was found to be violently insane and removed to an asylum. Overstudy was supposed to be the cause of her illness. She had just taken her degree and at the graduation ceremony delivered a capable valedictory address. *Cambridge Review*, 13th May, 1897.
[40] A. McLean to A. J. Balfour, mid-May, 1897. N.A.
[41] *St James Gazette*, May, 1897.
[42] Cam. H.41.
[43] Mrs Wilson, née Armitage (Newnham 1895–8) in a letter to the Principal, 13.2.1851. N.A.

Notes

44 *Cambridge Weekly News*, 28.5.97.
45 *Westminster Gazette*, May 1897.
46 *Morning Post*, 31.5.1897.
47 *Westminster Gazette*, 14,15.5.1897.
48 Rackham Papers. (See Chapter 2, Note 11.)

CHAPTER 9

1 *Reporter*, 1897/8, p. 273.
2 *Reporter*, 1914/15, p. 164, p. 256, p. 348.1.
3 *The Cause, op. cit.*, p. 197/8.
4 Cmd. 8137 and 8 XIX 1914–16. Education Reports. The total of part-time students was 16,492.
5 Miss Cooke held an Assistant Lectureship at Owen's College (later Manchester University). Information from University Calendars 1913/14.
6 Radio interview 24.6.1960. B.B.C. Sound Archives LP.26463.
7 Mrs L. E. Hertslet (née Jessie Winifred Baines Gould) in a radio interview, 8.7.1966. B.B.C. Sound Archives LP.30247.

Gwen Raverat, b. 1885, describes childhood memories of "drab Newnham girls (who) skurried to and fro". p. 45, *Period Piece*, Faber, 1952. A popular riddle circulating in Cambridge during the 1897 battle was "What is the difference between David's last wife and a Newnham girl? Answer: One is Abishag the Shunamite, the other a shabby Hag, the Newnhamite! Recounted by Mrs Herstlet.
8 This sketch of a talk given to her students is indistinctly marked 1904 or 1909, but the earlier date seems most likely. N.A.
9 Reported in most daily newspapers 27th July, 1919. Cam. H.41.
10 E.g. *Manchester Guardian*, 28.7.1919. *Times Educational Supplement*, 31.7.1919. *Daily Telegraph*, 2.8.1919.
11 James Mayo 1840–1920, described by R. F. Scott as "extremely eccentric". He lived in Cambridge from 1882 where he was "a continual attendant at discussions in the Senate House always contributing his remarks after stating "he knew nothing of the subject in question". In the early days of wireless he took legal action against his next-door neighbours alleging they were injuring him by sending "rays" through his person. From information given in *Alumni Cantabridgiensis*.
12 *Reporter*, 1916/17, p. 202, p. 234.4. and p. 234.5.
13 The term "young" and "old" defy definition but in this context it should be noticed that all able-bodied and non-exempted men under 41 years and, towards the end of the war, under 50 years, were eligible for conscription and might therefore be expected to have come in contact with a more modern appreciation of women's talents than they were familiar with in Cambridge.
14 Printed in *Reporter*, 26th May, 1919.

[15] A copy of this Memorial, signed by about 135 members of the University, appears in Cam. H.41 addressed to the Vice-Chancellor and date stamped 27.5.1918.

[16] Printed in *Reporter*, 26th May, 1919.

[17] *The Cause, op. cit.*, p. 370–1.

[18] *Daily Telegraph*, 2.8.1919.

[19] *Country Life*, 9.8.1919.

[20] *Manchester Guardian*, 28.7.1919.

[21] *Cambridge Daily News*, 9.7.1919.

[22] This account is taken from the *Times Educational Supplement*, 29.1.1920. See also A. M. A. H. Rogers *Degrees by Degrees*, O.U.P., 1938.

[23] *Daily Telegraph*, 21.2.1920.

[24] "Nothing in the Statutes or Charter of any University shall be deemed to preclude the authorities of such University from making such provision as they shall think fit for the admission of women to membership thereof or to any degree right or privilege therein or in connection therewith." 9 & 10 George V.

[25] See for example *Manchester Guardian*, 9.12.1919.

[26] *Daily Telegraph*, 11.6.1920.

[27] *Daily Telegraph*, 21.2.1920.

[28] Quoted in *The Cause, op. cit.*, p. 261.

[29] Associates Minutes. N.A.

[30] Report of the Committee appointed by the Associates to consider what would be the precise position of women under the present University regulations if the College became a Public Hostel and what would be the future prospects and possibilities. March, 1919. N.A.

[31] Letter from Alice Gardner (Newnham 1876–79) to Secretary of the Associates 21.3.1919. N.A.

[32] *Reporter*, 3.6.1919.

[33] Associate Minutes, 24.5.1919. N.A.

[34] Council Minutes, 8.2.1919. N.A.

[35] *The Times*, 30.10.1919.

[36] *The Times*, 5.11.1919.

[37] Joint Girton and Newnham Committee Circular to old students December 1919. N.A.

[38] *Observer*, 30.11.1919.

[39] *Reporter*. Discussion 11.11.1919; Vote 6.12.1919.

[40] *Reporter*, 1919/20, p. 935.

[41] R. St John Parry, H. McL. Innes, F. J. M. Stratton, C. R. Fay, Arnold D. McNair, J. R. M. Butler.

[42] Dr E. C. Pearce, Dr W. R. Sorley, Will Spens, J. D. Spittle, G. A. Elliott, R. V. Laurence.

[43] Council Minutes, 18.6.1920. N.A.

[44] June, 1920. N.A.

[45] Council Minutes, 23.6.1920. N.A.

[46] Royal Commission on Oxford and Cambridge Universities 1922 x Cmd 1588, p. 290.

[47] Flysheet, 8.11.1920. N.A.

[48] *Queen*, 13.11.1920.

[49] Flysheet, 1.10.1920. N.A.

[50] *Daily Graphic*, 5.10.1920, interview with Dr Winifred Collis.

[51] *Evening News*, 5.10.1920.

[52] See, for example *Daily News*, 27.5.1920; *Daily Mail*, 10.7.1920.

[53] *Evening Standard*, 7.10.1920.

[54] Council Minutes, 10.5.1919. N.A.

[55] Council Minutes, 8.5.1920. N.A.

[56] *Daily Mail*, 8.11.1920.

[57] *Daily Mail*, 8.11.1920.

[58] Letters from B. A. Clough, February 1921. N.A.

[59] *Spectator*, 17.10.1920.

[60] *Evening Standard*, 16.10.1920.

[61] *Observer*, 7.11.1920.

[62] This accusation had been more soberly made by J. H. Gray in a balanced speech during a discussion of the Syndicate's terms of reference 30.10.1919 (*Reporter* 11.11.1919). The carefully designed scheme for the English Tripos brought forward by Professor Chadwick and universally accepted as most satisfactory for men was "violently assailed by representatives of Girton and Newnham as unsuitable for women." The Principal of Newnham explained in answer to Ridgeway's attack that the English lecturers of Newnham only commented on the English Tripos after having been invited to do so and that the modifications suggested by them were designed to raise the level of the examination. *Evening Standard* 3.12.1920). Some, though not all, of the women connected with the teaching of English strongly opposed Professor Chadwick's scheme to limit the amount of attention paid to the study of Teutonic and Old English Philology and to emphasise instead the historical and cultural background of Old English and Old Icelandic. Miss Enid Welsford, then a research student and for many years a lecturer in English has commented, "it was a genuine difference of opinion on a subject of intellectual importance and like many such academic disputes, it did for a while generate a good deal of heat". (Private information.)

[63] Ridgeway to *The Times*, 22.11.1920.

[64] Flysheet. 23.11.1920. N.A.

[65] Harold Jeffreys undated flysheet (? Nov. 1920) N.A.

[66] *Reporter*, 1920/21, 28.10.1920.

[67] Report of the Joint Girton and Newnham Committee. 21.12.1920. N.A.

[68] *Evening Standard*, 3.12.1920 and others.

[69] *Evening Standard*, 3.12.1920.

[70] *Manchester Despatch*, 6.12.1920 and others.

[71] J. E. McTaggart to *Telegraph*, 6.12.1920.

[72] Letter from undergraduate to *Morning Post*, 8.12.1920.

[73] *Daily Mail*, 30.11.1920.

[74] *Daily News*, 6.12.1920.

[75] *Daily Mail*, 7.12.1920.

[76] *British Medical Journal*, 21.8.1920.

[77] *The Times*, 6.12.1920.

[78] See, for example, a later piece by Mrs Adam in *Education*, 2.1.1922.

[79] Mrs A. M. Adam, wife of Dr James Adam and mother of Barbara Wootton, worked on the history of the expansion of studies in the University since 1850. She wrote "If the Lady Margaret were to revisit her illustrious foundations [Christ's and St John's] might she not be more surprised to find in the lecture rooms Hindus, Japanese and Negroes, than to see there women of tastes akin to her own?" *Journal of Education*, 2.1.1922.

[80] *The Times*, 7.12.1920.

[81] *Daily News*, 9.12.1920.

[82] *Daily Herald*, 9.12.1920.

[83] See, for example, *Daily News*, 9. and 10.12.1920; *Telegraph*, 12.12.1920; *Oxford Times*, 10.12.1920.

[84] *Daily Chronicle*, 10.12.1920.

[85] *Manchester Despatch*, 14.12.1920; Bulletin 10.12.1920.

[86] *Times Educational Supplement*, 16.12.1920.

[87] *Daily News*, 10.12.1920.

[88] *Times Educational Supplement*, 17.2.1721.

[89] London Grace II Committee, October 1921, Draft flysheet. Cam. H.14.

CHAPTER 10

[1] The first Memorial was circulated on 1st February, 1921, the second on 14th February, 1921, see *Reporter*, 1920/21, p. 710.

[2] *Cambridge Review*, 25.2.1921; *Cambridge Chronicle*, 23.2.1921.

[3] *Cambridge Review*, 5.3.1921.

[4] *Reporter*, 1920/21, 3.5.1921, p. 903.

[5] *Reporter*, 1920/21, 3.5.1921, p. 903, Draft Statutes.

[6] Flysheet. 1.5.1921. N.A.

[7] *Church Times*, 29.4.1921.

[8] *Reporter*, 1920/21, 24.5.1921, p. 1028.

[9] Dr Clapham, *Reporter*, 1920/21, p. 1036.

[10] *Cambridge Review*, 20.5.1921.

[11] Flysheet. 4.6.1921. N.A.

[12] Flysheet. 2.6.1921. N.A.

[13] Flysheet. 6.10.1921. N.A.

[14] A. D. McNair to R. A. Wright, 11.10.1921. N.A.

[15] H. Bond to *Telegraph*, 15.10.1921.

[16] *Times Educational Supplement*, 15.10.1921. See also a Memorandum to the Royal Commission, November, 1921. Appendix 14.

[17] *Times Educational Supplement*, 15.10.1921.

[18] *Daily Graphic*, 17.10.1921.

[19] *Evening News*, 17.10.1921.

[20] *The Times*, 18.10.1921.

21 *The Times*, 19.10.1921.

22 *Newcastle Daily Chronicle*, 19.10.1921.

23 See, for example, *East Anglia Times*, 19.10.1921; *Daily News*, 20.10.1921.

24 *Westminster Gazette*, 19.10.1921.

25 *Daily Mail*, 20.10.1921.

26 Cambridge residents are often unfamiliar with these gates, as the part o Newnham most frequently viewed is that facing onto Sidgwick Avenue. The Porter's Lodge is there and this tends to be regarded as the front of the college. Until the construction of Sidgwick Avenue, there was a public footpath through the college grounds from Newnham Walk to Grange Road dividing Old Hall from Clough and Sidgwick Halls. This was a great inconvenience to the college and permission was long sought to close and replace it by a road round the boundary of Newnham's grounds. After three years of negotiations and public debate (described by Sidgwick as "tears and wrath and long letters in the Cambridge papers and, in short, a first-class row". Henry Sidgwick to H. G. Dakyns 19.12.1889. *Henry Sidgwick, A Memoir, op. cit.* p. 503) permission was granted in 1891. Sidgwick Avenue was constructed at the expense of friends of Newnham, especially the Sidgwicks, and an entrance gateway was then built joining Old Hall and Sidgwick Hall with rooms over it and on each side. In this gateway were placed beautiful bronze gates, designed by Mr Champneys and presented to the college by old students in memory of Miss J. A. Clough, the first Principal.

27 From the *Daily Chronicle*, report 21.10.1921 and others.

28 *Daily Chronicle*, 21.10.1921.

29 *Daily Telegraph*, 21.10.1921.

30 *Morning Post*, 21.10.1921.

31 *Daily Mail*, 21.10.1921.

32 For example *Evening News*, 21.10.1921; *Star*, 21.10.1921.

33 Undated but probably October 1921. N.A.

34 *Observer*, 23.10.1921.

35 *Cambridge Daily News*, 24 and 26.10.1921.

36 *Scotsman*, 31.10.1921.

37 *The Times*, 25.10.1921.

38 *The Times*, 26.10.1921.

39 *The Times*, 25.10.1921.

40 This paradox has been recorded many times: see, for example, the replies to interviews noted in *Women in Top Jobs*, M. Fogarty *et al.* P. E. P. George, Allen and Unwin, 1971.

41 *Times Educational Supplement*, 29.10.1921.

42 *The Times*, 29.10.1921.

43 *Times Educational Supplement*, 24.6.1922.

44 *The Times*, 27.10.1921.

45 *Times Educational Supplement*.

46 Royal Commission 1922 *op. cit.*, p. 290.

47 Royal Commission 1922 *op. cit.*, p. 291.

48 *Liverpool Courier*, 6.3.1922.

[49] S. R. Courtauld to B. A. Clough, 15.2.1922. N.A.
[50] Royal Commission 1922 *op. cit.*, p. 173.
[51] M. A. Adam. N.A.
[52] *Daily Telegraph*, 6.6.1922.
[53] *Times Educational Supplement*, 24.6.1922.
[54] Letter 8.6.1922. N.A.
[55] Flysheet. 5.12.1921. N.A.
[56] Flysheet. 21.6.1922. N.A.
[57] Flysheet. 19.2.1923. N.A.
[58] Letter P. Giles to B. A. Clough 15.11.1922. N.A.
[59] *Reporter*, 1922/3, p. 158.
[60] *Reporter*, 1922/3, 14.11.1922, p. 254.
[61] *Reporter*, 1922/3, 28.11.1922, p. 292.
[62] *Reporter*, 1922/3, 21.12.1922, p. 414.
[63] *Reporter*, 1922/3, 27.2.1923, p. 721.
[64] *Reporter*, 1922/3, 6.3.1923, p. 733.
[65] *Manchester Guardian*, 5.3.1923.
[66] *Manchester Guardian*, 16.3.1923. Full Library rights were given to women, equivalent to those held by men, in December 1923. By the end of the academic year 1923/4, 132 women had applied to receive titles of their degrees in retrospect. By the end of the academic year 1925/6, a total of 469 women had received degree titles. About 1650 women were eligible to apply for the title retrospectively. (Information from the University Registry, the *Reporter* and *Newnham* Hamilton *op. cit.*).
[67] *The Times*, 5.3.1923.
[68] E. Hubbock to P. Strachey, 23.1.1923. N.A.
[69] E. Hubbock to P. Strachey, 6.5.1923. N.A.
[70] *Time and Tide*, 27.7.1923.
[71] Statutes published in the *Reporter* 1925/6, 22.10.1925, p. 146; 29.1.1926. Discussed 16.11.1925, p. 286; 9.11.1926. Statutes approved by King in Council 20.12.1927.

CHAPTER 11

[1] *Reporter*, 1944/5, p. 199. Graces passed 16.12.1944.
[2] *Reporter*, 1946/7, p. 358. 3.12.1946. Memorial also reprinted.
[3] *Reporter*, 3.6.1947.
[4] *Reporter*, 1947/8, p. 295. 11.11.1947.
[5] Newnham College Roll *Letter*, 1948, p. 12. N.A.
[6] Letters, December, 1947. N.A.
[7] Letter, 8.12.1947. N.A.
[8] *Spectator*, 12.12.1947.
[9] *Cambridge Daily News*, 5.5.1948.
[10] *The Times*, 6.12.1947.
[11] Vice-Chancellor to Myra Curtis, 4.5.1948. N.A.

Notes

12 Darwin College, founded 1964, University (now Wolfson) College, founded 1965, Clare Hall founded 1966.

13 *The Times*, 1.11.1971, and *Reporter*, 21.12.1973. p. 466.

14 Figures calculated from "Officers in Institutions placed under the Supervision of the General Board". Michaelmas Term 1974 *Reporter* Special No. 2.

15 Report of Joint Working Party on Co-residence *and* First Report of the Standing Sub-Committee for Men and Women in Cambridge. Reprinted, *Reporter*, 23.10.1974, pp. 180–96.

16 *Ibid*, p. 186.

17 *Ibid*, p. 186.

18 *Ibid*, p. 181 and p. 190.

APPENDIX A

1 *Reporter* 1905/6, p. 649 for a historical outline of these exemptions.

2 *H.S. A Memoir, op. cit.*, p. 511.

3 *Reporter* 1904/5, p. 194, p. 354. Vote 3rd and 4th March 1905.

4 *Reporter*, 8.6.1914.

5 *Reporter*, 1917/18, p. 649. 1918/19, p. 249, p. 390.

6 *Reporter*, 12.11.1960.

APPENDIX B

1 *Reporter*, 1933/4, p. 663 and 915.1.

2 *Reporter*, 1944/5, p. 431.

3 *Reporter* 1944/5, p. 431. Discussion p. 526.

4 Some Colleges will not keep students who have been "allowed the Ordinary" for their first examination.

BIBLIOGRAPHY

BOOKS CITED IN THE TEXT

Bobbitt, Mary Reed, *With Dearest Love to All. The Life and Letters of Lady Jebb*, Faber & Faber, 1960.

Bradbrook, M. C., *That Infidel Place*, Chatto & Windus, 1969.

Brittain, V., *Testament of Youth*, Gollancz, 1933.

Clough, B. A., *Anne J. Clough*, Arnold, 1897.

Fogarty, M. et. al., *Women in Top Jobs*, Allen & Unwin, 1971.

Gardner, A., *A Short History of Newnham College*, Bowes & Bowes, 1921.

Glandinning, V., *A Suppressed Cry*, Routledge & Kegan Paul, 1969.

Glynne-Grylls, R., *Queen's College 1848–1948*, Routledge & Kegan Paul, 1948.

Hamilton, M. A., *An Informal Biography*, Faber & Faber, 1936.

Lloyd, E. M., *Anna Lloyd 1837–1925*, The Layton Press, 1928.

Manton, Jo, *Elizabeth Garrett Anderson*, Methuen, 1965.

Marshall, Mary Paley, *What I Remember*, Cambridge University Press, 1947.

Maynard, C. L., *Between College Terms*, James Nisbett & Co., 1910.

Megson, B. and Lindsay, J., *Girton College 1869–1959, An Informal History*, Heffers, 1960.

Mitchell, B. & Deane, P., *Abstract of British Historical Statistics*, Cambridge, 1962.

Raverat, Gwen, *Period Piece*, Faber & Faber, 1952.

Read Mumford, E. E., *Through Rose-Coloured Spectacles*, Edgar Backus, 1952.

Rogers, A. M. A. H., *Degrees by Degrees*, Oxford University Press, 1938.

Rothblatt, Sheldon, *The Revolution of the Dons*, Faber & Faber, 1968.

A.S. & E.M.S., *Henry Sidgwick, A Memoir*, Macmillan, 1906.

Sidgwick, E., *Mrs Henry Sidgwick, A Memoir*, Sidgwick & Jackson, 1938.

Sidgwick, E. M., *Health Statistics of Women at Cambridge and Oxford and their Sisters*, Cambridge University Press, 1890.

Stephen, Barbara, *Emily Davies and Girton College*, Constable, 1927.

Bibliography

Stephen, Barbara, *Girton College 1869–1932*, Cambridge University Press, 1933.

Stewart, J., *Jane Harrison*, Merton Press, 1959.

Strachey, Ray, *The Cause*, Bell & Son, 1928.

Tuke, Margaret, *A History of Bedford College for Women*, Oxford University Press, 1939.

Venn, J. & J. A., *Alumni Cantabrigiensis*, Cambridge University Press, 1922–27.

Webb, Beatrice, *My Apprenticeship*, Longmans, 1926.

White, Cynthia, *Women's Magazines 1693–1968*, Michael Joseph, 1970.

Winstanley, D. A., *Late Victorian Cambridge*, Cambridge University Press, 1947.

Wollstonecraft, Mary, *Vindication of the Rights of Women*, 1792.

OTHER PUBLICATIONS

The Cambridge University Reporter 1870–

Reports of Royal Commissions on:
    Secondary Education: 1867–8 xxxviii
    Secondary Education: 1895   xliii
    Oxford & Cambridge
    Universities: 1922   x
    Education Reports: 1914–16 xix

INDEX